MW00526539

"What Virtue There Is in Fire"

"What Virtue There Is in Fire"

Cultural Memory and
the Lynching of Sam Hose

Edwin T. Arnold

The University of Georgia Press
Athens and London

Publication of this book was supported in part by the
Kenneth Coleman Series in Georgia History and Culture.

Set in Ehrhardt by Graphic Composition, Inc.
Printed and bound by Maple-Vail
The paper in this book meets the guidelines for
permanence and durability of the Committee on
Production Guidelines for Book Longevity of the
Council on Library Resources.

Printed in the United States of America
13   12   11   10   09   C   5   4   3   2   1

Library of Congress Cataloging-in-Publication Data

Arnold, Edwin T.
   "What virtue there is in fire" : cultural memory and the
lynching of Sam Hose / Edwin T. Arnold.
      p.   cm.
Includes bibliographical references and index.
ISBN-13: 978-0-8203-2891-1 (hardcover : alk. paper)
ISBN-10: 0-8203-2891-X (hardcover : alk. paper)
   1. Hose, Sam, d. 1899. 2. Coweta County (Ga.)—Race relations—History.
3. Lynching—Georgia—Coweta County—History—19th century.
4. African Americans—Crimes against—Georgia—Coweta County—History.
5. Murder—Georgia—Coweta County—History—19th century.
6. Racism—Georgia—Coweta County—History.
7. Hose, Sam, d. 1899—Influence.   I. Title.
F292.C8A765 2009
323.1196'0730758—dc22   2008050471

British Library Cataloging-in-Publication Data available

For my granddaughters, Caroline Shade and Ashleigh Merrow

Sistren an' brethren,
Stop foolin' wid pray,
Sistren an' brethren,
Stop foolin' wid pray.
When black face is lifted,
Lord turn in' way.
Yo' head tain' no apple
Fo danglin' from a tree,
Yo' head tain' no apple
Fo danglin' from a tree,
Yo' body no carcass
for barbacuin' on a spree.
> —"SISTREN AN' BRETHREN," SONG COLLECTED
> BY LAWRENCE GELLERT IN THE 1930S

The monster fiend of all the fiends
*   That ever cursed the earth;*
The blackest devil of all his kind—
*   A devil from his birth!*

Then boldly say, "We've done no wrong
*   To burn the monster at the stake;"*
But join in peans [sic] and in song
*   For all that's dear—for woman's sake.*
> —"SAM HOLT," POEM PUBLISHED IN THE
> *NEWNAN HERALD AND ADVERTISER*, MAY 12, 1899

Let us try what virtue there is in fire.
> —"AN EYE FOR AN EYE"; OR THE FIEND
> AND THE FAGOT

Contents

"What Virtue There Is in Fire"

Introduction

On the night of April 12, 1899, Mattie Cranford, the young wife of a Coweta County, Georgia, farmer, stumbled through the dark to the nearby home of her father-in-law, her four children in tow. At the gate to the yard, she cried for help and then collapsed. When she was revived, she told Grippia Cranford a horrifying tale: his son was dead, brained from behind by an ax-wielding black laborer known locally as Sam Holt or Hose.[1] Hose had also hurt two of the children, one so grievously that the infant boy was disfigured and his condition critical. At some point she also claimed that Hose had raped her on the bloody dining-room floor, in the presence of the children, next to the body of her dying husband.

After rushing to his son's home, the elder Cranford reported finding Alfred's corpse as Mattie had described, his head split open and his blood and brains spewed on the table, in the food, and across the floor. Within hours, hounds were on the trail of the killer, and for the next ten days the state of Georgia was captivated by the search, the details of which were related by local and national newspapers. Many predicted that the monster Hose, when caught, would be burned at the stake, a punishment befitting the enormity of his crimes. The governor of Georgia, the leading state newspaper, and other local groups offered rewards for his capture.

After Sam Hose was finally found, over a hundred miles away, his captors crudely disguised him in an attempt to transport the prisoner secretly by train to Atlanta, where they would receive the rewards. However, at Griffin, Georgia, the train was met by a large gathering of armed citizens who searched the train and seized the suspect. Selected representatives of the city then escorted the chained Hose on a special express train to Newnan, the county seat of Coweta, located some fifteen miles from the Cranford plantation. A large crowd now awaited the train's arrival at the Newnan depot. There, in the early afternoon of Sunday, April 23, Hose was first turned over to the town's sheriff and escorted to the city jail, but then, once the quasi-legal formalities had been met, was once again taken by a mob now composed of people from both Newnan and Griffin. Efforts to control the crowd failed, and after a ritualistic procession through the streets of Newnan, the growing throng marched Sam Hose into a field on the outskirts of town and there mocked and mutilated him before chaining him to a tree, stacking wood at his feet, soaking him in kerosene, and setting him afire. For an agonizing time he writhed miserably in the flames while the crowd cheered his desperate contortions. A local photographer recorded his last moments. Members of the horde then dismembered what remained of his cooked corpse for souvenirs, pieces of which still circulated in the region as late as the 1970s.

I came to the story of Sam Hose's killing and the events that surrounded it by way of fiction, and the more I learned of it, the more like fiction it read. In my research on the southern writer Erskine Caldwell's campaign against lynching in his stories and reporting of the 1930s, I had found references to Hose's public execution in the Old Troutman Field, in the vicinity of Caldwell's birthplace of White Oak. Caldwell was born in 1903; his father, Ira Sylvester Caldwell, had come to the rural west Georgia community as preacher for the Associate Reformed Presbyterian Church in 1901. Although Erskine Caldwell lived in this area for only a few years before his father again moved the family, I wondered to what degree this horrific act of racial violence might have stoked his outrage and influenced his work. It now seems trite to say that as I delved deeper into the newspaper accounts of Sam Hose's lynching, I often could not believe what I was reading, but such was the case. Indeed, the primary (white) narratives often employed such melodramatic and sensationalistic style and projected such an unapologetic bias and assumption of guilt that any modern reader would certainly question the veracity of the events described in these contemporary reports. They read today as myth making of the most insidious kind, one that antagonizes prejudices and exploits fears in the dominant community in such a way that the most extreme reaction is both encouraged and expected. At the same time, they make for a terrifyingly compelling story that reveals a time and a people in complex and challenging ways. As Shreve McCannon tells Quentin Compson in William Faulkner's *Absalom, Absalom!* (itself an investigation of how narrative builds on and overwhelms the "facts" of history), "Jesus, the South is fine, isn't it? It's better than the theatre, isn't it? It's better than Ben Hur, isn't it?"[2] As a student of southern literature, I found myself drawn into a world I had known primarily through novels and stories, but that was here represented as "true" because it was being reported as the events occurred, in some form of "real time," with witnesses to support their veracity. And yet, as in Faulkner's novel, the gothic extravagance of the events as related made it something else, something essentially fantastic, although I could read the accounts and later visit the sites, stand by the graves, talk to the descendants.

Complicating my astonishment—and this is the best description I can give of the experience—is the fact that I was born and raised in this section of Georgia, lived there until I left for college, and had never heard of Sam Hose or of the events that led to and surrounded his death. As my research expanded, I discovered things about my own hometown that I had never known, its own racial notoriety and brief moments in the national news. My mother's family had moved into the small town of Hogansville, Georgia, from nearby rural Heard County around the turn of the twentieth century. Certainly her parents would have lived through these events. I have no sense of how they might have reacted, whether they were appalled by the brutal illegality or quietly approved of a restoration of order. I also have no idea if my mother, born in 1914, fifteen years after the event, would ever have heard of Sam Hose. If not, was it because of shame? Or was it because of the satisfied sense that the event was over and done and required no more discussion? Since beginning this study, I have learned from a few childhood friends that they, indeed, did grow up hearing stories of Sam Hose, but more as folktales, local yarns, even as gruesome humor, rather than as history. (The other killings and crimes explored in this work, as a rule, are rarely recalled, as either fact or lore.) But most to whom I have spoken or inquired had no notion of who Sam Hose was or how he died.

My ignorance, then, was in part a result of selected forgetting in my family and a public silence in my community. It may also reflect an even greater innocence or naïveté or simple blindness on my part, a failure to consider the realities of the conflicted southern world in which I was growing up in the 1950s and 1960s. In his book *What Else But Love? The Ordeal of Race in Faulkner and Morrison*, Philip M. Weinstein confronts his personal history as a liberal, white southerner attempting to write about race and acknowledges, "There will be readers for whom my positioning as white and male partially or entirely discredits this project, [but] silence would be more wrong than speech. I have a debt to acknowledge that outweighs rectitude."[3] I must also be aware of my "positioning" in this work, which has gone through several stages. At first I intended it to be a much more personal response to these terrible crimes, a form of memoir that used my (individual) "discovery" of these events as a way to examine the small-town southern world in which I lived. I later discarded this approach in distaste, feeling that my theme would essentially be that Sam Hose, Elijah Strickland, the victims of the Palmetto massacre, and many others suffered and died over a hundred years ago so that I could now talk about myself as a privileged southern white man "with issues." Nevertheless, I am aware that this self-centered approach has not been totally removed from this account, that the voice narrating these events is one influenced by sometimes unrecognized investments and even prejudices that skew my descriptions and responses. I am also aware that I base my study largely on white narratives, both in the primary newspaper sources I use and the present-day interviews I have conducted. Some early readers of the work recognized this unbalanced approach. My defense is that these sources make up the majority of the surviving accounts, and that when black newspapers challenged these accounts, I have shown the ways they did so. But both white and black newspapers of the time were prone to exaggeration, to misinformation, to error. Journalistic standards were variable, to be sure, but different publications had different agendas, and I have tried to note the ways different sources attempted to control the narrative for their own purposes. However, I trust that readers will understand that even the most sensational or repugnant telling might still reflect a worldview, a perceived reality, which should be considered in an effort to analyze the stories told.

This effort leads me to another potential misunderstanding about the book. Although the following is an in-depth study of a series of lynchings that occurred in a time of lynching fever and does, by necessity, describe several other lynchings and the world that not only allowed but often sanctioned them, it is not intended to be an examination of the practice of lynching itself. Others in this field, far more learned and authoritative than I, have written extraordinarily detailed and perceptive analyses of the varied purposes of lynch terror as employed in the South and elsewhere in the nation. My assumption is that readers will understand that, whatever cries of outrage, calls to honor, or other rhetorical flourishes were employed to defend both the necessity and the extravagance of these extralegal killings, the acts themselves were calculated, vicious, and inhuman deeds done by a dominant community to maintain and ensure its continued authority. However, I do attempt to understand how members of such a community, who pictured themselves as guardians of a threatened way of life, could perpetrate such acts and commend themselves for doing so. It is not that simple, of course. Many whites condemned the lynchings and called for punishment of the perpetrators. Their motives were mixed, but their outrage was real. Nevertheless, the society as a whole abided, even encouraged, these acts of terror and publicly justified them. Scholars such as Walter Benn Michaels and Scott Romine have explored this brand of southern nativism; my contribution is to examine the specific details of a set of events that illustrates this nativist impulse at its most virulent. In this attempt I look at the world these people inhabited, poised at the turn of the twentieth century but in far too many ways similar to our own today at the beginning of the twenty-first. Although I do not propose to draw out these comparisons, I hope that readers will recognize that, especially after 9/11, when the fears of terrorism and subversion overwhelmed our country, many of our leaders, politicians, and citizens rationalized racial targeting, the abridgement or flouting of laws, the sanctioned use of torture, the unsupervised actions of secret organizations. Others have already noted the similarities between the photographs taken at Abu Ghraib and lynching photographs from the late nineteenth and early twentieth centuries.[4] I do not mean to equate these actions unconditionally, but I do wish to point out that anxious times may result in similar responses. Thus, the world of 1899 Georgia may not be as foreign to ours as we might wish to think. Indeed, when the recent controversy over a memorial to Sam Hose, discussed in the final chapter of this book, arose, local reaction was at times indistinguishable from that of a century ago.

Perhaps for me, as a student of literature, the greatest danger is becoming so wrapped up in the drama—it is, as a colleague said almost apologetically, "a hell of a story"—that I misapprehend or minimize the brutal truths that caused it to happen. The distancing of years plays its part, to be sure, but the grandiloquent language of the accounts, the shameless manipulation of emotions, and the raw power of narrative also seduce the reader with a terrible aesthetic pleasure even as the events themselves grow ever more awful in the telling. It is similar to a viewing of *The Birth of a Nation*, in which the brilliance of the cinematic creation threatens to overwhelm the moral repulsion of the underlying thesis.[5] I have sometimes found myself, in recounting the details of these events, too caught up in narrative delight, too willing to indulge in the very melodrama that distorts the stark truth of the world it portrays. As with Quentin and Shreve in *Absalom, Absalom!* it is all too easy to "play" with these events and thus to become complicit in the myth making.

By this time it should be clear that I am not approaching this material in the guise of a historian. Nor am I attempting to establish the "facts" of these events. There is much that remains unknown, and unknowable, in this account. Did Sam Hose kill Alfred Cranford in self-defense or for revenge or out of blood lust? Did he rape Cranford's wife? Were there connections between the Palmetto shootings and the Cranford murder? Was Elijah Strickland a coconspirator or a collateral victim? These are all questions with no definite answers. At the time and over the years that followed, different commentators have shaped the narrative to fit their positions. First reports pictured Sam Hose in the already conventional role of the "black beast," and there was no question of his guilt. He deserved to die, and to die horribly, for the sake of white society. Investigations instigated by Ida Wells-Barnett, Reverdy Ransom, and others quickly created a counternarrative in which Sam Hose was yet another southern black man falsely accused of the rape of a white woman. His killing of Alfred Cranford was not disputed, but his motives were. Still other versions offered an even more complicated portrait in which Hose took on the role of insurgent, his murder of Cranford an act of political and racial revolt. In this identity, Hose became a revolutionary hero cited by guerrilla fighters in the Philippines as a martyr in the worldwide struggle for freedom from imperialist rule. I have attempted to explore Sam Hose in all these roles, recognizing that the "truth" has likely been impossibly lost. At the local level, in Newnan today, many still believe unconditionally that Sam Hose viciously killed Alfred Cranford and raped his wife. Conversely, in most present-day examinations of these events, scholars tend to accept Wells-Barnett's version without question and conclude that Hose killed Cranford in self-defense and was innocent of rape. My study is not intended to settle this question, but it will, I hope, represent the complexities too often ignored by both sides.

What, then, is the purpose of this book? First, to give a close reading of the accounts that created the narratives of Sam Hose, his crimes, and his public death. I examine the use of language, the appeals to sectionalism, the unabashed sensationalism that provided entertainment as much as information. Grace Elizabeth Hale has labeled spectacle lynchings "Deadly Amusements," and although I question the reductionism of this position, it is evident that newspaper accounts were often written in order to thrill and hold the audience much as a penny dreadful would.[6] I quote at length from newspapers, in part for this reason but also because I am fascinated with the audacious vocabulary, the melodramatic verve, the bold disregard for "truth" in many of these accounts. Papers contradicted themselves from one day to the next, or even within the columns of the same page, with a kind of boisterous indifference. I feel that it is important to read these newspapers as they would have been read in 1899. The pages are visually very dense: they are tightly packed, although sensational headlines followed by explanatory subheads did serve to direct the readers as they negotiated the sheet. Moreover, although an edition was obviously limited by what was known at the time of its production, as one read down the columns and across the page, it might well update itself, contradict itself, give wildly different versions of the same story. In other words, the paper was alive in a way newspapers aren't today. Compare, for example, twenty-four-hour news channels or the Internet, where the flow of information is constantly updated and the viewer or user adjusts from hour to hour or minute to minute as new "facts" are presented, old "facts" corrected or discarded or discreetly forgotten. A century ago, as readers made their way through the columns of a page, they might find themselves interrupted by a bulletin that visually "refreshed" the news, brought it forward in time. In the case of Sam Hose, whose pursuit lasted some ten days, reporters were able to create story lines that became the equivalent of a serialized novel, each day bringing a new chapter of information related through dramatic settings, invented dialogue, recognizable character types, and a constantly developing plot. A reporter like Royal Daniel of the *Atlanta Journal* or Goode M. Guerry of the *Macon Telegraph* might even become a figure in the narrative. When the *Atlanta Constitution* offered a reward for the capture of Sam Hose and also predicted that he would be burned alive when caught, it not only inserted itself into the proceedings but actually began to manipulate the outcome. Occasionally, however, the awful facts could at least temporarily overwhelm the narrative, as happens, I argue, with Daniel, whose correspondence becomes increasingly conflicted and accusatory of the white community when he experiences firsthand the horror of the public burning.

Second, I have attempted to place these events in the context of their world, not to defend or excuse but in some way to make them understandable. It is all too easy to remove ourselves from the possibilities of these actions, to view them as so aberrant, so linked to a particular time and place, as to be unthreatening to us today. Obviously, I take a dimmer view. That these were some of our ancestors, perhaps our direct ancestors in a lineage that is only a couple of generations removed, may make for some difficulty, but what is more challenging is to see the complexities, to recognize that sensitive, thoughtful, spiritual people can do awful things and can justify them with the frailest of excuses. In his book *Imagined Communities*, Benedict Anderson examines the idea of nationality or a national identity that may have little to do with borders or geography. Anderson credits newspapers as essential to the construction of these fanciful communities, the daily reading of them as an "extraordinary mass ceremony" performed by "communicant[s]" throughout the extended community at more or less the same time each day. He quotes Hegel's observation that newspapers "serve modern man as a substitute for morning prayers."[7] So, what would be the "imagined" world of this southern "nation" as told by its newspapers to readers throughout the region? During the first months of 1899, in this part of west Georgia, it would be one of anxiety and fear, a land feeling beset without and within. Having experienced defeat and gone through an insulting (to most whites) occupation and Reconstruction, the South was in the process of redefining itself as it anticipated the new century, but the continued animosity it felt toward the North, even as it grudgingly joined forces with it, was constantly played out in the daily papers. Southern voices simultaneously rebuffed or rejected northern admonitions and yet sometimes sought northern approval. When a man from Pennsylvania joined in the burning of Sam Hose, carrying the kerosene that ignited the pyre, southern papers underscored this point. They insisted that once a northerner truly understood what it meant to live in the South, to experience on a daily basis the racial threat under which the white community perceived itself as suffering, then that northerner would behave just as a southerner might. When the *New York Herald* sent its correspondent Dr. George Hepworth to Georgia to investigate the Hose lynching, his sympathetic reports (he abhorred lynching but accepted as fact the fears that supported the practice) were taken as further justification. But in general the North simply did not understand, southern papers told their readers, and it had no right to criticize or propose solutions until it did. It was this hypocrisy of the North that so infuriated southerners, that put southern noses so out of joint.

What the North didn't understand, the papers reminded their readers, was that the white South was under siege. Race war was in the air at the end of the century, in part because the United States was deeply engaged in an imperialist and blatantly racist conflict in Cuba and the Philippines in which the white man's obligation to subdue and rule people of color was a primary motivation and justification. But rumors of local black rebellion here at home were also constantly reported in the daily papers. These stories stood juxtaposed, it must be said, to condescending, often sentimental, or viciously comic representations of blacks, whether in Joel Chandler Harris's "Uncle Remus" tales that ran in the Sunday *Atlanta Constitution* or in amused reflections on black behavior recorded in letters to the paper and sententious editorial observations and cartoonish illustrations of blacks in various modes of outlandish dress. Blacks were a primary source of hilarity for white readers, especially in their speech, which was often recorded in exaggerated eye dialect even in ostensibly serious news items. Reporters indulged themselves and their white readers in these representations, just as they would fall back on melodrama and theatricality in presenting noble white southern speech and action. At the same time, the specter of black threat also filled the pages, the fear that beneath these smiling, joking, humble, childlike performances the brute was lurking. One must be constantly alert, the papers told their readers, and prepared to take action. Blacks were becoming increasingly assertive in public, but who could imagine what they were further doing in secret, plotting, scheming, preparing for who knew what outrage? Just as the country was obligated to impose white rule on the world, so this community of white southerners had to be vigilant and ready to protect social order in their own region.

My third objective is to examine how different groups did and have continued to appropriate Sam Hose for their own purposes and thus have created such vastly divergent versions of the man. Even before his death, Sam Hose was physically taken apart, ears and digits exchanged, sold, distributed as commodities. Other pieces of his body, scraps of his clothes, splinters from the tree to which he was chained, links of the chain itself, all had commercial value. As is often noted, his knuckles were displayed in a storefront window as a sales promotion within twenty-four hours of his death. These relics soon gained a more symbolic power, and for years they were—and perhaps still are—kept by some as fetishes that emblematize the force of the mob. In this way, Sam Hose physically took up residence in individual homes throughout the communities of Newnan and Palmetto and Griffin. Although the specifics of the events were soon erased from official local history, the stories, like the relics, lasted, translated into other forms of narrative, sometimes subversively so. Sam Hose became a figure that amused and frightened children both white and black, something uncanny, inspiring tales that grew separate from the actual facts of his life and death. Although a kind of local social propriety, engendered in part by a respect for the Cranford family, soon made it inappropriate to discuss openly Sam Hose's assumed crimes or his death, elements of both found their way into such popular works as Thomas Dixon's *The Leopard's Spots* and from there to D. W. Griffith's *The Birth of a Nation*; possibly into Margaret Mitchell's *Gone with the Wind* and Erskine Caldwell's lynching stories such as "Saturday Afternoon," "Kneel to the Rising Sun," and *Trouble in July*, and most definitely in Michael Harper's "Dear John, Dear Coltrane," his poetic tribute to the jazz artist John Coltrane in which Harper conflates Coltrane and Hose into a mythic vision of black martyrdom. The resurgence of scholarship on lynching has also resurrected Sam Hose, making his horrendous death a centerpiece illustration of the awful extravagance of mob violence while often oversimplifying both him and the circumstances surrounding his execution. This renewed attention has recently forced the local community to face its history and its responsibility, and the book ends with a portrait of a place still trying to reconcile itself, a century later, to its past.

I owe debts to many people for their help and support in the writing of this book. In Newnan, Winston Skinner has guided me in invaluable ways and has shared his knowledge of the region and its people without stint. I am also grateful to those in Newnan and Palmetto who have spoken to me about difficult, unpleasant, and often personal subjects, most specifically Carole Harper, Robert Wood, and John Herbert Cranford and members of the Cranford family. Among my colleagues, I would like to acknowledge Susan Donaldson and Noel Polk, both of whom have read and commented on versions of this work. John Inscoe has supported this project almost from the beginning, as has Nancy Grayson, who has shepherded me along the way and shown great patience during those periods of fretful inactivity. My thanks also to project manager Jennifer Reichlin and copyeditor Barb Wojhoski for their careful work on the manuscript. The advice of all these people has been invaluable. I have also asked my friends Peter Josyph, Robert Morgan, and Jerry Williamson to read this work at different times in its development; their responses encouraged me to continue when I wondered what in the world I was doing.

It is impossible to list all my other colleagues with whom I have, sometimes obsessively, discussed this material, but among them would be Dawn Trouard (always the voice of skepticism, thank you very much), Jay Watson, Michael Zeitlin, and Tom and Pearl McHaney, good friends all. From the English department at Appalachian State University, I have made a captive audience of my best friends and long-time companions Emory Maiden, Tom Mc Laughlin, and Gene Miller. Susan Staub has often put down her own work to let me rehearse aloud some narrative, examine some approach, and for that I am tremendously grateful. Fred Hay and Sandy Ballard most generously provided me with information on lynching that they came across in the pursuit of their own studies. I also offer my appreciation to the students in my graduate class The Literature of Lynching, taught in spring 2006. They helped me reconsider a number of my assumptions and did what good graduate students do: made the class much more challenging than I had expected. My thanks, then, to Connie Bracewell, Robert Canipe, Lori Beth DeHertogh, Ron Funderburke, Andy Hill, Kathryn Langston, Audrey McCloskey, Brad Prestwood, Paul Robertson, Sarah Vanover, Kyle Warner, and Kevin Young. I also value the support of my department and of the two chairs who served during this time: Dave Haney and Jeanne Dubino. A research grant from ASU Graduate Studies and Research helped to underwrite several of my trips to Georgia, and the exceptional library services provided by Georgie Donovan and my former student Dianna Johnson, who has been a lifesaver more than once, were invaluable. It is a pleasure to work with such professionals.

I have also drawn heavily on other relationships during the writing of this book. I have renewed contact with old friends with whom I grew up and from whom I have recovered a sense of time and place that I had forgotten. I thank Dick Austin, Steve Boswell, Bill Martin (who gave me a legal term that I forgot to use), and John Strain (who provided the stunning anecdote about "Sam Hose's knuckles") for their influence and long-lasting friendship. I would also like to express my respect and admiration for Mrs. Jane Strain, historian of Hogansville and Troup County, Georgia. My sister and I spent a remarkable morning visiting her in the summer of 2006, and in that brief time I realized how much fragile history resides in a select number of special people and what a treasure these people—exemplified by Mrs. Strain—are.

While in Georgia, I have discussed my ideas, shared my findings, and questioned my conclusions with my sister, Ellen, and my brothers, Richard and Frank. They have kept me grounded. Finally, I would like to thank my wife, Ellen, and our children, Matthew and Elizabeth. Ellen's advice and support, and her understanding as the years passed, have been very important to me. She knew this project was something that, in terms of career, I did not need to do and probably was foolish to attempt, but she also gave me the encouragement to consider it, to try it, and then to finish it—this while following her own demanding and productive career at East Carolina University. Both of our children read versions of the work, offered insightful suggestions or recommended revisions, kept up with its progress, showed enthusiasm for my enthusiasm. That they would take the time to do this is more satisfying to me than any other aspect of the experience.

The title of this book, *What Virtue There Is in Fire*, comes from a particularly odious pro-lynching publication describing the torture-death of Henry Smith in Paris, Texas. A few readers have expressed consternation that I have used it because of its source and because it might be interpreted as somehow suggesting that there could, indeed, be "virtue" in burning someone to death. I, too, find it a vicious and appalling phrase, and I trust that most will realize I am using it to shock and to condemn. If it represents a failure of sensitivity, I accept the criticism, acknowledging that the subject matter of this book is and must be an affront to us all.

Chapter One

War Fantasies

Within a twenty-four-hour period covering April 12 and 13, 1899, two unrelated killings took place within twenty-five miles of each other in the state of Georgia. On the evening of Wednesday, April 12, just outside the small community of Palmetto, Sam Hose slew his white employer Alfred Cranford by striking him on the head with an ax. He then fled, setting in motion a massive manhunt that would eventually culminate in one of the first spectacle lynchings in the nation.

The following night, near the town of Woolsey, in neighboring Fayette County, George W. Kerlin, a well-known and highly respected white farmer, a deacon and Sunday-school teacher in his Baptist church, a "through and through gentleman," took a young woman named Pearl Knott to the banks of the Flint River, shot her in the forehead, and then sank her body using axes and plows as weight. Five days later, two men fishing in the Flint snagged and brought up her corpse. After Kerlin was arrested, word spread that the girl had been pregnant, presumably by Kerlin himself. The *Atlanta Constitution*, employing its usual hyperbole, proclaimed the murder "one of the most revolting in the criminal record of the state."[1] It was a scandalous, shameful crime, to be sure, but in comparison to the horrific deeds by that time being attributed to black Sam Hose, Kerlin's actions could seem almost understandable. People were upset and repulsed by Kerlin's "demented" behavior, but they were terrified by Hose, who was quickly made into a demon, a monster of incredible depravity.

Kerlin had been only recently arrested when Sam Hose was finally hunted down and brought to Newnan, Georgia. While Kerlin was housed in Atlanta, in the Fulton County jail known as the Tower, to await trial, the crowd that met the train carrying Hose was intent on its own brand of justice, one that later apologists thought best fit the brutal nature of his deeds. On the night of Sunday, April 23, after Sam Hose had been mocked, marched, beaten, stabbed, mutilated, and burned to death by the mob, Georgia governor Allen D. Candler sent the Fifth Regiment of the Georgia militia to the Tower to protect George Kerlin, something he had chosen not to do for Sam Hose earlier in the day, even though he had been notified of Hose's capture and the crowd's illegal intent. The governor feared that people returning to Atlanta from Newnan, some of them carrying spoils and human remains from the execution, might in their enthusiasm and excitement attempt to seize and lynch Kerlin as well. The *Athens Weekly Banner* later speciously editorialized in defending Hose's lynching: "This punishment is not directed against the negro in particular. . . . If the same mob could have secured the seducer and murderer of Pearl Knott they would have tied him to the same stake with Sam Hose and sent them to a warmer climate together."[2]

But they did not. Instead, after Sam Hose was dead, these Georgians extended their anger not to George Kerlin but to other black men, known and unknown, who also suffered abuse and death before the night was over. Kerlin, protected, was eventually accorded a trial in keeping with the law, defended by Thomas E. Watson himself, the prominent politician and Populist Party leader.[3] Although Kerlin's crime was clearly premeditated, he was allowed to make a plea for mercy, a "Rambling Talk of Half an Hour," before the jury sentenced him to life imprisonment.[4] By this time, Sam Hose, Elijah Strickland, and other black victims of this "lynch holiday" were dead and gone, although not, as many would have hoped, totally forgotten.

Obviously, George Kerlin was fortunate to be a respected white man in Georgia when he was arrested for the murder of Pearl Knott. He had the protection of the legal system, and Tom Watson was able to reason with the jury of Kerlin's peers—white men all—and secure his life.[5] It could easily have gone otherwise. Georgia freely practiced capital punishment—death by hanging—and accounts of executions of both whites and blacks made for sensational and entertaining reading in the daily newspapers. An example that held the public's attention in Georgia during the first months of 1899 was the hanging of Robert Lewis, a white construction worker who in July of the previous year had shot and killed the foreman of his work crew on the streets of downtown Atlanta. Lewis had been found guilty at trial despite serious questions concerning his sanity, and he went to the gallows on March 15. The *Atlanta Constitution* followed in lurid and excruciating detail the horror of his final days as he awaited execution: his lawyers' frantic appeals, his wife's pathetic personal plea to the governor for clemency, Lewis's growing terror of death and his howling collapse in the cell as he anticipated the rope, his frantic attempts to avoid the noose as it was placed around his neck and to delay the moment with pathetic last minute requests, even the final disposal of his body in potter's field.[6] These articles provided fascinated readers with all the macabre information they could have hoped for, including the crowning irony that Lewis, while working on the construction crew, had helped to build the very scaffold on which he died.

Despite the unseemly relish that fueled these articles, they provide an extended description of the legal process surrounding death by hanging, including legal procedures, prison rituals, and the overall treatment of the condemned in Georgia at the end of the nineteenth century. The electric chair had been in use since 1890, when William Kemmler was the first human intentionally put to death by electrocution. This occurred in New York, but many other states maintained that hanging was a more humane form of capital punishment (Kemmler's execution had been a shameful, appalling botch), and Georgia continued legal execution by hanging until 1924, when the electric chair was finally employed.[7] Although poor Robert Lewis, unlike George Kerlin, was deemed unworthy of mercy, and his death sentence was ultimately carried out in accordance with the law, he was nevertheless given every opportunity for appropriate redress, and the execution itself was done in a respectful, professional, and even kindly manner.

But what of the accused who were outside the system? How did justice work for the disaffiliated? Certainly many blacks were also processed through the existing legal system and executed following the rules of law. But since blacks could not serve on juries, and white juries and judges routinely gave harsher sentences to blacks than to whites, the justice system for blacks was often a sham and sometimes a vicious travesty. And there was also that shadow justice that operated outside the law, a form of mobocracy with its own rules and rituals that substituted for legal proceedings. "If the lawful authorities failed to measure up to community demands, the initiative for law enforcement could easily pass into the hands of private citizens," Jacquelyn Dowd Hall wrote in her pioneering study of Jessie Daniel Ames's campaign against lynching, and although the victims of this parallel justice could occasionally include whites, it most often was used as a form of racial intimidation and control.[8] And that societal demand for intimidation and control allowed this form of enforcement to employ atrocities that the official legal system would never permit. Indeed, the more horrible the punishment, its adherents would argue, the greater its effectiveness.

The French philosopher Michel Foucault examined "The Spectacle of the Scaffold" in his study *Discipline and Punish*, in which he discussed the role of torture, of *supplice*, in corporal punishment, observing: "Torture is a technique; it is not an extreme expression of lawless rage." To be effective, pain must be controlled, "measured," and "calculated," else the subject of the torture would likely die before the full effect of the punishment could be experienced, and the subject's premature death would defeat the purpose for both the subject and, in cases of public executions, the audience. The "gravity" of a crime determined the profundity of the pain. A crazed mob bent only on quick, savage death demeaned both the seriousness of the crime and the purpose of the punishment itself. Certain crimes demanded greater degrees of pain and thus careful management of the torture. The "duration of the death agony" not only prolonged the audience's participation in this communal action but validated its cruelty. As Foucault summarized, "The very excess of the violence employed is one of the elements of its glory: the fact that the guilty man should moan and cry out under the blows is not a shameful side-effect, it is the very ceremonial of justice being expressed in all its force."[9]

Sociologist David Garland, in his essay "Penal Excess and Surplus Meaning: Public Torture Lynchings in Twentieth-Century America," argues that one way to understand the possibility of these "public torture lynchings" is to see them as "collective criminal punishments," "staged public events with a conventionally understood form, a recurring sequence of actions, and an accompanying normative discourse" that provided a "preferred alternative" to "'official' justice." While they were obviously an audacious form of "race repression," they also reflected the southern white community's "anxieties about status, authority, and personal security." Thus, they served a communal function that the courts, with their pretense of fairness and objectivity, could not provide. Indeed, according to Garland, "this self-consciously excessive retributive ritual ('penal excess') was a strategic means adopted by political actors to communicate meanings and sentiments that went well beyond the bounds of criminal justice in their intended significance ('surplus meaning')."[10]

It is within this context that we must approach the violent Georgia spring of 1899. In the early hours of March 16, two days after Robert Lewis was legally hanged in the Fulton County Tower, nine black men, accused of arson and attempted assassination and therefore considered terrorists by the local white community, were lined up against a wall in a stone warehouse in the middle of Palmetto, Georgia, some twenty miles southwest of Atlanta, and shot down by a crowd of self-appointed vigilantes. Five weeks later, Sam Hose was tortured, castrated, and burned alive just outside nearby Newnan. Within hours of Hose's death, another black man, Elijah Strickland, was strangled repeatedly by a crowd, again in Palmetto, which demanded a confession that he steadfastly refused to give, then was indifferently mutilated and left hanging by his neck from the limb of a persimmon tree until he also was dead, a note affixed to his chest warning other blacks in the area to watch their actions. These incidents occurred in the larger context of extreme racial unrest that beset not only the state of Georgia but the country at large.

While this is primarily the story of three small Georgia towns—Newnan, Palmetto, and Griffin—it is also the story of a region and, ultimately, of a nation. Localized race issues were often interpreted through and compared to larger national and international events, which were themselves motivated by imperialist and racist assumptions of white Christian superiority. In April 1898, the United States, led by Republican president William McKinley, had declared war on Spain, with Cuba and the Philippine Islands as primary sites of confrontation. After relatively quick U.S. victories, Spain had sued for peace. Shortly thereafter, the country took control of Spain's colonies in Guam, Puerto Rico, and the Philippines. The "enemy" now became the Filipino rebels, led by Emilio Aguinaldo, who declared the islands' independence from the United States through the formation of the Philippine Republic on January 23, 1899. These Filipino fighters were often portrayed in overtly racist fashion as primitive blacks, and defenders of the racial status quo in the southern United States would argue that local actions simply reflected what the nation was doing on a larger scale. A *Washington Post* political cartoon typical of the time showed a determined Uncle Sam, switch in hand, chasing a small, bushy-haired, barefoot, grass-skirt-clad, rifle-wielding native through the reeds and palm trees while Europe watched in detached amusement from a farther shore. "Not in Position to Give Up the Chase," the caption read.[11]

When the United States first entered the Spanish-American War, it had only a small regular army, organized largely for peacetime activities. By the time conflict had spread to the Philippines, this army was already stretched thin. Therefore, most of the actual fighting was being done by state militias, made up of "volunteer citizen soldiers." As Brian McAllister Linn described it in his history of the Philippine War,

> The declaration of war with Spain . . . and the subsequent call-up of Volunteers [were] greeted in most communities with an enthusiasm that appears almost unbelievable a century later. A decade of economic convulsion and social turmoil had left many eager for any noble cause that would take the nation's mind off its internal problems. The Yellow Press portrayed Spain as fanatical, merciless, wicked, and corrupt, and it reinforced American views of their nation's role as the great liberator, destined to bring freedom and civilization to the oppressed people of the world.[12]

These troops were sometimes led by combat veterans, northern and southern, from the Civil War. As Linn notes, "Indeed, the Civil War was a powerful inspiration for young Americans determined to prove they had the courage and manliness of their fathers."[13] Many southerners especially saw this overall conflict as an extension of the great War between the States, but one in which the enemies were not northern brothers but clearly identified racial "others" whose defeat could almost be seen as a vindication of earlier southern beliefs.

While these external conflicts were predicated on religious, imperialist, and racist tenets, they also revealed a set of national anxieties that beset the United States and other Western countries between the 1870s and the beginning of the First World War. The British literary scholar I. F. Clarke has examined at length these uncertainties as expressed in frightening "invasion" stories that described these nations as threatened or overrun by insidious and merciless enemies. In England, the invading force was most often another Western nation like Germany (*The Battle of Dorking* [1871]) or France (*Pro Patria* [1901]), although H. G. Wells, in 1898, could extend these fears to Mars in *The War of the Worlds*. As Clarke observes:

> Most of the hundreds of imaginary wars that appeared between 1871 and 1914 presented idealized visions of the heroic nation triumphant over all enemies and set for ever on a course to increasing power and prosperity. Moreover, even on those occasions when authors chose to describe the defeat of their nations, the forecasts of the coming disaster fell into the pattern of the admonitory terrors of the dystopias, since the propagandists sought to achieve their objectives of political or military reform by demonstrating the catastrophic consequences of wrong principles and chronic national failings. For better or for worse, in war or in peace and in hope or in fear, the authors of all these stories about the future respond to the problems and possibilities of their society.[14]

Although Clarke concentrates on British invasion stories, he notes a similar history of predicted or imaginary wars in American fiction of the nineteenth and early twentieth centuries. Among the earliest of them is Edmund Ruffin's *Anticipations of the Future*, which, published in 1860, anticipated the American Civil War, which would begin the next year. In this novel, Ruffin, a Virginian, predicts the South's seceding from the Union because of slavery. In the one-year war that follows, Ruffin imagines that the North employs such "means of war" as blockades, invasion, and the encouragement of "servile insurrections." Nevertheless, as Clarke summarizes, this "hypothetical history demonstrates the justice of the Southern cause, and in the manner of so many of these projections an ideal South emerges from a just war."[15]

H. Bruce Franklin, in his study *War Stars: The Superweapon and the American Imagination*, explores in greater detail American "war fantasies" near the turn of the century. Although many of these stories, like their British counterparts, pictured invasions from without, especially in the form of "yellow peril" literature that imagined the United States overrun by Chinese or Japanese invaders, Franklin also explores the "black peril" subgenre that both frightened and entertained by imagining an "invasion from within." He gives as an example a novel by King Wallace titled *The Next War: A Prediction* (1892), in which eight million southern "Africans" join forces with twelve million "Mulattoes, Quadroons and Octoroons" to accomplish the extermination of the white race. These "four divisions" are finally not only defeated but eradicated, resulting in a thorough removal of the black race from southern soil. "Cleansed of its darker population, America becomes a more wholesome society, reaping unanticipated benefits," Franklin summarizes. In William Ward Crane's story "The Year 1899," published in 1893, the racial threat against whites is global when "a grand alliance of Asians, Africans, and nonwhite Americans," including Native Americans, begins a war seeking total white annihilation.[16]

Franklin further notes that the beginning of the Spanish-American War in 1898 inspired several novels published in that very year that celebrated the white imperialist "Anglo-Saxon" triumph over lesser races. S. W. Odell's *The Last War: Or, The Triumph of the English Tongue* is set in "the mid-twenty-sixth century," at which time the English-speaking peoples, who have neared "human perfection," engage in a final, decisive battle with Russian-Asian forces led by the czar. In Benjamin Rush Davenport's *Anglo-Saxons, Onward! A Romance of the Future*, the Spanish-American War is seen as the beginning of a global war in which the United States joins with Great Britain and achieves domination over the world. Stanley Waterloo's *Armageddon* also postulates the final triumph of the Anglo-Saxon race and the English language.[17]

The point here is that fear of and fascination with race wars were ingrained in the public imagination at the end of the nineteenth century. Such suspicions of black insurrection strike us today as either shameless fearmongering or paranoid racist ranting. Indeed, whites instigated most of the actual violent conflicts in an effort to assert social control. For example, on November 10, 1898, the white citizens of Wilmington, North Carolina, killed as many as sixty blacks, destroyed black establishments, including the leading black newspaper office, and seized control of the city government, ousting legally elected officials. The Wilmington Race Riot Commission, established in 2000 by the North Carolina General Assembly, observed in its 2006 report that "the violence of 1898 was a conspiracy of a white elite that used intimidation and force to replace a duly elected local government, that people lost their lives, livelihoods, and were banished from their homes without due process of law; and that government at all levels failed to protect its citizens."[18]

In March 1899, at approximately the same time that the Palmetto shootings occurred, there were reports that a "race war" had broken out in Little River

County, Arkansas, after a "carefully laid" black "plot" to kill whites had been revealed. Twenty-three blacks were named as insurrectionists, and the leader, identified as General Duckett, was said to have murdered a man named James Stockton as the inauguration of a "General Massacre of Whites." Duckett and six other "ringleaders" were quickly captured and hanged, but the subsequent murders of other accused participants continued for several days. The *Macon Telegraph* reported, "The work of wiping out the entire list continues without relaxation. All implicated in the plot are known and parties of white men varying in numbers from twenty-five to fifty are scouring the country for them. Whenever one is found he is quickly strung up and his body perforated with bullets."[19] The *Newnan (Georgia) Herald and Advertiser*, which told its readers that Arkansas whites had "positive proof" that Duckett and his followers "had planned a race war," further quoted the coroner's report on one of the victims. "He was frozen to death; his head, however, had a hole in it, and his neck was broken."[20] The *Macon Telegraph* felt it necessary to explain, "The verdict is regarded as a gruesome joke," but the attitude expressed indicated a kind of white glee in eradicating unruly blacks.[21] As these and subsequent examples like the Atlanta race riot of 1906 show, black "rebellion" usually resulted in the indiscriminate killing and violent subjugation of the blacks themselves.[22]

By 1899, southern concern over potential race war had found another source of worry in the number of black militia now stationed in the South. Some of the regiments organized to fight in Cuba and the Philippines were made up entirely of African Americans, usually but not always led by white officers. Some seven thousand of these volunteers were quartered in southern states. In late 1898, for example, approximately four thousand black soldiers were stationed at Camp Haskell near Macon, Georgia, and stories about the Negro Third North Carolina, the Sixth Virginia, and the Tenth Immunes regiments regularly fed the suspicions of the nearby communities. As Willard B. Gatewood Jr. explained in his study of black militia, Macon businessmen had originally campaigned for the establishment of this military base but had not expected it to be "manned primarily by Negro soldiers. In fact, the concentration of so large a contingent of black troops at Camp Haskell caused fear and alarm among whites, who increasingly viewed themselves as a beleaguered people." As Gatewood notes, "The fears of whites were continually nourished by rumors that the black troops at Camp Haskell planned to invade Macon and 'take over the city.'"[23] White newspapers such as the *Macon Telegraph* regularly carried stories ridiculing the black soldiers and picturing them as comic characters while also warning against their unruliness and the corruptive effect they might have on local blacks.[24]

In truth, many of these soldiers who came from other parts of the country did refuse to follow local traditions or even laws distinguishing between the races. They were determined "not to tolerate insults from whites": in Gatewood's words, they could "insist upon respect for their rights, because they were armed and numerous enough to risk forceful action against those who attempted to enforce 'the ancient, barbaric customs' of the South."[25] For instance, in November 1898, soldiers from the Sixth Virginia chopped down a tree pointed out to them as the "hanging tree" and tore down a sign that read "No Dogs or Niggers Allowed" at a public park. Some demanded service in "white only" saloons and restaurants. Macon authorities had hitched trailers to the regular streetcars to accommodate blacks, but many of these soldiers refused to use them, and there were "a series of disturbances" resulting in the deaths of several black volunteers.[26] These black men in uniforms, armed with guns and trained in their use, gave further credence to fears not only of local violence but ultimately of the possibility of outright race war.

By late 1898, political pressure from the South was so great that the military had decided to muster out these regiments, and in early January 1899, word came to Camp Haskell that its black troops would be paid and discharged.[27] These orders came as a disappointment to many of the soldiers. The Third North Carolina, for example, which was commanded entirely by black officers and was recognized as one of the finest regiments at the camp, requested a delay, in part because its men had little desire to return to their home state. The recent Wilmington riot was still fresh in their minds, and they knew that their state government was even then considering outright disenfranchisement of black voters. As one of their officers put it, "[if we returned to North Carolina] just now, during the sitting of the [Democratic] legislature, they would enact even worse laws than now anticipated. Our very presence on the streets of the different cities would simply inflame them against the entire race."[28] These concerns were well founded, for in February both the North Carolina House and the Senate passed an amendment to the state constitution effectively ending black suffrage in the state.[29]

The mustering out of these black troops produced mixed feelings in the local white communities. The *Atlanta Journal* reported that the commandant at Camp Haskell was "anxious to get the regiments off his hands, as they ha[d] been nothing but a thorn in the side of the first corps since they ha[d] been attached to it," but continued, "Among the citizens a considerable amount of anxiety is felt. There is fear that the members of the regiment, when they are once out from under the military control, may attempt to show their independence and become disorderly."[30] The *Macon Telegraph* bluntly expressed these worries:

> It has always been the case that even where white regiments were mustered out there was more or less hilarity, and which often resulted in trouble, and the people of Macon as a rule are afraid to have all of these darkies turned loose here at once.

However, the article continued,

> Though there is some fear expressed as to the results of turning all of these men loose here, there will be a large amount of money which will be given to them at the time of their discharges spent here for clothing as there are very few of the men who will be willing to wear their uniforms away from here, though it is a natural inclination of the darkey to wear brass buttons and blue clothes. They have become tired of the uniforms now, for they have been under such close guard for the past few months that they are as a rule glad to get out of the service.[31]

Under the mustering-out orders, each soldier was given mileage and ration money and was also compensated for the traditional thirty-day furlough that was part of his service term. Thus, it was estimated that each soldier would have $125–150 in final pay. The idea, then, was to encourage the black soldiers to spend their money as quickly as possible on clothes, liquor, and other goods and then immediately to remove them from the area on special trains.[32] In another effort to control this procedure, the army agreed to release the soldiers by companies, two at a time, spaced over a period of weeks. The first regiments selected were the Third North Carolina and the Sixth Virginia.[33] The *Atlanta Constitution*, like the *Macon Telegraph*, assured its readers that these black troops were anxious to leave the military. "They say that they don't care how they are mustered out. Just so they get out."[34]

Although earlier reports, made before the black troops began to leave Camp Haskell, stated, "Their conduct is proper, and there is no more reason to expect any breach of the peace from them than from any one else," once the men started their journeys home, stories of misbehavior spread through the white papers, quickly developing a set of narrative conventions that was then repeated, with slight variations, for months to come.[35] The Third North Carolina, for example, was a well-trained regiment that, according to Gatewood, had "achieved a degree of efficiency which the ridicule and bombast of the state's white press tended to obscure." The volunteers in this regiment were often reminded that they were examples for others of their race to follow: "Such units were never allowed to forget their special responsibility to perform in a manner that would disprove the notion that Negroes made good soldiers only if commanded by white officers, while at the same time reflecting credit upon all black Americans."[36] Nevertheless, when a train carrying members of the unit left Macon on the afternoon of January 31, 1899, the *Macon Telegraph* reported that "more than half" of the four hundred to five hundred soldiers were "drunk and boisterous," that they had taken over the special train and "soon had things their own way. The soldiers quarreled and fought in the coaches and several of them fired their pistols. Three or four of the coaches were riddled with bullets. There was a caboose on the rear of the train, which had been coupled on as a place of safe retreat for the [white] train crew."[37] The report maintained that these soldiers shot at both whites and blacks on the roads near the tracks as the train carried them away from Macon. By the time they reached Union Station in Atlanta, a squad of policemen was waiting, "pistols and clubs freely shown." Word had come that some soldiers meant to "tear Atlanta up." As the *Atlanta Constitution* continued the story, the black "ring leader" of the group, identified as Charles Greely, leaped from the train as it pulled into the depot and drunkenly confronted the police: "He began to curse and talk about killing somebody before he left the 'damned old town that Sherman burned down,'" the *Constitution* quoted him provocatively. He "resisted" when the police grabbed him, prompting "four or five" other soldiers to come to his aid, at which point "there were as many bloody heads in a very few seconds." Greely was arrested and, the *Constitution* assured its readers, "This produced a quietus on the turbulent Atlanta-demolishing colored troops, and when the four or five bloody heads disappeared into the coaches no other heads showed themselves for a similar reception."[38]

On February 2, another train carrying more companies of the Third North Carolina left Camp Haskell. According to the *Constitution*, these soldiers had read of their comrades' reception and were determined to exact revenge by killing policemen when they arrived: "They will show Atlanta policemen how to make arrests," a telegram sent from Macon to the paper warned. But the primary purpose of this article was again to reassure the paper's white readers that Atlanta could handle any such riotous behavior on the part of black troops. This time, the paper reported, the depot was filled with police and with undercover agents who wore ordinary clothes but were prepared "at a moment's notice to quell any disturbance that might arise." The soldiers were warned to remain orderly, and the article gave a comic example, complete with exaggerated black dialect, of the Atlanta police's success:

> As the train rolled into the depot a negro had his head poked out of a window, and when he saw all the police he cried out:
> "Dis nigger ain't been home sence last May, and I'se gwine ter stay on dis car, fur I sure wants to see my folks."

The other soldiers remained "as quiet as mice," and the only injury reported was a soldier who supposedly had accidentally shot himself in the head as the train was leaving Macon. He was removed from his car and taken to Grady Hospital.[39]

There were occasional reports that white soldiers committed the same sorts of misdeeds attributed to the black companies. The Atlanta Police Reserve was called out on February 3, the day after the North Carolina troops had passed through Union Station, to "restore order" when members of the Fifth Infantry, who had been discharged at nearby Fort McPherson, arrived drunk and shooting their pistols.[40] More seriously, members of the white Second Ohio caused a "melee" at Camp Haskell a week later when they were discharged and then looted the wagons of local merchants who had come to the camp to sell their goods.[41] However, in both cases, the papers clearly identified these rampaging whites as "northern" soldiers. Nevertheless, most accounts of unruly behavior were focused on black soldiers and quickly developed their own folklore, despite arguments that they were often exaggerated or simply untrue. As Capt. Amos Brandt, a white officer who led the Negro Seventh Immunes stationed in Macon, commented after his regiment's return to Iowa,

> Speaking of Georgia, all I want to say is that whenever that state asks anything of our congressmen or senators, I hope they will vote against it. The treatment we received in that state was the most hellish one can imagine. They arrested our men without cause and gave them heavy fines. They lied about our men, perjured themselves to get our money and threatened our second lieutenant with a year on the chain gang for an offense he was not responsible for. Georgia is as black as hell and the city of Macon is a trifle worse.[42]

Throughout the months of February and March 1899, as the mustering out continued, Georgia papers filed repetitive stories detailing the outrageous, sometimes comic, sometimes frightening, behavior of black troops, which forced stalwart white citizens to resort to arms and violence for the protection of their community and the restoration of order.[43] The two most dramatic of these episodes were reported in early March, both dealing with companies of newly discharged black "Immunes." The Immunes were regiments created in 1898 specifically for service in Cuba and the Philippines. According to Gatewood, these units were originally to be made up entirely of blacks from the Deep South, who were considered more likely to be immune to the diseases that had afflicted so many American troops in the tropical climes. They were, however, also judged as more primitive, and thus even more threatening, than their fellow black soldiers in other state militias. While the states could create all-black regiments, at times led by black officers, the War Department held that in the Immune regiments blacks could hold no commission higher than lieutenant. Thus, the Immunes were identified in the white public mind as lower-class blacks without ambition, as more naturally savage, as the "'dregs of negrodom.'"[44]

The first episode involving the Immunes took place in Chattanooga and Nashville following the mustering out of the Eighth Immune regiment at Chickamauga on March 7. In Chattanooga, approximately one hundred of these soldiers were said to have filled the "negro saloons and low dives" of the city, causing "much disorder and rioting." At the depot, other discharged soldiers were reported to have fired indiscriminately in the air and then at houses as the train left, wounding a white car inspector.[45] By the time the train reached Nashville, that depot was filled with "a detail of forty policemen and a number of armed citizens" who went through the cars searching the men and taking their guns. The *Atlanta Constitution* reported, "The negroes who were inclined to resist were toppled over with billies, and some who attempted to draw pistols were severely handled. When both trains had been handled there were thirty or forty very bloody heads."[46]

In this report, the *Constitution* congratulated its state readers that "Negro Troops Wait to Get Out of Georgia to Kick Up," but on the day this article appeared—Wednesday, March 8—a similar scene took place in Griffin, Georgia, a town that considered itself "hard on race" and would very soon play a major role in the lynching of Sam Hose. The story as reported in state papers followed the same outline as the narrative of the Eighth Immunes in Tennessee, repeating many of the same details in similar language. Now the soldiers were members of the Tenth Immunes, discharged at Camp Haskell. The first group that came through Griffin in the middle of the day was reported to be "filled up on cheap whiskey . . . firing their pistols and yelling like Indians." The *Constitution* explained that Griffin was taken entirely by surprise. "Over two hundred shots were fired and the police were powerless to resist. The city was at the mercy of the howling mob, who kept up a fusillade of shots until they were carried beyond the city limits." The *Griffin Daily News and Sun* reported that "the discharged soldiers . . . were firing their pistols from car windows at men, women, children, cows, hogs, cattle, and chickens." As the city waited for the arrival of other transports, Griffin mayor W. D. Davis telephoned Georgia governor Candler for permission to order out the town militia, known as the Griffin Rifles. When Candler asked for time to discuss the situation with "military authorities," Davis acted "on his own responsibility" since the second train was now on its way. He ordered Lt. M. J. Daniels to take charge. Each member of the Rifles was given five rounds; the mayor also deputized "over one hundred citizens to assist the officers in preserving the peace and protecting the city from a repetition of such outrageous behavior on the part of the soldiers." When the second train arrived just after 5:00 p.m., it was met at the Griffin station by a large crowd of armed men, both militia and civilians. "The negroes were awed and with a few exceptions were as docile as lambs. Those who proved the exception received cracked heads, and but for the failure of a cartridge to explode one of them would have received a bullet in the brain." According to reports, as the train left the depot and the soldiers considered themselves out of range, they again began firing their pistols. "At the first shot a volley was poured into the retreating train by the infuriated citizens and it is known that one negro at least was shot. It was learned later that a [white] brakeman, George Agee, was [also] seriously shot." Agee died later that night in Atlanta.[47]

The next day, March 9, the *Griffin Morning Call* claimed, "Not since the civil war has Griffin seen such exciting times as was witnessed yesterday."[48] The *Griffin Daily News and Sun*, under the editorship of Douglas Glessner, an irascible figure who would become a prominent provocateur in the events to follow, carried on its front page a more elaborate account of this incident. As was so often the case, the article offered a sensational version of the event that emphasized the stalwart heroics of the white citizenry and the comic foolishness of the black soldiers. Titled "What City This Is," the report included a supposed exchange between one soldier and an armed keeper of the peace.

> "What city is this, boss?" was the respectful question of one of Uncle Sam's experiments in the ways of a negro soldier yesterday afternoon, as the train stopped here.
>
> "Griffin," was the reply of the quiet citizen with a Winchester.
>
> "I thought it must be," answered Corporal Cuffy, as he ducked his head in and closed the window.
>
> There is nothing that the true Griffinite delights in more than to give instructions to all sojourners in her midst, and if two sections of the 10th Immune Regiment did not learn a lesson here yesterday it was only because Booker Washington is mistaken in the idea that his race is capable of the most rudimentary instruction.

Following the now-established narrative, the paper reported that, as the second train stopped at the station, a "big negro with a gun at his shoulder walked out upon the platform with an oath and proposed to clean up the town. But very much to his surprise he found it was already a clean town."

> "Get back into that car at once!" came from a dozen throats, with the click of as many revolvers, one or two sounds being those of snaps that missed fire. And he got, and turned over his comrades behind him in getting.

As this train left, "the expected happened": the black soldiers ("insatiable brutes") began to shoot their weapons, and the white citizens returned their fire, at which time the brakeman Agee was hit. When the third train arrived with the last of the Immunes, the citizenry immediately took over the cars, walking through and imposing order on the men, who, having been warned, now offered no resistance.[49]

Over the next few days, the Griffin incident was debated in local and state papers. One of the white officers of the Tenth Immunes, Lt. Col. Charles Withrow, wrote Governor Candler to object to his men's treatment in Griffin, giving quite a different description of the event. It was a "cowardly, dastardly and entirely unnecessary attack," he maintained.

When our train reached Griffin we found soldiers lined up on both sides of the track under arms. When we inquired the cause, we were told that another train had preceded us several hours before and had fired pistols, and that they wanted to protect themselves. Not a shot was fired while we were in Griffin at the station, and our men were perfectly orderly. After the train started and the rear end of it was about two hundred yards from where soldiers were standing, a pistol was fired by some one at the head of the train. Immediately the soldiers opened fire upon the sleeping car which contained my officers and their wives. G. L. Agee, the rear brakeman, was standing in plain sight of the soldiers at the rear door of the rear car, and he is dangerously, if not fatally wounded. Four ladies were seated at the windows of the car fired upon, and were in plain sight of the men a minute before they fired.

Withrow ended with an angry rebuke to the governor and the men of Griffin. "We are an orderly body of men, peaceably making our way home, and we demand protection from the assaults of cowards who disgrace the uniform of your state and demonstrate their total unfitness to bear your commissions and your arms. Men never fire on women." Governor Candler responded to Withrow's "imperious and ill-natured" letter by noting that Withrow himself "admits that this first shot was fired by one of his own men, then the fire was returned." He concluded, "The occurrence was deplorable, but those disorderly negro soldiers alone are responsible for it."[50]

Withrow's account was soon confirmed by Col. Charles Jones, commander of the regiment, in a statement made to a reporter in Raleigh, North Carolina, after the train had safely left Georgia. Repeating much of what Withrow had maintained, Jones insisted that his men "were full of good spirits and had no intention to harm any one," insisting, "No shots were fired when we went into the town of Griffin." He admitted that as the train left shots did come from the front of the train but were fired only in celebration. The Griffin militia then sent a volley into the rear car, fatally wounding Agee, the brakeman. He also repeated, "As the officers' car passed a body of the militia, a volley was fired into it, notwithstanding the fact that four ladies were at the windows." Jones then issued his own denunciation:

> The action of the militia in Griffin was the most cowardly that I have ever seen human beings guilty of. Had they fired into the car from which the one shot was fired, it would have been bad enough, but to fire a volley into a car, when the officer who had charge of the men who fired the volley knew there were ladies in the car who were unable to protect themselves and who had not been guilty of any breach of law, was beneath men.

In response, Griffin mayor Davis reasserted that the town's militia had acted "in a manner that was above reproach," and Lieutenant Daniels, the commander of the Griffin Rifles, insisted that his men had merely "done their duty." "Upon the departure of the train the negro troops fired several volleys directly at the citizens and military. Their fire was not returned by my men, but the citizens did return the fire. I had given positive orders to my men not to fire and they most positively did not."[51]

Although both the *Constitution* and the *Macon Telegraph* presented both sides of this incident, on March 10 the Atlanta paper made clear its understanding of the events. "Griffin Men Did Their Duty in Checking Drunken Negroes," the headline read, and any pretense of objectivity was forgotten. Withrow now became the chief target of the paper's freewheeling attack.

> Withrow's statement was contained in a letter he wrote Governor Candler, asking for protection for himself and the black desperadoes whom he was accompanying to North Carolina. As long as the negroes were allowed to fire their guns in every village they passed through, shooting down innocent men and endangering the lives of women and children, Withrow sets [*sic*] quietly in his car surrounded by his negro officers and their wives.
>
> But when the law-abiding citizens of Griffin—forced by desperate circumstances to use desperate means—rise in righteous indignation and stop the lawlessness of these half-drunken fiends, the craven-hearted lieutenant colonel pleads to the governor for protection—and his petition is but a fabrication of lies. . . .
>
> It was not the drunken negroes under the command of Withrow that needed protection, but the women and children of Griffin, and they got it.

The article then quoted Professor Charles M. Neel, "one of the most conservative citizens of Griffin," who again challenged Withrow's account and concluded, "Had Colonel Withrow been a very brave man he would have been more conspicuous at the depot and at the points of danger. If he had a proper regard for the safety of his family, he would not have placed them in the rear of a train of drunken negroes who amused themselves shooting at the homes and persons of innocent Georgians."[52] Withrow finally took his protest to the U.S. assistant secretary of war, but the War Department insisted that, since the men were volunteers and had been discharged when the incident occurred, it had no authority to pursue the case.[53]

In March, after most of the black troops had been discharged and returned home, the War Department did finally speak out, explaining that these now common reports of black soldiers' misconduct rarely had basis in truth and that constantly having to issue denials had become a "burden" to the department.[54] By this time such a denial was largely beside the point, but the *Macon Telegraph* nevertheless ran an editorial commenting on the "experiment" of enlisting black men as soldiers. While acknowledging that "the negro ha[d] not disappointed those who [knew] him and [understood] him," the paper argued that his "instincts are apt to lead the mass of ignorant negroes to lawlessness and defiance of the simplest rules of society." The paper concluded, "Is it wise then to put guns in the hands of ignorant, lawless men? The proposition was absurd and illogical from the start. If the government had consulted those who understand the average negro best, it would never have made the mistake. . . . An individual with such a nature is the best citizen when he is least armed."[55]

Although these stories emphasized a surface confidence in the white southerner's ability to control unruly blacks, they also reflected the siege mentality and sense of victimization these same white southerners affected. They claimed that while the country was at war abroad against what were perceived as barbaric and primitive peoples of other races, the threat of another, undeclared war—a race war of outright terrorism played by no standard rules of engagement—threatened them in their very towns and homes. A *Baltimore Sun* editorial, "A New Crop of Northern Slanderers," clearly expressed these anxieties. Referencing the race riot—the "white revolution"—in Wilmington, the editorial spoke of the "bitter hostility" and "savage desire" of "the negro" against "Southern white people" that "rendered the situation at Wilmington intolerable and made revolution a necessity." The "heroic measures" of the whites were demanded to regain control of blacks, who were not yet ready for freedom and responsibility. The *Sun* continued:

> The false teachings of the past thirty years has done infinitely more moral harm to the negro than all the generations of slavery through which he has passed. Slavery found him a savage, and in multitudes of cases made him a Christian, and in many instances gave him the refinement and good form which were developed even in dependents of the high social standards of the old South. The political education which he has received from New England sources since emancipation has confused his brain, perverted his heart and corrupted his manners, and instead of really progressing, there is danger, under the baneful influence of the morbid and unprincipled guidance to which he has been exposed, that he may revert to the original type from which slavery rescued him, except that this renaissance of barbarism in him will be accompanied with the vices of civilization, and the power for mischief which civilization confers upon those who are in it, but not of it.
>
> If the negro is to avoid this danger and develop into a higher manhood and citizenship, he must free himself from the evil influences and teachings under which he has

been degenerating since the war. As long as he suffers himself to be abused by bad counsel and kept in a false attitude toward the Southern white people, just so long will he continue to retrograde in character and respectability.[56]

This editorial was reprinted by the *Newnan Herald and Advertiser* on December 2, 1898. It told the white people of Newnan what they wanted to hear. Although Baltimore was essentially a southern town, it was also located outside the Deep South, and its statement gave support to those who argued that they were in the middle of an undeclared but increasingly brutal racial conflict. The next four months would witness more acts of "black insurrection," leading up to the spectacular convulsion that would occur on the afternoon and evening of Sunday, April 23, when the people of Newnan, Griffin, Palmetto, and other nearby locales would join forces to purge their communities of this insidious menace once and for all.

Chapter Two

Lynch Sunday

In the May 5 edition of the *Newnan Herald and Advertiser*, which appeared almost two weeks after Sam Hose's death, "Ripples," the pseudonym of Coweta County squire J. P. Reese, who regularly commented on local events, proclaimed,

> The 23rd day of April, 1899, will be remembered as "Lynch Sunday" in Coweta. Already the wail of the hobgoblin and the rattle of chains are being heard at dead of night in the vicinity of the spot where Sam Holt was cremated, and but few darkies will go near the place after nightfall. There still remains about twelve inches of the stump to which the victim was chained, and every day people stop and whittle off a chip as a souvenir—not in memory of the brute, but in remembrance of the lynching.[1]

By most accounts, the killings of Sam Hose and Elijah Strickland were the first lynchings to take place in or around Newnan, but the state of Georgia and the country itself were in the middle of a prolonged "Lynch Sunday."[2] In 1901, Mark Twain would call the nation "The United States of Lyncherdom" and even considered writing a history of lynching in America before deciding against it, fearing that he would alienate too many of his readers who accepted or even approved of the practice.[3]

In addition to the Wilmington coup d'état, stories of "race wars" in Arkansas and elsewhere, and the ongoing confrontations with black militia, newspapers at the turn of the century carried weekly reports of whites' usurping the justice system and at times defying the federal government itself. A story much in the news during the first months of 1899 concerned the consequences of the killing, a year earlier, of a black federal postmaster, Frazier B. Baker, in Lake City, South Carolina. Republican administrations had routinely made black federal appointments in the South, and the position of postmaster was at first considered to be a relatively nonoffensive one for blacks to hold in a white community. But the government underestimated southern white outrage, anger that a black appointee would handle, perhaps even read, their personal mail, letters and correspondence that would then reach the hands of wives and daughters.[4] There had been sufficient warning, most notably from this section of west Georgia where Sam Hose would meet his death. In 1890, a black man named John Clopton had been appointed to serve as postmaster in Hogansville, a small town twenty miles south of Newnan. The *Atlanta Constitution* offered the following description of Clopton: "A negro of little more than ordinary intelligence [who] has rendered himself very obnoxious to the community by his mischievous course in politics. His only qualifications for office, as far as known, are the prerequisites to republican favor nowadays."[5] Clopton held the office for only a short time, over the protests of the town's white residents. After "the door had twice been shot to pieces and his office once burned to the ground, he considered that the microbes of disorder hereabouts were too plentiful to suit him and he went to work as a Pullman car porter on a route running between Boston and New York," the paper later related.[6] A white postmaster named J. W. Hardaway then served until, in 1897, the McKinley administration named Isaiah H. Loftin, described as a schoolteacher of good character, a college graduate, and "a high grade specimen of his race," to the political position. But Loftin also was controversial. Not only was he well educated, but he was "interested in teaching [black residents] the young idea how to shoot and the old idea how to vote." Moreover, only the year before, his brother Augustus, who had served in federal positions with the post office and the Internal Revenue Service in Atlanta, had been shot to death while visiting in Hogansville.[7]

Once appointed, Loftin was denied an office in the downtown area and forced to perform his duties from a building near his home on the west end, the "colored section" of town.[8] Hogansville's white community boycotted this office, and J. W. Hardaway, with the white community's approval, continued to serve as unofficial postmaster in direct defiance of the federal government. In a further affront, Hardaway used a white "half idiot" to serve as his "letter boy." The *Constitution* explained with some amusement that the boy "had just enough sense to go to the houses of the white citizens and get their mail which they wanted to send off and then carry it to the train and shove the letters and packages into the letter box on the car." For a time this scheme worked. "Some of the citizens openly speak of the crazy boy's agency and laugh at the inability of the government to prosecute the idiot," the paper reported.[9] Hardaway and Loftin soon reached a compromise in which Loftin would receive the mail, separate it, and then send all white correspondence and packages to Hardaway, who kept his office at the Grand Hotel in downtown Hogansville.[10]

Although Loftin had received numerous threats against his life, this arrangement seemed to work until, on the night of September 16, 1897, he was ambushed and shot.[11] First reports indicated that he had been killed, but his wounds turned out to be minor, the result of "bad marksmanship," according to one report.[12] Hogansville was at this time a town of fifteen hundred, with almost nine hundred of those identified as black, and talk of race riots quickly grew. As the *Constitution* remarked,

> There are more negroes in the town than there are whites. . . . Usually the negro population is very quiet, but since the shooting of Loftin war-like demonstrations have been made. Every night large crowds of negroes collect in the colored section of the town and discuss the shooting. There is but one feeling among the negroes. They say that there is no doubt that the shooting was the result of a plot to kill Loftin because he was a negro and had been appointed above the protests of the white public.[13]

After the shooting, the McKinley administration sent federal Secret Service agents to Hogansville, and two "prominent citizens" were quickly identified as perpetrators (although not by name in the newspaper accounts). On the advice of U.S. postmaster general James Gary, President McKinley decided to "take up the gantlet thrown down by the Georgia Democrats." According to one official,

> From this time on it will be a fight between the 500 [*sic*] people of Hogansville and the whole power of the government at Washington. . . . The people of Hogansville will either get their mail through the regular post office or not at all. If they want to do without their mail, that is their privilege, but they will not receive or send letters except through Loftin or his successor. If the ex-postmaster or anybody else presumes to handle the mail he will be arrested and sent to the penitentiary. . . . There will be no half way measures because the president is convinced from the preliminary reports that an attack has been made on the authority of the federal government, which amounts almost if not quite to treason.[14]

Despite such declarations of "treason," the fact that Loftin was not badly injured—Hogansville's mayor, R. H. Jenkins, gained momentary national attention when he declared, "There is not a word of truth in the published statements about the shooting of the negro postmaster at Hogansville except that he was shot"—helped to defuse the confrontation, and by the end of the month the government had closed the investigation with no arrests.[15] Soon after, Loftin resigned his position. But the next year, the Lake City killings drew a clear connection. As one northern paper put it, "If stern measures had been taken at the time of the Hogansville outrage, there would probably have been no murders at

Lake City. The former has been allowed to pass unpunished, and the lawless mob at Lake City believed that a greater crime was admissible."[16]

Postmaster Baker's story was similar to Isaiah Loftin's. Baker had also been appointed to his position in Lake City in 1897, over the objections of the white community. In January 1898, the post office was burned to the ground, and Baker moved the mail operation to his home just outside town. On February 22, a mob of some three hundred people gathered at his house during the night, set it on fire, and then shot at Baker and his family as they tried to escape. Baker and one of his children, a baby girl being carried by his wife, Lavania, died in the gunfire. President McKinley, at the urging of Ida Wells-Barnett, among others, again ordered an investigation, and on April 7, 1899, thirteen men were indicted. As Philip Dray notes, it was the first federal response to a lynching to result in arrests since Reconstruction.[17] U.S. Circuit Court judge W. H. Brawley declared Baker's murder a crime against the government and "one of the blackest ever perpetrated in South Carolina." This time, the men arrested, local merchants and farmers of Lake City, were identified by name in the papers.[18] Although the trial ended in a hung jury and all the accused were set free (Judge Brawley openly wept at the verdict), the case did show that under extraordinary circumstances white men in the South might be brought to court if they took on the federal government. However, it also showed that southern white communities protected their own, especially against what they considered outside influences, and that, as in Hogansville, they were "not losing any sleep over their fear of a [federal] prosecution."[19]

If the federal government proved unwilling or unable to prosecute illegal mob action successfully, how much less did white southerners have to fear from state and local authorities? In the years leading up to the events of the spring of 1899, a series of lynchings took place in Georgia that illustrate the variety of incidents that could cause men to take the law into their own hands. As these examples show, although race was almost always at the core of the decision to lynch, its role was not as simply defined as one might expect.

Of the three towns—Newnan, Palmetto, and Griffin—that spearheaded the violence that spring, Griffin had the worst reputation concerning racial intolerance. In 1890, a gun battle between blacks and whites had erupted outside town at a fish fry; two black men were killed and some fifteen others, black and white, were wounded.[20] Griffin's newspapers recorded numerous racial incidents over the years, including whippings, shootings, and hangings. On October 15, 1896, a black man named Henry Milner was charged with the assault of a Miss Blanche Gray, who asserted that Milner had caught her "near a clump of bushes," had choked her unconscious, and then had raped her. Milner was shot while running from deputies and, after being identified by Gray, taken to the office of Dr. T. J. Collier in town to have his wound treated. There, after "some one remarked to him that he ought to be hung," his captors placed Milner in a buggy and drove him outside town, where observers gathered, arriving on foot, on horseback, and even on bicycles to watch the lynching. In the woods near the county prison, the crowd "deliberated as to the method of taking the negro off." They offered to take him to jail for trial if he would swear that he was not guilty of the rape, but he refused to do so, at which point he was "strung up and his body perforated with bullets." The *Atlanta Constitution* noted, "[This event marked] a new epoch in the criminal history of Spalding county. Since its establishment, there have been murders and arsons, as well as crimes of a less degree in abundance, but never before has a negro committed an assault, as on yesterday, while today occurred the county's first lynching."[21]

A second one was soon to follow, this time more sensational and oddly suggestive of the events that would later be played out in Sam Hose's case. Indeed, in essential ways the reports on the pursuit and execution of Oscar Williams in July 1897 laid out a narrative that would be repeated, at times almost verbatim, in the later news articles describing Hose's crime, flight, capture, and death.

According to first reports, on Saturday, July 10, Williams had been directed by his white employer, Samuel E. Campbell, to plow a field some distance from the Campbell residence. Campbell's property was located in Clayton County, near the town of Lovejoy. According to reports, Williams was a trusted worker. Late in the afternoon Mrs. Campbell sent her eight-year-old son and six-year-old daughter to the field with water for the worker. After drinking, Williams complained of a headache and asked the boy to hold the plow lines to the mule while he and the girl, Jewell, went to the spring nearby so that she might pour more water on his head. Shortly after, the boy heard his sister scream. Dropping the lines, he ran back to the house to alert his mother, who then hurried to the spring where "the sight that met her view was terrible to her, and for a moment she was dazed." By the time she had recovered her senses, Williams had fled. At first thinking her daughter dead, Mrs. Campbell carried her quickly to the home and gave the alarm. By early night, crowds of men, some with bloodhounds, had arrived, and the search was on. Led by the sheriffs of Clayton and Henry counties, the posses, made up of "brave, law-abiding men . . . determined to slay the man who had ruined their neighbor's home," scattered throughout the countryside. At one point Williams was spotted and shot at but nonetheless continued to avoid capture.[22]

By the next day, the fugitive was reported near Griffin. The city had already prepared itself for action. "The streets were full of armed men, who marched around with their guns and pistols in ready view . . . and they talked freely of how

Chapter Two

they expected to hang Williams when he is caught," the *Constitution* reported. Some of the hunters had vowed not to return home until Williams was dead. The Atlanta reporter predicted, "The negro's body may be found hanging from some limb this morning. The discovery would create little surprise and the news from Griffin is that the people there expect nothing else."[23]

Despite the number of men, estimated at over four hundred, chasing Williams, he was still at large on Wednesday of the next week. He was now being described as "a tall, ginger cake colored negro, who stammers while talking and when excited finds great difficulty in making himself understood," characteristics that would later be applied to Sam Hose as well. No one considered that Williams's "difficulty" in talking might have played a part in his fleeing from his accuser, Mrs. Campbell, nor that she might have misconstrued Williams's actions toward the little girl, who was now recovering. Instead, efforts were under way to prove that, despite Samuel Campbell's long-time reliance on his worker, Oscar Williams was essentially "shady and untrustworthy." Indeed, he was now described as having "a vicious cast of countenance," although, oddly, "he does not look wicked enough to create a distrust," as Farmer Campbell had discovered to his grief. Moreover, Williams was said to come from a "bad family." "The father of the negro has the reputation of being a good old darky," the *Constitution* related, "but all of the sons are reckless characters." One of his brothers had been lynched several years earlier "for a crime similar to the one for which Oscar Williams is wanted," and another brother had served time in the state penitentiary. Members of the posse declared that when the hunt was over, "the old man [would] have at least two sons to die at the end of a rope."[24]

Oscar Williams was finally captured by a farmer named Ben Perdue in the early morning hours of Thursday, July 15, at Williams's sister's house near Barnesville, Georgia, fifteen miles south of Griffin. Although he admitted to being "Oscar Williams," he insisted that there were two men with that name and that he was not the one they sought. The mayor of Barnesville, fearing a lynching in his small town, telephoned then-governor William Y. Atkinson, asking for permission to call out the local Barnesville "Blues." Atkinson, who would later figure prominently in an attempt to prevent the Sam Hose lynching, had already offered a $250 reward for Williams, stipulating that the fugitive be remanded safely to the authorities in either Atlanta or Macon for a proper trial. Atkinson now feared that the prisoner might easily be taken from a small-town jail such as the one in Barnesville, and when Mayor Huguley called, the governor agreed to protect Williams with the local guard until he could be transported to a more secure cell in Macon, to the south, rather than attempt to bring him to Atlanta. Atkinson had heard that there was still confusion over the prisoner's actual identity, and both he and the mayor worried that moving Williams through

Griffin or Lovejoy, rail stops on the way to Atlanta, could result in his seizure and death, since both places were outspoken in their determination to hang Williams. Men from Griffin had already begun arriving in Barnesville before daybreak, and "all of them seemed determined to take Williams' life." Only the presence of the local troops, who "walked around the guard house with fixed bayonets," prevented this from happening.[25]

Barnesville authorities took other precautions to avoid an unlawful hanging of their prisoner. Before daybreak on Friday, the sixteenth, two guards, Ben Perdue and Z. T. Evans, secretly shuffled Williams, who was "heavily shackled," into a buggy and began a circuitous twenty-five-mile route to a stop on the Macon–Birmingham railroad, which they felt would not be as closely watched by potential lynchers as the Central or the Southern, more direct ways of reaching Macon. There they flagged down a passenger train and boarded with their captive. One of the men sent a telegram to the Macon authorities: "Meet me at Macon and Birmingham depot at 11 o'clock with Black Mariah [a police wagon]. Have a prisoner." Williams supposedly confessed to the crime during the trip, even correcting first reports by saying that the attempted assault on the little girl had taken place in the field and not at the spring.[26]

After Williams was placed in the Bibb County jail, the girl's father, Samuel Campbell, his brother-in-law, and several other men, some of them armed, appeared before the Macon sheriff. Campbell asked to see Williams so that he might identify him, and this was allowed. According to reports, the two men acknowledged each other, and Oscar Williams again confessed his crime. Rumors that the jail would be stormed by men from Griffin and Lovejoy continued to grow during the day, and Governor Atkinson ordered that members of the Macon Hussars and the Macon Light Infantry report to the local armories as a "precautionary measure."[27]

At this point Williams seemed secure enough in the Macon–Bibb County jail. He was not the only desperate character being housed there. Among the other prisoners were a white condemned murderer, Tom Allen, an outlaw who had previously escaped from the jail, and an interracial couple: Elizabeth Nobles, a white woman in her early fifties, and Gus Fambles, a black man with whom she had conspired to kill her husband for his insurance.[28] All had been sentenced to hang and were awaiting execution. But other events now intruded, complicating what was already a tense situation and illustrating how difficult maintaining legal authority had become in Georgia.

Three days after Williams was placed in his Macon cell, an unrelated, truly unique lynching occurred in Talbot County, near the city. The victim was both a white man and, according to one account, "the first university graduate in the history of the country who has been lynched." This honor went to Dr. W. L.

Ryder, a young dentist living in Talbotton and a member of one of Georgia's leading families (one brother was superintendent of public schools in Columbus, Georgia, another was a doctor, and his sister, who was the widow of a former state senator, was "credited with being the largest woman landowner in the south"). Several years earlier, Ryder had courted a young woman named Sallie Emma Owens, who discouraged him from further wooing. On the night of Easter Sunday, April 5, 1896, Ryder called on her at the home of her friend Jennie McCoy, with whom she was spending the night, and found her in the company of Augustus Persons, a young attorney. Humiliated and furious, Ryder went to his room at the Weston Hotel, took a dose of morphine, got a shotgun, retraced his steps to the McCoy home, and with two blasts shot Sallie Owens dead and wounded Gus Persons. He then ran to his office, took more morphine, and fled by a back stairway into the countryside. A pursuing crowd found him a half mile away trying to drown himself in a pond. When they dragged him from the water, they discovered he had also hacked at his throat with a knife. A local doctor pumped out his stomach and treated his wound. Although there were calls for his immediate execution, he was instead sent temporarily to the Bibb County jail.

Despite the fact that Ryder's sanity was in serious question—he was often described as "nervous," given to angry outbursts, and suffering severe depression and pain from deafness—in September 1896 he was found guilty at trial and sentenced to hang. After the verdict, the Georgia Supreme Court ordered a new trial due to numerous errors made by the presiding judge. Many felt that Ryder's prominent family had a hand in this reversal. This second trial started on Monday, July 19, 1897, but was delayed because of missing witnesses and the proclaimed illness of Ryder's lead counsel, which caused the judge to grant a continuance but also led him to wonder aloud from the bench whether the defense was dealing honestly with the court. He ordered Ryder returned to the Muscogee County jail in Columbus, where he had been kept while awaiting this second trial.

As authorities transported Ryder to the railway where he would board the train to Columbus, his buggy was overtaken by a mob near Waverly Hall, Georgia. These masked men easily overpowered the deputies and dragged Ryder "like a sack of corn" from the buggy and dropped him on the ground, where he lay prostrate and silent. They put a noose around his neck and asked if he wanted to pray, but according to witnesses, Ryder did not respond and seemed unaware of what was happening to him. At that point, one of the lynchers remarked, "He's dead to the world. We'd better string him up and have done with it." Two men then lifted him on their shoulders until the body was raised to the desired height while others in the crowd pulled their end of the rope "hand over hand" over a tree limb until the line was taut. At a signal, the two men supporting the prisoner let him drop, and he slowly strangled to death.[29] The corpse was left hanging from the tree during the night, but the next day it was brought at first to Talbotton and from there to Macon, where it arrived on the night of July 20.[30]

This hanging, which received massive coverage in Georgia papers, complete with dramatic front-page illustrations of Ryder's lynching—masked men in black suits standing and kneeling around his recumbent body as they placed the rope around his neck—was bad news for Oscar Williams. If a respectable white man, a college graduate (one illustration of Ryder frequently used in papers had him wearing his mortarboard), a professional, and a member of a prominent family whose influence had apparently allowed it to manipulate the state legal system, could be summarily executed by locals who had grown exasperated with the perceived failure of justice, then why should a black, self-confessed child molester (Jewell Campbell's age changed in various reports, ranging from six to nine years) be allowed to live? As the *Constitution* observed, "The arrival of the lynched body of Dr. Ryder in the city Tuesday night added to the determination of the mob to lynch Williams. It seems to have had the same effect as the taste of blood to the famishing lion."[31] By Thursday, July 22, the word was out that an attack would definitely be made on the Bibb County jail to seize Williams and hang him. The crowd had dynamite, it was said, and intended to blow up the building if necessary to get to the prisoner. It was also suggested that friends of the outlaw Tom Allen were stirring up the crowd on his behalf as well, hoping to free him during the ensuing melee. Others also proposed to use the opportunity to lynch Elizabeth Nobles and Gus Fambles, who had so offended the sensibilities of the community.[32]

Thus, Bibb County sheriff Wescott had a dilemma on his hands, or so he later explained. Attempting to transport Williams from Macon to Atlanta, the safest place to move him, carried definite risks for the prisoner, especially since the fastest and most direct means of travel would be by train, which would of necessity pass through Griffin, whose citizens had been clamoring for his death by rope. This was the reason Williams had been brought to Macon in the first place. On the other hand, to keep him in the Macon jail would invite almost certain destruction of the building, result in the likely deaths of other prisoners and possibly the freeing of Tom Allen, and cause general bloodshed between the mob and the soldiers who would be expected to guard the jail, "for both [groups] would have assembled at the jail with loaded guns." Such were the reasons later given by Sheriff Wescott.[33]

Therefore, in the early hours of the morning of July 22, Oscar Williams was once again hurried from jail by two deputy sheriffs, placed in a hack, and driven to the Macon depot for transportation by train to Atlanta. The train passed safely through Forsyth and Barnesville, but at Griffin the crowd had gathered at the station to await its arrival as daylight was breaking. Some later speculated that observers had been stationed to watch the jail in Macon and telephone ahead to their contacts in Griffin if they saw Williams being moved. Others wondered if some authorities had intentionally let slip the information. "It had been predicted, time and time again, that if Williams was ever brought to Griffin, he would be lynched," the *Constitution* commented after it was over, adding, "In fleeing from one mob he ran into the arms of another, not quite so large, but just as determined."[34]

By whatever means the news was related, Griffin was prepared. At the depot, the train carrying Oscar Williams halted, and a group of some fifty Griffin men boarded and began their search. The deputies had hidden Williams in a "closet"—a lavatory—in one of the cars for protection, but an elderly white man gave the prisoner away when he asked the searchers for permission to remove an invalid with whom he was traveling before they made their seizure of the black prisoner being escorted to Atlanta. After he identified the specific car, the man was allowed to detrain with his companion, at which point the Griffin crowd rushed down the aisle, overpowered the "big, burly deputy sheriff," and "swept, with him and his prisoner, out of the door, down the steps and onto the ground before he could breathe a second time."

A procession then took shape as the crowd marched Williams down Griffin's main thoroughfare, Broad Street, gathering more participants and observers as it went. Although the news "spread like wild fire," the crowd was described as orderly, with no "boisterousness"; however, women and children hurried to doors and windows to watch the early-morning parade pass. A group of black men, "bent on seeing the terrible work accomplished," was said to have followed the crowd until they were warned away for their own safety. Williams, who was being held by each arm and propelled at the head the mob, "was too frightened to talk, and the people were in too big a hurry to listen to anything he had to say." At the edge of the city limits, the crowd veered from Broad Street into a clump of trees, and there Williams was made to confess his crime. Immediately they put a noose around his neck, and "[w]ithin fifteen minutes his body was swinging in the air from a limb of the big redoak, while his body was being filled with lead." The firing continued for some ten minutes, and when it was done, Williams was described as "literally shot to pieces." More precisely, as the reporter put it, "There is not a piece of skin six inches square that is not punctured with a bullet hole. . . . As it swayed in the morning breezes, turning first one way and then another, it presented a sight that was truly horrible." But not so horrible that it should be taken down. Instead, Oscar Williams was left hanging throughout the day while trains brought spectators from throughout the region to see his remains. His place of death was not far from the site of Henry Milner's lynching the year before.[35]

Given that Griffin had made clear its intention to lynch Oscar Williams, Sheriff Wescott's decision to smuggle him to Atlanta through that city was immediately questioned, although "the conservative people of Macon" were pleased that the killing had not taken place in their town and that a possible riot and siege had been avoided. "Considering the excitement and danger prevailing here, the sheriff solved the problem in the only way open to him," the *Constitution* concluded. Others questioned whether Williams's delivery into the "arms" of his executioners was prearranged, although local authorities expressed nothing but amazement and consternation over the way that the Griffin men had discovered their stratagem. Editorials again condemned the lynching but, with the cases of Dr. Ryder and Elizabeth Nobles in mind, blamed the slowness and ineffectiveness of the court system as a contributing element. "The people have seen murderer after murderer, self-confessed, slip through the hands of the law until they have been educated to look upon that result as the usual outcome of murder trials. They stand aghast at the opportunity offered by the law for new trials and for final escape by the process of appeals to the state and to the United States courts, and to the interminable plea of insanity with all its tortuousness."[36] Although the mob's actions were clearly illegal and should be condemned, the editorials suggested, its actions were based in understandable frustration. In any event, no member of the Griffin party could be identified, although none of them was masked (as was the case with Dr. Ryder's executioners), and they had brazenly marched down the main street of the city in full view. And while Dr. Ryder's brothers were demanding of Governor Atkinson that his killers be brought to justice—they now charged that the courts had colluded with local authorities to hand their brother over to the lynch mob (a scenario that might very well have inspired Bibb County officials to do the same with Oscar Williams), and, moreover, provided Atkinson with the actual identities of some of the lynchers—no one made a similar effort on behalf of Oscar Williams.[37] Instead, although Atkinson did offer a reward for the identification and arrest of members of the Griffin mob, the Spalding County coroner's jury declared that "the deceased came to his death by hanging and shooting at the hands of parties unknown to the jury."[38]

The story of Oscar Williams's crime, capture, and lynching as related in the newspapers followed an established "lynch narrative," a protocol that would be expanded on in the Sam Hose killing almost two years later. This narrative, predicated on a horrible, sexual (black) crime, exonerated both the authorities, who were represented as trying to do their duty, and the self-appointed mob, which was pictured as having been forced to take the law into its own hands because of the failure of the official legal system. The mob had to be shown not as a crazed lot of vengeful renegades but as citizens acting responsibly. Thus the emphasis on their deliberate action, their seriousness, even their regret at having to take these unfortunate steps. The community might observe and applaud, but a certain decorum was also expected of them as they watched this solemn ritual take place. Thus, the white newspaper accounts provided their readers with a reassuring self-image. Even as they described the horrors of the crime and the lynching, which made for sanctioned sensational (and entertaining) reading, they put the events in the larger context of the need to protect communal order. The narrative always ended with the sense that things had been set aright, at least momentarily.

One more lynching helped set the scene for the events of 1899, another provocative tale of sexual assault that anticipated the salacious nature of the Cranford story of murder and rape. On December 18, 1898, a Mrs. J. S. Maruney (also spelled as Maroney and Meroney) had, according to a report in the *Atlanta Constitution*, been raped and abused by "a burly negro" near Albany, Georgia. She was the wife of John Maruney, a "well-known school teacher" in the county. The assailant had forced his way into the Maruney home and, armed with either a pistol or a shotgun, had instructed Mrs. Maruney to "bind [her husband] hand and foot" and tie him to the bed. After searching the house "for booty" and taking thirty dollars, the intruder "then turned his attention to the defenseless woman, who had been forced to render her husband and protector helpless, and committed the most hideous crime which the mind can conceive." The assault took place before the bound husband's eyes. The article assured its readers, "The white men of two counties—Worth and Lee—are scouring the country. . . . The determined men who have set to work to apprehend the inhuman being who is the object of their search are leaving no stone unturned to run him to earth." The main headline anticipated the outcome: "Will Stretch Rope If He Is Caught."[39]

The story, with its elements of bondage and exhibitionism, was designed to provoke both anger and titillation. A later report noted that Mrs. Maruney was "subjected . . . to outrages that only savages could think of."[40] There are clear similarities between the Lee County invasion and rape and the stories that would later circulate concerning Sam Hose's assault on the Cranford family. What made this story different was that the Maruneys themselves were black, "highly respectable colored people [who] stand well in the community where they live." Their race was mentioned only in the first report, however, and during the following months, as the conventions associated with the lynching narrative played themselves out, readers would not necessarily know that the "brute" had "Assaulted a Woman of His Own Race." In this case, the "White People" sought to avenge the "dastardly deed" done by a black criminal to a well-regarded black couple. It was black rape that they intended to punish, no matter against whom the rape had been committed.[41]

As was so often the case in these accounts, "facts" changed from one report to the next, and this extended to the identity of the suspected rapist(s). The first article cast suspicion on a Jule Henderson, "against whom there [was] a strong chain of circumstantial evidence." A detailed description of the assailant was provided: black, around thirty-five years of age, a height of five feet nine inches, a "scattering beard on his face," a "blue blouse and light brown shirt," and, as a last detail, a "number nine shoe." But it was also now suggested that the assailant had a companion who had remained on guard outside the home during the assault.[42] By the next day, the *Constitution* had identified the intruder as "Bill Holt," and Jule Henderson was no longer mentioned. A posse had tracked "Holt" with bloodhounds to a swamp, where he was possibly wounded before escaping deeper into the darkness. "All the streams are full and the dogs are unable to enter," the paper reported; nevertheless, the men had surrounded the area, "guarding every outlet." "The whole country for miles around the scene of the crime is intensely excited, and the horrible affair, think indignant white men, must be avenged. . . . It is safe . . . to predict that the tomorrow will furnish material for a lynching, which will be but a humane punishment for the terrible crime committed by the fiend. The rope is already prepared."[43]

And then nothing. The next day was Christmas Eve, and perhaps the posse went home. Whatever the case, the fugitive "Bill Holt" remained at large until he was reported killed, sometime in January, in the swamps near Leesburg. But by that time he, too, had been replaced as the primary suspect. Now the chief assailant was identified as "Cupid" Redding, also know as "Geechee," and he further was said to have had two accomplices, identified as George Blevins and George Fort. Although Blevins and Fort were well known around Leesburg, "Geechee" or "Cupid" Redding was from outside the area, and according to the *Macon Telegraph*, "evidence against him was hard to accumulate." He had first been arrested, "after a hard fight and a long chase," in Cordele, Georgia, on charges unrelated to the rape. The arresting officer, N. Y. Peavy, had then sent Redding to Macon, where he was wanted on still other charges. When Peavy learned that Redding might be connected to the Maruney assault, he arranged for Mrs. Maruney to come to Macon, where she identified Redding as the rapist. Redding then, according to reports, made a "complete confession" in a letter, in the hopes that he would not be returned to Lee County but kept in Macon.

As the *Macon Telegraph* explained, his thinking was that if he were prosecuted in Macon, "he would only go to the chain gang and stand a chance to get away when, if he went to Lee county, he was sure to hang."[44] Despite his maneuverings, Redding was taken to Leesburg on Friday, February 11, and there incarcerated with the locals Blevins and Fort, who had already been arrested.

Although the fact that the Maruneys were black had now been largely dropped from these accounts, there were hints in the reporting that this case was somehow less horrible to the white newspapers than, for example, the Sam Hose case would be. One indication was the barely disguised delight in "Cupid" Redding's name, which got full play in the headlines: "'Cupid' Confessed It." "Cupid" and his companions would be lynched shortly before Valentine's Day, and although the connection was never directly noted in the papers, the allusion would have been hard for readers to miss. It is highly unlikely that the rape of a white woman by a black man would have permitted any such levity.

Otherwise, the traditional lynching scenario played itself out. Thus, according to the newspaper accounts, once the men were placed in jail, the talk of lynching began. Leesburg sheriff Jones notified Governor Candler on Saturday afternoon that there were rumors of a "party of lynchers" coming from Smithville, Georgia, on the train. They would arrive that night in Leesburg. Candler ordered the Smithfield train held up, and forty-five state militiamen stationed in Albany were ordered to Leesburg to protect the jail. In the meantime, however, locals had already begun to gather there to await the anticipated Smithfield train. When word came that this party had been stopped, "the people . . . , who had been gathering from all parts of [Lee County] and surrounding counties . . . organized themselves into a mob, and, appointing a leader, were not long in doing the work." The "leader" exhorted the crowd of some three hundred not to fear the militia but to act decisively. He was quoted as follows:

> The people of Lee county have already shown all the patience that can be expected. With perpetrators of this, the most dastardly crime ever committed against a civilized race, already in jail and within easy reach of your avenging hands, you have gone on gathering evidence and guarding against the possibility of a mistake as long as you ought. Now is the time to act. If these men are guilty, they should pay the penalty, which is none too severe. Contemplate the enormity of their crime, and then think of what slight punishment they must suffer for it. Consider what they will suffer at your hands, and what poor Mrs. Meroney endured at theirs. Is it not enough to drive a people to madness?[45]

With this justification (as quoted "in substance" by the correspondent), the mob moved to the jail. Taking the sheriff completely by surprise, "as he had no idea but that those who had come in from the country were merely sightseers and curiosity seekers bent on seeing others do the work, but not caring to take any part themselves," the crowd forced its way into the building and demanded to see the prisoners. The sheriff and his men were overpowered, but according to the accounts, "the plucky official refused to surrender the keys. He said he would die first." The mob began to beat at the cell doors. Then someone produced "a package of dynamite" and, as with Oscar Williams in the Bibb County jail, threatened to blow up the building if the men were not turned over. To save his other prisoners (there were either two or three other black men also being held on unrelated charges) and to avoid destruction of the jail, the sheriff agreed to get the keys, which he claimed were in a different location. He hoped, he said later, that this delay would give the militia the opportunity to arrive and disperse the crowd. Unfortunately, "the mob did not give him a chance to waste time. A number of them went with him and forced him to make haste."[46]

Back at the jail, the crowd demanded that all the prisoners be turned over to them, but the sheriff argued successfully that the other men were innocent of this crime and should not be included in the inevitable lynching. The three men accused of the Maruney attack were then marched from the jail into nearby woods, tied to trees, and shot "full of holes" in a continuous volley. The mob then dispersed, "firing their pistols into the air."[47]

Later accounts attempted to correct or clarify initial versions of the lynching. One early report had it that six men had been taken from the jail and killed; but even when this was corrected, the names of the three lynch victims were given as Blevins, Fort, and the supposedly dead "Will Holt" instead of Cupid Redding, which led to further "confusion."[48] Moreover, subsequent stories indicated that the lynch party was composed of men who had initially intended to take the train from Smithfield but had found other conveyances once the train was ordered held by the governor. "Americus sent the largest delegation—probably two hundred coming from that point," the papers reported, deflecting suspicion from local citizens. Sheriff Jones's actions were now represented as somewhat less heroic in the retelling: "Under cover of several large-sized revolvers, [he] unlocked the cage in which the negroes . . . were confined." His earlier delaying tactics were forgotten, although the revised reports still credited the sheriff for protecting the other prisoners not involved in the Maruney rape.[49] The mob, in these later accounts, first intended to hang the three men in the town square, but "the sheriff and citizens begged that the prisoners be taken out of town, on account of the women and the children." The crowd agreed, marched outside the city limits, "and hanged all three to one tree and riddled their bodies with bullets. Their bodies were literally shot into doll rags," the account explained, adding:

After the shooting the mob quietly dispersed, and today our little town is as quiet as if nothing had happened.

The three bodies are still hanging in the limb of the tree.[50]

Learning of the lynching, Governor Candler announced that he would offer a "large reward" for the apprehension of the lynchers ("Governor Did His Best" one headline read), but, as always, no one was arrested.[51]

On Thursday, April 27, four days after Sam Hose was burned at the stake, a postscript to the Leesburg lynching took place. On that day a black man named Alf Thurman was shot down as he traveled near the town. Thurman was identified as an informant, and his killers were said to have been friends of the three executed men. The name "Cupid Redding" had entirely disappeared from the public record: the victims were now identified with certainty as Bivins, Fort, and "Bill" Holt (the surname also given as an alias for Sam Hose), who apparently had not died in the swamps after all.[52] According to this account, the murdered Thurman had aided authorities in the initial arrests and had claimed that these men were leaders of a "band of outlaw negroes" who had intended to kill "prominent white men in the county."[53] This, then, was a revenge killing, a public signal that other black outlaws remained at large.

Although no newspaper would draw a direct connection between the Leesburg hangings and the lynching of Sam Hose, there were enough similarities between the crimes and the punishments that readers were likely to relate them. Both events presented proof of the insurgent race war that threatened white society. The difficulty in naming these "outlaw negroes," whose identities changed from day to day in newspaper accounts, only added to white paranoia, whether in Leesburg or Palmetto or Newnan: how could you protect yourself against an "enemy" that might lurk all around you, even live on your land or possibly in your home, but could not be confidently named or individualized? Published descriptions of black criminals often contained the same, almost generic descriptors—ginger-colored skin, tendency to stutter, missing teeth, evasive eye or body movements—that offered little help in terms of actual identification. Names and ages obviously meant nothing, nor did family relations or place of work or other common affiliations. All too often to the white mind, at least as indicated by these public reports, the black race was simply fluid, sourceless, and unknowable. A "Cupid Redding" could hold the headlines and provide both fright and/or amusement and then simply drop from sight, replaced by a "Bill" or "Will Holt" who had already been declared dead. And yet, ironically, there was rarely the worry that the wrong man had been taken (as Oscar Williams had insisted when he was first arrested). It was almost as if *all* blacks were guilty, if not of the specific crime for which they were punished, then for some other that they had somehow escaped. Such would be the argument soon used to defend the lynching of Elijah Strickland, for example. Although most would admit that Sam Hose's accusation of Strickland's connection to the murder of Alfred Cranford was at best suspect and that Strickland had been rashly hanged, his reputation would nevertheless be challenged in other ways in order to mitigate the possibility of gross injustice. Besides, sometimes it was necessary to act first and sort through the facts later to keep order, and if apologies then needed to be made, some sort of restitution could follow.

Chapter Three

The Palmetto Massacre

The town of Palmetto, Georgia, located twenty-five miles southwest of Atlanta, got its start in the land lottery of 1827. As described in *Palmetto: A Town and Its People*, the first building in the settlement was John H. Johnson's general store, built in 1833. In the 1840s, Maj. Willis P. Menefee moved to the area and established a plantation. As local history tells us, "the 'Major' saw to it that the settlement would grow into a cohesive and lasting community by donating land for churches, schools, and parks."[1] In January 1847, a volunteer regiment of South Carolina soldiers led by Gen. William O. Butler camped for two weeks near the Menefee plantation on their way to fight in the Mexican War. Major Menefee's hospitality led the soldiers to present him with a sword in gratitude, and the good will was such that the locals decided to name their community in honor of the Palmetto Regiment.[2] In 1851, the Atlanta and LaGrange Railroad was laid through town, a station was built, and three years later, in 1854, the state legislature granted Palmetto its charter.

During the Civil War, Palmetto escaped major destruction. Its most notable brush with Confederate history occurred when, in September 1864, President Jefferson Davis visited the troops of Gen. John B. Hood, who had retreated from General Sherman's northern army near Atlanta. As related in *Palmetto*, "Davis reviewed the troops and made a short speech in an attempt to boost the morale of both the soldiers and the civilians. Davis assured the audience that they would make Sherman's retreat 'more disastrous than was that of Napoleon from Moscow.'"[3] Bold words. After the war, the town reorganized itself, elected a mayor and a set of councilmen, and prospered. In the 1880s, Palmetto gained renown as a summer resort with the establishment of the St. Elmo Hotel, named after Augusta Jane Evans's enormously popular sentimental southern novel *St. Elmo* (1866). The hotel was built by Dr. Henry Lafayette ("Hal") Johnston, a dentist, and run by his sister, India Estes. Industry also arrived with the establishment of the Palmetto Cotton Mill in 1896. Two warehouses were built to hold bales of cotton for shipment on the railroad. One of these, locally known as the Granite Warehouse, was partially constructed of rock taken from the Stone Mountain area east of Atlanta. Built in 1898, the warehouse also was owned by Dr. Johnston and, located as it was in the middle of town, quickly became the city's "most visible and lasting landmark" until it was torn down in the 1960s.[4] Thus, by the late 1890s, Palmetto was by most measures a thriving and growing town.

Any sense of well-being enjoyed by Palmetto's white citizens, however, was shattered in January 1899. Around 3:00 a.m. on Monday, January 23, several buildings in the middle of town were set ablaze. According to reports, the fire started in the drugstore owned by C. B. Moseley and occupied by Dr. Paul Peniston, who lost his stock of medicine. It then spread to T. P. Zellars's hardware store and on to Moseley and F. H. Steed's dry-goods business, the two buildings adjacent to the drugstore. The upper rooms of the drugstore and the dry-goods store made up the Palmetto Hotel, run by Sallie Abrahams. The fire destroyed all three businesses, although some of the goods were saved from the flames. "The fire at one time threatened about half the town," the *Constitution* reported, "but owing to the dampness [of the weather] and hard work of the people, it was finally got under control."[5]

Four nights later, on January 27, in the middle of a rare snowstorm that left several inches on the ground, a second fire broke out. The *Atlanta Journal* noted, "It seems that an incendiary is trying to burn Palmetto, and he is succeeding."[6] This time there were two sites where the fires started, Mrs. M. A. Garrett's store, "the largest and finest in the town," and the store owned by C. B. Moseley that had been saved from the first fire. Mrs. Garrett's building was totally destroyed, and the fire spread to two other buildings on the west side, into one of which the unfortunate Dr. Peniston had moved his remaining stock of drugs, now completely lost. If the first fire had possibly been an accident, this second round appeared deliberately set, evidenced by a pile of wood soaked in oil at the front of Moseley's store.[7] "There is no question but it was the work of some incendiary," the *Constitution* excitedly explained, adding, "The calamity has cast a gloom over the entire town, and many hardly know what to do."[8] As the *Journal* further noted, the arsonist could possibly have been followed through the snow except that "his tracks were obliterated by the hurrying feet of the citizens" fighting the blaze. "The people are greatly excited over the attempts to destroy their town, and detectives from Atlanta will be employed to discover the dastard and bring him to justice."[9]

Chapter Three

The *Newnan Herald and Advertiser* reported on February 3 that a black man identified as Boston Frederick Brown was "arrested on suspicion" and jailed, but despite the "strong circumstantial proof," he was eventually released.[10] As the weeks passed, tensions grew higher in the town. The *Macon Telegraph* commented, "Since the recent burning there have been few people in Palmetto who have felt safe to retire at night and leave their property unprotected, and every citizen has constituted himself a committee of one to hunt down the perpetrators."[11] Governor Candler offered a reward of three hundred dollars for the arrest of "the first incendiary" and one hundred dollars for each subsequently arrested member of the gang.

As the *Journal* had reported, after the fires Palmetto merchants pooled their money to hire a black Pinkerton detective from Atlanta. It was later said that this man successfully infiltrated a black gang and learned of its plans. Another Palmetto citizen would also testify that he had overheard the conspirators' plot by crawling under the floor of the house in which they were meeting and eavesdropping on their scheming. However the information came to light, on Wednesday, March 15, a black man named William ("Bud") Cotton was reported to have given his confession to the prominent Palmetto dentist and businessman Dr. Hal Johnston. Johnston, who would play an increasingly important role in the events that followed, related Cotton's confession to Dr. T. P. Bullard, who then arranged for a posse to arrest Cotton and the eight coconspirators he had named. According to Johnston's account, Cotton and his gang of incendiaries had carefully plotted these arsons, robbery being one of their motives. They had met in the woods near Palmetto and had drawn cards "to see who would apply the torch." However, the story then shifted into a more conspiratorial context: three of the men were chosen because they were "bright mulattoes." They were told to "dress in good clothes" and "to say that they were white men who worked at the factory near the town" if they came under suspicion. Robbery thus became a secondary purpose. Absolute destruction of the town, carried out by black terrorists passing as whites, was now the primary motive the citizens of Palmetto attributed to the group.[12]

As late as the 1970s, there were people in Palmetto still alive from those days who remembered even more alarming versions of these events. One recalled the belief that radical blacks from Atlanta had infiltrated Palmetto to incite local black residents, telling them that the town had been built through the slave labor of their ancestors or even themselves and that the town therefore actually belonged to them. Since it was unlikely that present owners would offer restitution, the Atlanta agitators argued, local blacks needed either to take the town by force or to destroy it. Thus, the fires had been started with the intention of wiping out the prosperous white merchants and others who had unfairly benefited from black servitude. Whites soon began to suspect their black workers. One Palmetto housewife claimed to have overheard her maid singing to herself, "The whites is going down, and the blacks is going up" as she cleaned the house. Although the white woman did not fully understand the meaning at the time, she was alarmed enough to tell others of this unusual ditty.[13]

Also, according to lore still accepted even today by some Palmetto residents, the black gang further intended to murder selected citizens of the town. The first so marked was said to have been Tom Daniel, a wealthy businessman who owned mercantile stores in Palmetto and the nearby towns of Tyron and Fairburn. As related, the intention was for a group of assassins to hide in a ditch that bordered the road on which Daniel normally traveled on his way to and from work. As he passed by in his wagon, they would ambush and kill him. Learning of these plans, local authorities, with the assistance of leading Palmetto citizens, decided to set a trap. Daniel was told to take a different path to his home while a lawman, disguised as Daniel, drove his wagon down the original route. Thus, when the assailants revealed themselves, they were easily captured by the white men who were waiting nearby.[14]

However the arrests occurred—and there are no newspaper stories that support this second, local version of the events—after Cotton's confession (given to Dr. Johnston "with a grin," according to one article), the eight other men were quickly rounded up.[15] Ostensibly because of damages caused by the recent fires, the prisoners were incarcerated in Johnston's Granite Warehouse rather than in the jail. They were to be transported the next day to nearby Fairburn and there held for preliminary trial. Arson was at this time a capital crime, and the men could be sentenced to death if found guilty. Yet, despite the seriousness of the offenses with which the men were charged, the authorities set only a small contingent of guards—the number varied from two or three to six in different reports—to watch them.

According to the dramatic renditions that filled the next day's papers, between midnight and 1:00 a.m. on March 16, a party of "masked whitecaps," first described as "a gang of fully two hundred men," boldly rode into Palmetto, forced their way into the building, overpowered the guards, lined the prisoners against the stone wall, and summarily shot them down where they stood. The frightful noise of repeated gunfire, angry shouts, and pained screams rudely aroused the sleeping town, and as men in their night clothes or hastily donned trousers ran into the street, the first reports they heard were that the prisoners had overpowered and killed the guards, followed by equally alarming reports that all nine prisoners and their white guards had been slain by the band of masked vigilantes. The bulletin that appeared early the next morning on the front page of the *Atlanta Constitution* tried to make sense of the confusing event. The guards, it

Chapter Three

now explained, had been "overpowered without difficulty" and were unharmed; however, the "nine negroes were shot down while they were calling for mercy. Six of them were killed outright; the others will die." It continued, "Everybody is awake and armed, and fearing an outbreak on the part of the negroes of the community, who are threatening to avenge the blood of their race. The people are in a frenzy, and a riot on the part of the negroes is believed to be dangerously near."[16]

The Thursday-morning edition of the *Macon Telegraph* headlined its initial bulletin "Great Slaughter at Palmetto." It informed its readers that "Nine Negroes Were Killed by Citizens of That Place Last Night," and it increased the size of the vigilante party to "300 enraged citizens." The *Telegraph* continued, "Further trouble is expected, and it is probable that others who are supposed to belong to the gang of incendiaries will meet with the same fate," since "it seems certain that there was an organized gang of incendiaries banded together for the purpose of burning every house owned or occupied by white people in Palmetto."[17]

The next day, under the headline "Night of Horrors at Palmetto," the *Telegraph* continued its melodramatic narration and indulged its readers with a novelistic setting of the scene:

It was just past the hour of midnight. The guards were sleepy and tired of the weary watch and the little city of Palmetto was sound asleep, with nothing to disturb the midnight hour to interrupt the crime that was about to be committed.

Without the slightest noise the mob of riders approached the door to the warehouse. Not a false step was made, not a dead leaf was trod upon, and not even the creaking of a shoe or the clearing of a throat broke the stillness of the night.

The guards dreamed not of danger, and the prisoners laughed and sang and watched the fire flicker in the big rock fireplace.

With a noise that shook the buildings and threw every man to his feet, the big fireproof door was thrown open as if with the force of a battering ram.

The guards sprang to their guns, and the negroes screamed with terror.

But there were rifles, shotguns and pistols everywhere.[18]

Obviously, this version of the story, stirring and suspenseful in its telling, strained credulity. The idea of two or three hundred masked men riding on horses into the middle of this small town after midnight without either immediately rousing the local populace or alerting the guards was more entertaining than believable. The paper and its readers were, on one level, engaging together in the construction of an acceptable and even necessary scenario that could relate the essential facts—a group of masked men had taken the law into its own hands and shot down nine unarmed, bound black prisoners—as a stirring revenge narrative that mitigated or disguised the awfulness of the deed in romantic folderol.

This was a pattern often followed in the journalism of the day, especially those articles describing rape and murder. Reporters gratified their eager readers with explicit descriptions of violent death, with salacious suggestions of unspoken sexual outrages, with histrionic renderings of contemptible and craven behavior. The second or third day's paper might correct, without apology, the misstatements of the first account, but that first narrative would have by that time served its purpose, no matter how implausible the story line might be.

Thus it was with the Palmetto killings. A more detailed report by correspondent Frank Fleming, which appeared in the Friday, March 17, edition of the *Atlanta Constitution*, offered revised information and impressions. Four men—Henry Bingham, Tip Hutson (Hudson), Ed Brown, and the first arrested, Bud Cotton—were now listed as dead, and another, John Bigby, as dying. The remaining four—John Jameson, Isom Brown, George Tatum, and Clem Watts—suffered minor or no injuries at all. Also, the overblown story of 200 or 300 masked horsemen riding into town—the sort of melodrama that Thomas Dixon Jr. would incorporate into his novels and that D. W. Griffith would film so effectively fifteen years later in *The Birth of a Nation*—was quietly deflated. Although two of the guards subsequently reported the number of vigilantes at between 75 and 150, one of the victims, Clem Watts, put it at closer to 20 men, and Frank Fleming himself reported that "the self-constituted executioners consisted of no more nor less than fifteen men, evidence of the guard before the coroner's jury to the contrary." The room, according to Fleming, could not have held more than this number in addition to the prisoners and the guards already inside.[19]

There was also the question of who constituted this group. A section of Fleming's report was titled "Where the Mob Came From," and he acknowledged that this issue had not been "satisfactorily answered." The most grievously wounded of the survivors, John Bigby, held that the horsemen were from Campbell County, where Palmetto was located. The county sheriff, J. C. Aderhold, disputed this assertion and argued that the whitecappers came instead from the south, pointing out that a mask had been found on the road in that direction from the warehouse, thus exonerating men from his region. Neither of the two guards who later testified admitted to having recognized any of the party. All were masked, and the leader, they said, was a "large man" with a "hoarse, totally strange voice. They had never seen him before."[20]

Whatever the number of men, they had gone about their business "orderly and coolly and [had] exhibited a determination seldom equaled under similar circumstances," the correspondent Royal Daniel wrote in the *Atlanta Journal*. Daniel was relying on a staff correspondent for his information, but in keeping with journalistic conventions of the day, he (unlike Frank Fleming) freely attributed dialogue to the participants. He quoted the leader as saying, "You guards, move, and move quick, if you don't want to get your brains blown out."[21] The unnamed reporter for the *Macon Telegraph*, who apparently relied on the same correspondent, gave an even more dramatic version: "'Hands up and don't move: if you move a foot or turn your hands I will blow your damned brains out,' came the stern and rigid command from a man of small, thick stature, his face wholly concealed by a mask of white cloth and holding in his hands a couple of dangerous horse pistols." He then warned one guard who hesitated, "I'll blow hell out of you in a minute if you don't put that hand up."[22] In Daniel's report, the "trembling, pleading, terror stricken negroes" were then marched to the front of the room near the door. There they crouched, tied together with ropes, "begging for life and declaring that they were innocent." The whitecappers then paused. The prisoners at first thought that this hesitation meant they would be spared, but as the masked men raised their guns, the victims renewed begging for their lives. "Oh, God have mercy! . . . Oh, give me a minute to live," one, apparently Bud Cotton, the accused instigator, cried, arousing laughter from the masked group. The leader then ordered the nine prisoners to move to the back of the building. "Stand up," he called, adding strangely, "and we will see if we can't kill you out if we can't burn you out." Whatever the leader actually meant by this, since white establishments had been the primary objects of arson, another vigilante picked up the idea of fire and cried, "Burn the devils!" "No, we'll shoot 'em like dogs," the leader declared. Daniel continued his reconstruction of the events:

"My men, are you ready?" asked the captain, still cool and composed and fearfully determined to execute the bloodiest deed that has ever stained Campbell county.

"Ready," came the unanimous response.

"One, two, three—fire!" was the command, given orderly, but hurriedly. . . .

"Load and fire again," shouted the captain of the mob, and his voice was heard above the screaming and death cries of the wounded and dead.

The men rapidly loaded their guns, then fired at the given command.

"Now, before you leave, load and get ready for trouble," came the captain's order, and the men loaded their guns and got ready to leave the bloody room.

Before the men departed, several of them were "sent forward into the blood and brains and into the twisting mass of dying men to examine if all were dead." Those discovered still living were shot again in the face or the chest.[23] The *Columbus (Georgia) Enquirer-Sun* reported that the bodies were turned over and examined for life. If the men were breathing, groaning, or begging, the whitecappers would place the barrels of their pistols on the men's chests "and every chamber was emptied." "He's dead now," one vigilante laughed after finishing off one victim.[24]

The *Constitution*'s Frank Fleming gave a less dramatic account but offered one significant difference. In his version, after the men were lined up and the first volley fired, some prisoners, "infuriated by the pain of the bullets," ran at their executioners and fought "with their bare hands" but were repulsed. One, supposedly, "frantically tore the mask" from the head of a shooter, revealing the man's identity, before having his jaw broken by a rifle butt. "The victim now lies on the floor with his jawbone curiously dislocated," Fleming observed, then commented gratuitously, "He was not satisfied with what came to him naturally."[25]

As the mob fled, on horse or by foot, the people of the town ran to their windows or into the streets. As some raced to the Granite Warehouse, they encountered members of the shooting party. "No questions were asked; silence was demanded on the part of the citizens, and it was not denied," Frank Fleming reported, and then concluded, with barely subdued skepticism:

> No citizen was found who recognized any member of the party. A few said the party was on horseback, but as a matter of fact they were on foot. It was necessary in order to come and go silently.
>
> Even what road they left by is not remembered by those who saw the flight—a curious fact, but no one would think for a moment of imputing complicity to the people of Palmetto; they were distraught and terrorized; they ran on toward the scene of the firing without knowing where they were going.[26]

One of those who met the "desperate horsemen," according to Fleming, was the dentist Hal Johnston, the owner of the Granite Warehouse and the man to whom Bud Cotton was said to have first confessed. Johnston now spoke for the town as he "expressed regret that such a calamity should have fallen on a community [that] had hitherto borne such a good reputation." He continued:

> Where the parties came from that did the deed, we cannot say. I do not believe they came from this place, and am at a loss to locate them anywhere.
>
> The negroes here have been very aggressive in their recent conduct; in addition to the work they have done for us in this town, they have made open threats to burn the town of Fairburn.
>
> You will find that the people of this place, in spite of the conduct of the negroes or some of them here, are down on any such summary action as was taken this morning.

Reporter Fleming concluded, "The well disposed people of Palmetto, an element made up of the large majority, express the deepest regret at the unfortunate occurrence and point without irony and with simple truth to the good conduct of the community in the past."[27]

What was strongly suggested but left unsaid in Fleming's account was the likelihood that the Palmetto shooting was planned by a small group of the town's leaders. Many years later, one resident who had been a boy at the time of the massacre remembered being told not to go into town that night because "something would take place." The day before, several men, it was said, had gathered north of town at the Ramah First Baptist Church, the area's central meeting place since it was located at a crossroads: "All roads lead to Ramah," was a local saying. There they had planned the attack. Members of this group were also reported to have gone to a local mercantile store to buy white sheeting for disguise. The merchant later related that some of this material came from the last of a stock and thus bore distinctive markings that were later seen on at least one of the outfits worn at the warehouse. The men had then boldly marched or ridden in wagons into downtown Palmetto, entered the warehouse, and shot the prisoners. The description of anonymous hooded horsemen as offered by Johnston and others gave these men some degree of protection, but most locals were aware that their own people, including some of their most prominent citizens, officials, and spokespeople, had taken a direct hand in this deed.[28]

The next day Palmetto mayor Thomas P. Arnold called for calm, and Governor Allen Candler, who was by now an old hand at expressing his outrage at the unlawful killing of blacks, maintained that "the interposition of this mob was entirely unnecessary, since with the proof in the hands of those who had made the arrests conviction and punishment were absolutely certain." He put forward a reward of five hundred dollars for the "apprehension and delivery of the first member of said unknown mob and further reward of one hundred for each additional person so implicated, with sufficient evidence to convict."[29] But Candler also knew where to lay the blame. "Until recently there was no race friction in the state," he declared. "The Georgia negro is not naturally vicious nor predisposed to the commission of atrocious crimes. . . . Such outrages as this never or seldom occurred in this state till regiments of insolent, drunken negro soldiers, the scum of the dives of the cities north and south, were quartered here and there in the state and in the south." He listed as specifics the race problems in Macon, Chickamauga, Tampa, "to say nothing of the Griffin episode," before summarizing,

> The Leesburg outrage, the Palmetto burning and many other similar crimes committed in Georgia by negroes during the last few months are due to the baleful influence and example of these lawless rowdies who disgraced the uniforms they wore. This is the primary cause of all these troubles. Still, this does not justify the bloody and barbarous retaliation of Leesburg and Palmetto.[30]

At the further request of Dr. Johnston, who now warned of an outright revolt from Palmetto blacks, Governor Candler sent a detachment of some fifty soldiers from the Fifth Georgia Regiment, the "Capital City Guards," to impose martial law. Under the initial command of Capt. W. W. Barker, the leadership shifted when Col. John S. Candler, a superior court judge and soldier who had recently served in Cuba with the Third Georgia Volunteer Infantry, "readily consented to lay aside his judicial duties for a time and to put on his uniform again."[31] Until the troops arrived, Mayor Arnold had local whites, armed with shotguns and rifles, patrol the streets of the town. "The negroes stood with bulging eyes and scattered about the place, being warned not to congregate," the correspondent Royal Daniel wrote. Many of the black citizens of Palmetto, he added, had "left the town in droves . . . weeping and screaming and dogged and revengeful," although, as he made clear, "the lives and property of citizens will be protected at any cost, and the white people, while condemning the act of lawlessness of the mob, are determined to meet any attempt the negroes may make for revenge." Colonel Candler had ordered a curfew hour of 9:00 p.m. Nevertheless, Daniel played up Palmetto's continued fear of retaliation, especially when the next morning local blacks gathered at the warehouse, which still contained both the dead and the wounded. "There was danger lurking in every corner, and the negroes were sullen and defiant and the white people were anxious but determined. An outbreak was momentarily expected, and it looked as if there was sure to be a clash between the races."[32] In this way, the black inhabitants of Palmetto were again identified as the source of destructive violence, although they were the ones who had been shot down. The white mob, on the other hand, was essentially excused for its actions. The killings might be described as a "Bloody Tragedy," but the blood spent was necessary, forced upon the community by the outrageous behavior of the blacks themselves. Thus, Palmetto had replicated in miniature the actions of the Wilmington, North Carolina, mob, seizing control of justice and forcing an exodus of its black residents.[33]

Over the next few days, both Atlanta papers provided their readers with an array of front-page sketches that represented several of the survivors (George Tatum, Clem Watts, and Isom Brown), members of the Palmetto Guard, the Granite Warehouse, a "Domino [mask] Left Behind by Whitecappers," and spent shells from the rifles. Both also included drawings of the shooting locale, with bodies strewn on the floor, women weeping and praying, a child observing quietly. The *Constitution*'s artist was more skillful, but the illustrations from both papers were similar enough to indicate that each recorded actual scenes. Both papers also emphasized the horror of the massacre with such gory descriptors as "Brains and Blood and Moans" and "Blood and Brains Were Spattered on the Walls and Floors." Nevertheless, in the midst of such reporting, Royal Daniel included a moment clearly meant to amuse his white readers. In a section titled "Hauled Home for Dead," he related that when Clem Watts was found unconscious among the bodies, he was assumed dead and taken to his home, where mourners gathered

Chapter Three

and "his old mother was moaning and pulling her hair." Several hours later, when Watts revived and asked for water, "the negro mourners fled in dismay and superstitious horror." Upon examination, it was discovered that Watts "had not been scratched nor even bruised." Instead, according to Daniel, "he had been frightened into unconsciousness and to all outward appearances was dead." This episode, a variation of numerous comic tales of revived "corpses" found in southwest humor such as George Washington Harris's "Sut Lovingood" yarn "Frustrating a Funeral," presented the paper's readers with a racist "skeer" story often associated with the Ku Klux Klan. As Andrew Silver, in *Minstrelsy and Murder: The Crisis of Southern Humor, 1835–1925*, observes,

> The humor of fright and flight is central to these tales. . . . The black body in these sketches is relentlessly dehumanized in such moments of terror, and it is precisely this dehumanization which amuses racist nineteenth-century audiences. Comic narratives such as these served both to condition the reception of terror as comic and to temper the tone of articles detailing real instances of Klan torture and murder, often appearing on the same pages as these practical jokes.[34]

Thus, Daniel's comic aside allowed white readers a smile at the victims' expense and strongly suggested that black grief was less profound than white, more easily translated into burlesque and superstition. It also mitigated and distanced the horror of the surrounding account, turning it into yet another form of entertainment.[35]

While also capable of an unseemly quip, Frank Fleming showed greater overall sympathy for the black victims and their families. He devoted part of his article to "A Sight Not Forgotten," which, in its own fashion, challenged his readers as Daniel's did not. "What is seen upon entering the small room of the warehouse, where the prisoners were confined, and while its grewsome inhabitants yet remain, is a sight that can only be felt. The view touches the emotions deeply," he wrote, "not however on account of the dead and wounded lying on the crimson floor, but at the aspect of the living":

> There, crowded in the narrow space left by the lifeless trunks, are kneeling the women people of the dead. Old women, born in slavery, mourning for a son, in a low, meaningless, savage chant, now in low, unnatural voice and now in high treble; no patent sorrow on the face, but with the same meaningless lost look, as of voice. Sorrow personified and unfathomable.
>
> Young wives and sisters, with perchance a lighter sorrow, stand up swaying their arms and bodies in frenzy and calling on God, after the latter day fashion, for retribution. It is all sad, even the curses of the young women.

When the women were forced by doctors to leave the room, Fleming reported, they stood outside the windows and watched. "The women was the worst part of the select parties' work and the part unforeseen," Fleming noted.[36]

Of this group, the "most striking" was one of the mothers, whom Fleming described in a way that was both patronizing and conflicted.

> She chanted her soft lullaby of goodby in her savage way by [her son's] side and then staggered to the door to return to her cottage. As she passed the curious crowd at the door the woman threw up her arms with a wild maniacal laugh and wabbled on over the hill, swinging her arms and laughing the laugh of sorrow. No face in the crowd smiled and if a whitecapper happened to be present his small heart must have smote him with a great stroke.[37]

Royal Daniel subsequently reported that when the militia train arrived in Palmetto on the morning of the sixteenth, a woman stood in front of the warehouse shouting, "Oh Lordy! Oh Lordy! my son is gone! My poor boy's dead!" Colonel Candler's first order was to have the women silenced. "Tell that woman that this is no place and time for a public demonstration," he commanded, and she was removed from the spot.[38] There is no way to know if this was the same woman described by Fleming, but it might well have been. One wonders how white newspaper readers reacted to these scenes. Would they have seen Colonel Candler's orders as mean-spirited—identifying the woman's grief as a "public demonstration"—or as a necessary step in maintaining order? Fleming surely meant to prick at his readers' feelings, and perhaps at their consciences, as they absorbed the results of these killings. His reference to a whitecapper's "small heart . . . smote . . . with a great stroke," while a neat turn of phrase, also undercut any romantic idealization of the vigilantes that his readers might have formed.

The Fifth Regiment, reinforced on Saturday, patrolled the streets of Palmetto for the next three days. Royal Daniel praised the effect these "Brass Buttons" had in restoring order. "It looked as if all the soldiers in the state had been turned loose in the town and that they were trying to find something that had been lost. Up and down the street they marched and back and forth, the constant step, step, step, the stern commands of their superior officers and the blast of the bugle was too terribly realistic for the negroes, even if they had ever dreamed of revenge." The white citizens "could not do enough for the soldiers" and brought them cigars, cigarettes, and food. Colonel Candler assured the town, with a flourish, "There'll be no mob in Palmetto tonight. . . . You may go to your homes and throw off all anxiety and know that your property will be safe so long as the militia is here."[39] Once again, it was the fear of black retribution that was being addressed. On Monday, the twentieth, most of the militia returned to Atlanta, leaving a temporary contingent of fifteen soldiers. Although the town still feared rumored uprisings by blacks, Daniel reported that after the killings "not a negro was seen in Palmetto after sundown," noting, "Where they went or where they spent the night has not been ascertained, but it is known that they were not in town, and none dared return until after the sun was up this morning."[40] The white community at first maintained a nervous vigilance, and the sense was that, despite some vague sympathy with the "slaughtered prisoners," a "general and indiscriminate massacre" of blacks would result if they "offered any show of fight."[41]

Palmetto now wished to put this unpleasantness behind it as soon as possible. "As the excitement and terror of the situation dies away the people are gradually realizing the awfulness of the crime that followed in the wake of the armed mob," the *Constitution* reported. Colonel Candler, in his alternate role as judge, had decreed that since the victims had died while in the custody of the law, the state should be responsible for their burial, and on the afternoon of Friday, the seventeenth, Bingham, Hudson, Brown, and Cotton were interred, their pine coffins and the wagons that carried them to a cemetery outside town provided "by the community." "Weeping women, mothers, wives and sisters of the dead followed behind with a grief that had not been spent. The service was simple at the grave and was soon over, and the disinterested left, leaving the women behind."[42]

The explanation now given for the mob's action was the unlikely suspicion that although Bud Cotton had supposedly confessed and named the others as coconspirators, they might still have been acquitted by a jury. This lack of faith in the legal system was temporarily underscored after the shooting, when four of the five survivors—Brown, Jameson, Tatum, and Watts—were released from custody, although still held under warrant for trial. The *Constitution* wondered why the law had grown so lenient. "It is not presumed that the death of their companions had any effect on the legal obligation to hold them for trial," the paper observed, although another interpretation might suggest that evidence against them was simply not that strong. Indeed, one explanation was that since Bud Cotton, the primary witness, was now dead, it would be easy for the other men to dispute his allegation. Nevertheless, the four were rearrested the following day, largely on the insistence of Dr. Johnston, and placed in the jail at Fairburn. But clearly Palmetto, at least for the moment, had lost its taste for further vengeance. It was generally agreed that the whitecappers had numbered no more than fifteen and that they had most likely walked rather than ridden to the jail. Although the "best people" in Palmetto continued to voice their determination to find and punish the perpetrators, no member of the mob had yet been identified. Isom Brown, who had broken his arm during the shooting, made it clear that he had nothing to say. "I did not recognize any member of the party and wouldn't know one again if I was to see him," he told the *Constitution*.[43]

At noon on the sixteenth, although the county coroner could not be found—he was reported "out of the city"—a jury of six men was impaneled, with Dr. T. P. Bullard (to whom Hal Johnston had first related Bud Cotton's confession) as foreman. The coroner's jury, presided over by Justice of the Peace Cummings, heard testimony from four witnesses, two of the guards and two of the victims. The first guard, R. E. Baker, swore that there were between 75 and 100 men in the gang that took over the warehouse but insisted that he did not recognize any of them. J. J. Conger or Conner put the total at between 75 and 150, but he agreed with Baker that the members could not be identified. Clem Watts, following Isom Brown's lead, also said that he did not know any of his attackers.[44]

Of the survivors, John Bigby was the most horribly wounded. Bigby had been shot nine times and left untended among the corpses in the warehouse for many hours. He was reported paralyzed below the waist. Nevertheless, according to the *Constitution*, "While lying in the warehouse after the shooting he implicated a number of the most prominent men in Palmetto in the lynching, but his word is not taken for anything." Despite his deteriorating condition, Bigby was brought before the coroner's jury, and there he boldly identified two local men as members of the mob, one of them being Tom Daniel, the merchant supposedly picked out for death by the black gang and who was now a member of the jury itself. Bigby's testimony was quickly discounted because, as was shrewdly pointed out, he had been "shot in the back, and none of the shot that entered his body entered from the front," which meant, in the opinion of the jurors, that he could not have actually seen the shooters to identify any of them. Also, there was "sufficient evidence that Bigby had a spite" against Daniel.[45] After this testimony, Bigby "ceased to be communicative on the subject of the men who composed the mob."[46] The jury's verdict read:

> We, the coroner's jury, empaneled in the cases of the death of Harrison Hudson, William Cotton, Jr., Ed Brown and Henry Bingham, find that they came to their death from gunshot or pistol shot wounds from a crowd of masked men to the jury unknown, a little after midnight, or on the morning of the 16th of March, 1899.
>
> T. J. Bullard, Foreman

The other members of the jury were listed as F. T. Mixon, W. C. Smith, H. T. Daniel, J. L. Giles, and R. G. Mixon.[47]

When the state militia left town on Monday, the twentieth, they took the wounded John Bigby with them to Grady Hospital in Atlanta. Some of Bigby's friends and relatives had voiced fears that he "would be killed by the whites in twenty-four hours" if he remained in Palmetto after the troops withdrew. Governor Candler advised that Bigby be transported with the militia, "provided

Chapter Three

the civil authorities of the town did not object to his removal."[48] Bigby died at Grady Hospital the next day, "After Five Days of Horrible Agony."[49] George Tatum, who had suffered minor wounds, also left Palmetto when he was released from custody, and like Bigby, he went to Grady Hospital for treatment. There he wrote a letter to a black preacher in Palmetto in which he named men who made up the mob. His correspondence, however, was deemed "wild, incoherent," and Captain Barker, who now commanded the state militia in Palmetto after Candler had returned to Atlanta, "stated that the letter contained nothing more than a few lines of illegible, indiscriminate scribbling that could not by any means be deciphered."[50] The preacher to whom Tatum wrote was most likely a man named Thorp, who was "believed by many of the people in Palmetto to be at the bottom of much of the mischief taken part in by the negroes of the community." The white citizens of Palmetto, concerned that black preachers would use their Sunday services to "stir up the passions of the negroes on the subject of lynching," had "warned [them] in a friendly way" not to do so. So advised, Thorp and his family gathered their belongings and also left for Atlanta on Sunday afternoon with Captain Barker and some of the troops.[51]

Thus, by Monday, order appeared to have been restored in Palmetto. The victims' testimony was either discredited or dismissed, and the "prominent men" of the town, with the help of the Atlanta newspapers, had been able to package the event as they saw fit. The *Constitution*, for example, explained, "Probably the negro element in Palmetto is the worst to be found anywhere in the state. A prominent citizen stated today that the town had new additions to its colored population every week; that outlawed negroes came in from surrounding counties, and refusing to work, fell into all forms of devilment and moved about in gangs, which the town authorities could not control."[52] Of the nine victims, four were identified as repeat offenders, "indicted by the grand juries of this county and tried on various charges such as burglary, assault to murder and many misdemeanors." Bud Cotton had been charged with "assault and battery, simple larceny, assault to murder, larceny from the house and selling whiskey," while Bigby, now identified as a "shrewd mulatto," had paid fines for selling "blind tiger whiskey" and had "always been considered fortunate in getting out of trouble." After his death, Bigby was accused of other misdeeds. Some locals acknowledged that, after the first fire, they had secretly hired the black Pinkerton agent to "work up evidence" against the guilty parties. "It is positively known than John Bigby . . . searched the town for this negro we employed, trying to find him to kill him," one insisted. As for the others, Watts and Brown had records of misdemeanors, but Brown had served time on a chain gang. Only Tip Hudson, one of the dead, was assumed an innocent victim: an inoffensive "old negro," he was identified as Bud Cotton's father-in-law, "which probably accounts for the old man being charged with helping to burn the town."[53]

Palmetto, on the other hand, was now established as the properly aggrieved party. In support of an application to Governor Candler for permission to organize a company of "Palmetto Guards," the proposed commander, Dr. Bullard, explained the need for a local militia:

> Since the first burning we have guarded the town day and night: men have slept in their clothes, expecting every moment to be called out to meet a mob of incendiaries and armed negroes. It has been impossible to rest from the anxiety. Negroes have poked their heads in at the windows of residences, frightening the women and threatening the men. It is impossible to describe or to imagine the feelings of the people of Palmetto, for we dreaded, like death, something that we knew not what. . . .
>
> The citizens of Palmetto are peaceable and attend to their business. There was no bitterness between the races and we have treated the negroes kindly in all our dealings with them. We regret the visit of the mob, and I do not believe the people of Palmetto had anything to do with the mob's work.
>
> The negroes lay in wait for the white people and nearly all of us have been threatened with death.[54]

Thus, although Palmetto was by nature a quiet, simple retreat—"There is nothing in the peaceful, bucolic air of the village that breathes of riot or an armed mob on the outskirts or that would induce any but the most pleasant feelings," as one report put it—nevertheless, it had reached a breaking point. As another "well-to-do and highly respected citizen" further explained, "You see, the people in the community here are human in this respect, that they will not be overrun, even if the outside world is not willing to grant that we are human in other respects."[55] This was as close as Palmetto spokesmen came to admitting that the masked vigilantes were in all likelihood members of the community.

Despite these attempts at justification, many of the state's leading newspapers now criticized the shootings. The *Augusta Chronicle* headlined its report "Uncalled For Lynching of Several Negroes" and added "Most Shameful Violation of Peace and Good Order of the State of Georgia," the kind of condemnation usually reserved for descriptions of black crimes. In an editorial, the *Savannah Morning News* stated, "There is not a single extenuating circumstance from any point of view that can be urged in defense of those who committed the cowardly crime at Palmetto. . . . The Palmetto lynchers made themselves greater criminals than the negroes they lynched, assuming that the negroes were guilty of the crimes for which they had been arrested."[56] On March 17, the *Atlanta Constitution* ran an editorial titled "The Palmetto Mob" that condemned the killings: "But the verdict of all sensible men and of all law-abiding citizens will be that it was a very cowardly thing to do," the paper stated. While admitting that "there are crimes in their nature so hideous and revolting as to seem to call for immediate reprisal regardless of legal proceedings . . . there is no justification for this murderous assault of a mob on helpless prisoners already in the clutches of the law and certain to have their desserts dealt out to them in a manner at once peaceful and legal." The editorial even acknowledged, "It may be that some of the prisoners were innocent of the crimes laid at their door. If so the mob has been guilty of as foul a piece of injustice as ever blackened the records of disorder. And if every one of the prisoners is guilty of incendiarism, that is no excuse for the murderous action of the mob."[57] The *Macon Telegraph* was even more critical in its assessment of the lynching. "The suggestion that it behooved 200 masked men to fall on and massacre the prisoners after midnight, in a community where a resort to lynch law is not regarded as a necessity, would probably have been too absurd to occur to anybody, but for the question of color. The horrid tragedy would therefore appear to be the result, not of alleged necessity, but of race antipathy." It also disputed the often-stated fears of race war.

> Were the blacks powerful, dreaded, challenging the other race to battle, the matter would have a different aspect. As it is, compared with the whites, they are weak and practically helpless, and therein is the chief horror of these wholesale slaughterings. The men who take part in them bring more evil upon themselves than upon their hapless victims. That they are ready to dip their hands in human blood lightly and recklessly, without any just provocation, implies a moral obliquity of mind and a brutal perversion of all humane instincts that should be a source of grave concern for their friends and their community. . . . The wretches lying dead at Palmetto have suffered less perhaps than their executioners are likely to suffer from the injury done their own moral fiber, to say nothing of the damaging effect of example upon youthful and unstable minds.[58]

In Washington, D.C., W. Calvin Chase, editor of the black newspaper the *Washington Bee*, offered his own scathing response. "The recent, blood thirsty murder which took place at Palmetto, Ga., last week displays at once the cowardice, brutality, and hatred of the whites of that section. . . . The boasted bravery of the South is a myth. The scoundrels who committed the murders were not only masked, but they were so chicken-hearted as not to dare to make an attack upon eight [*sic*] imprisoned, defenseless persons without being assisted by 150 fully armed men." Chase continued his furious assault on southern courage:

> There was once a boast on the part of the Southern white man that one of his kind could whip three yankees. And this boast was knocked out when the yankees made

them turn tail and run like curs. But it was for the colored people to outdo even the yankees. It takes twenty white Southern men to successfully defeat one colored man. There are no epithets in the English language to adequately express the incomparable meanness, treachery, and cowardice of the Southern white man.[59]

But on March 24, the *Newnan Herald and Advertiser* offered its own assessment in an editorial titled, like the *Macon Telegraph*'s, "The Palmetto 'Affair.'" Its placement of "Affair" in quotes indicated a judgment quite different from that of its sister publication. Editor James Brown wrote:

> We do not wish to be understood as defending the bloody work of the mob. . . . It would have been infinitely better for the good order and welfare of the community if the victims of the tragedy had been tried in the courts and made to expiate their crime in accordance with the forms prescribed by law. The moral effect would have been more salutary, unquestionably; but there have been similar crimes in other communities, at other times, where persistent and malicious aggravation on the part of a lawless element has been known to make demons of peaceable men, who, grown impatient at the law's delay, have taken the law into their own hands. It is a desperate recourse, and is usually fraught with tragic results, but in many instances the general effect has proven beneficial to the community.[60]

———

In early July, Tatum, Jameson, Brown, and Watts were among a group of ten prisoners who broke out of jail in Fairburn, where they had been held since the shooting. Watts soon gave himself up. Jameson and Tatum were caught, but Brown remained on the loose for a time. After their captures, Tatum, Jameson, and Brown were sent to the Tower in Atlanta for safekeeping until their court date.[61] In August, George Tatum and John Jameson (or Jemison or Jimmerson, as his name was sometimes spelled in the papers) were brought to trial in Fairburn, Georgia, with John Candler, who had commanded the militia in Palmetto, as presiding judge. No one raised objections as to his impartiality. Judge Candler insisted on his respect for the law and his ability to render justice in an honorable manner.[62]

The case against Tatum and Jameson was based on their confessions and what was called "circumstantial evidence of rather strong character." One of the witnesses against Jameson and Tatum was J. R. Minx, who testified that he had crawled under John Bigby's house and listened to a gang of seventeen men boast of the arson and their plot to do more burning. Minx related that he heard the men threaten Bud Cotton if he told, saying that any traitor would be killed by the others in the gang.[63] Jameson offered an alibi, stating that he was asleep when the fires occurred, and further claimed that "one of the principle witnesses for the state was in the crowd that killed five out of nine in the warehouse in Palmetto, stating he recognized him at the time."[64] Nevertheless, both Jameson and Tatum were found guilty and sentenced to life imprisonment in the penitentiary. After the trial, the court stenographer was quoted in the *Constitution* as saying, "There is no doubt in my mind but many of the men who were witnesses in the trials of these cases were in the gang that did the killing of these negroes." He also indicated that the full story had not been reported by the papers.[65]

John Jameson's allegation and the stenographer's suspicion concerning the state's witnesses may have been a reference to Hal Johnston, who was described in later articles as the man "at whose insistence the two convicted men were arrested and rearrested and who furnished evidence to convict them."[66] The state had first offered its four-hundred-dollar reward for the capture of the Palmetto arsonists at Johnston's urging, and after the trial Johnston, J. R. Minx, and H. K. Beckman made claims for that money. In January 1900, Johnston received the reward. Bud Cotton's confession to him was deemed the most important break in the case. Johnston then generously split the money with Minx and Beckman.[67]

By this time, however, others were questioning not only the guilt of the arrested men but the entire story that had been constructed around the charges of arson and terrorism. In September 1899, Isabella Webb Parks, a leader in the Woman's Christian Temperance Movement and an editor of its newspaper, the *Union Signal*, published an essay titled "Our Responsibility to the American Negro" in the *Methodist Review*, in which she recounted the events of the Palmetto massacre and the subsequent burning of Sam Hose. While acknowledging that Palmetto had a reputation as "an ideal spot, where the race problem was being worked out in the most happy manner," she declared that the stated "grievous provocation that had excited the lynchers" was "utterly false":

> The truth was that the first fire was clearly not incendiary, and no one thought of suggesting that it was until after the second one. The other so-called fires were set the same night in different parts of the town. One was kindled conspicuously against an outer door, where it was seen at once and extinguished, probably for the purpose of diverting attention from the other, which was started inside a store where, by a peculiar "coincidence," the owner of the goods had taken out insurance in great haste, having received his papers the afternoon before the fire.

Mrs. Parks's allegations supported the idea that these men had been innocent of the crimes attributed to them. She doubted that the accused would have boasted of having set the fires to facilitate a robbery. She furthermore maintained that "the arrested negroes had been previously taken before the judge" on the charge of stealing, that the case had been dismissed, and the white accusers made to pay the court costs. The angry white men, protesting that "'it made niggers impudent to arrest them and not punish them,'" had, she reported, threatened,

"'The next time we arrest any niggers for those fires Judge Candler won't have any trouble with them.'"[68]

For all its melodrama, the notoriety of the Palmetto lynchings would shortly be eclipsed by events even more horrible and ultimately more controversial. The shooting of these black men set the stage for an even greater paroxysm of violence. The connection between the Palmetto "Affair" and the subsequent public execution of Sam Hose would make clear how far the white community was willing to go to assert its authority in a world perceived as growing more and more unstable.

Preparations to hang Dr. W. L. Ryder near Waverly Hall, Georgia (*Atlanta Constitution*, July 21, 1897)

The lynching of Oscar Williams, Griffin, Georgia (*Macon Telegraph*, July 23, 1897)

Dr. Hal Johnston's Granite Warehouse, the "Scene of the Bloody Tragedy"
(*Atlanta Journal*, March 16, 1899)

Scenes following the Palmetto massacre, Palmetto, Georgia
(*Atlanta Constitution*, March 17, 1899)

ALFRED CRANFORD AND HIS WIFE
The Victims of Sam Hose, the Negro, Near Palmetto Wednesday Night.

Alfred and Mattie Cranford
(*Atlanta Constitution*,
April 15, 1899)

Mattie Cranford standing outside the Cranford home
(*Atlanta Journal*, April 18, 1899)

Mattie Cranford and three of her children near the home (*Atlanta Journal*, April 18, 1899)

Sam Hose at the coach window on the ride to Newnan
(*Atlanta Constitution*, April 24, 1899)

Recived of J.B.
Jones, R.A. Gordon,
Wilson Mathews,
P. F. Phelps. Charles
Thomas and A Rogow-
ski, one Sam Holt
or Hose (alias) or Tom
Wilks in a live
condition and
unharmed = Delivered
as the murderer of
Alfred Cransford of
near Palmetta, also a
rapist.   J S Brown
              Shff Coweta Co
April 23/1899

FACSIMILE OF SHERIFF BROWN'S RECEIPT FOR HOLT.
It was on Presentation of This Document That J. B. Jones was Able
to Collect the $1,350 Reward which Had Been Offered
for the Arrest of the Negro.

Sheriff Brown's handwritten receipt for Sam Hose (*Atlanta Constitution*, April 24, 1899)

Governor William Y. Atkinson
(Courtesy of Georgia Archives,
Capitol Museum Collection,
1992-23-0046)

Preparations for the torture and burning of Henry Smith, Paris, Texas,
February 1, 1893 (photograph by J. L. Mertins, in R. W. Shufeldt, *The Negro,
A Menace to American Civilization* [Boston: Gorham Press, 1907], 168)

"Sam Hose: The First Picture of the Negro Yet Printed" (*Atlanta Journal*, April 24, 1899). In this illustration, the representation of the light-skinned Hose was rendered so dark that the image is difficult to reproduce clearly.

He Slipped In Behind the Unsuspecting Man and Brought Down the Axe on His Head.

The murder of Alfred Cranford as represented in the *National Police Gazette*, May 13, 1899

Details from an illustration of the burning
of Sam Hose as represented in a halftone
supplement to the *National Police Gazette*,
May 13, 1899

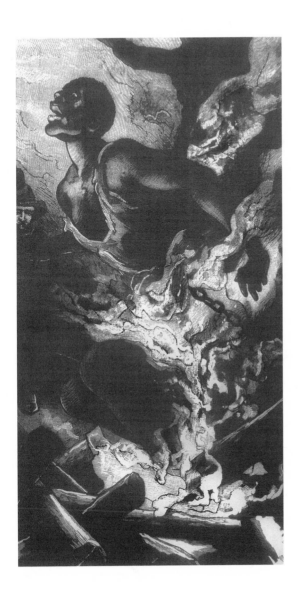

"Representation of Elijah Strickland's hanging, taken from a photograph,"
Atlanta Constitution, April 24, 1899

Chapter 4

A Carnival of Blood and Lust

Although the Palmetto killings held the front pages for a short period, the story was rather quickly lost to other events, both local and national. One of these was the visit of U.S. president William McKinley to Georgia for a restful vacation in Thomasville, located in the extreme southern part of the state near the Florida border. On March 10, it had been announced that McKinley, accompanied by his wife and a small party including the vice president, Garret (Gus) Hobart, Hobart's wife, Ohio Senator and Mrs. Mark Hanna, and a few other dignitaries would be making the trip to Georgia to stay at the plantation owned by Hanna's brother Mel. "The president goes south to get the benefit of the magnificent Georgia weather to rest, and he does not care to make any plans with anything else in view," the *Constitution* noted. "There are to be no receptions and no speeches. It will be the quietest kind of a social visit."[1] The special train, made up of five Pullmans, a dining car, and a combination smoking/baggage car, left Washington's Union Station at 6:00 p.m. on Monday the thirteenth and arrived in Thomasville twenty-four hours later. "It is entirely fortunate that the president should have chosen Thomasville as the point at which to seek repose," an editorial in the *Constitution* remarked.

> He will find the mockingbirds singing there, and the pungent odor of the pines will fill his nostrils and soothe what Old Aunt Minervy Ann calls the "mukyous membrine." If he does not find spring in Thomasville, he will find a semblance of her, a fairly good imitation.

Reflecting on the unusually cold and wet weather the South had experienced in the first months of 1899, the paper continued, in a slightly eroticized mode:

There are times too, when spring shows herself to be as shifty and as tantalizing a trollop as ever teased man withal. . . . Her reputation is gone in these parts, and we are waiting now, not for spring, but for summer—for those glorious days when the mercury stands at 98 degrees in the shade, and the whole body glows with a generous warmth that is mitigated now and again by light breezes that blow softly through the ivy leaves on the veranda.[2]

Georgia papers divided their attention between the shootings in Palmetto and McKinley's vacation (and, for a few days, the hanging in the Tower of Robert Lewis), sometimes producing odd juxtapositions. On March 16, Palmetto got the headlines, but McKinley shared the front page in articles that emphasized Old South charm. "Mark Hanna seems determined that President McKinley shall pump ozone into his lungs until they reek with it," the *Constitution* reported.[3] McKinley told the *Atlanta Journal*, "I have always enjoyed my trips to Georgia. Your balmy climate is delightful, and I always find it pleasant here. Georgia possesses many attractions, and I consider this place a fine one in which to rest for a time."[4] He made no mention of the incidents concerning black militia or of the recent lynchings in Lee County and then in Palmetto. McKinley would spend two weeks in the state, leaving Thomasville for Jekyll Island and other resort spots on the coast.

By Saturday, March 18, a second story had pushed Palmetto from the front pages. In New York City, the burning of the Windsor Hotel presented a scene of horror and derring-do that immediately captured the attention of the reading public. Located at Forty-sixth Street and Fifth Avenue, the Windsor was one of the city's finest, a luxury hotel that filled an entire block of Fifth Avenue. The fire started on Friday afternoon as the city's annual St. Patrick's Day parade was passing below the building. It spread so rapidly through the interior of the building that some who were watching the parade from windows or the roof were forced to jump into the streets, some to their deaths. "Windows were thrown up on every side of the building and guests, mostly women, in all stages of terror, made their appearance and uttered frantic appeals for assistance to the crowd below," the *Constitution* recounted:

> As the flames gathered about them they became more and more terror-stricken, and presently some of them stood upon the narrow window sills and beckoned to the spectators that they were about to leap. The men collected upon the sidewalks ready to render any assistance they could, and in the meantime some of the women left the window sills and dropped to the streets. In most cases the efforts to catch them and break their awful fall were unavailing, for they struck the sidewalk and in frequent instances broken limbs were the result.[5]

Among the ninety-two dead were the wife and the daughter of the hotel's owner, Warren Leland. Other notable guests who escaped were the president's brother Abner McKinley and his family, and Georgia governor Allen Candler's sister-in-law, Alice Price, who broke her leg when she jumped.[6]

If these events were not enough to divert attention from the Palmetto shootings, that weekend in March also brought rain, hailstones, and even a tornado into this area of west Georgia. Buildings were blown down in nearby Grantville and Hogansville, and as the line of storms passed into Alabama, they grew stronger and caused greater damage by wind and rain. At least sixteen people were killed by a series of cyclones in that state.[7]

For the most part, the white citizens of Georgia were now ready to turn the page on the unpleasant events that had consumed them since the beginning of the year. There was the sense that awful but necessary, even heroic, actions had been taken to restore order between the races. On April 7, the *Newnan Herald and Advertiser* published an essay titled "The Ante-bellum Darkey," which nostalgically recalled (or invented) a safer, simpler time to comfort its readers but also sadly to remind them of what had been lost. "As we stand on the verge of a new century and gaze down the dim vista of the past, we behold the decrepit and trembling figure of the old ante-bellum darkey as he slowly marches to the grave," it read:

> What pleasure it would be could they who were children during those days recall for a few short hours the times when they sat and listened to stories from the lips of an old white-haired darkey, whose originality and dialectic speech could add a charm which can never be equaled.
>
> When once this negro formed an attachment for his master he would lay down his life for him. No stronger love ever existed than that of old "Uncle Ned" for his master. No sweeter songs were ever sung than those which came from the lips of old black "mammy," by which we were lulled to sleep, and we closed our weary eyes in sweet slumber with a confidence which she alone could inspire, never fearing for a moment the intrusion of some nocturnal marauder as long as old "mammy's" watchful eye was over us, and the faithful old darkey keeping a sleepless vigil over his "chillum" whom he loved and for whom he would consider death a small sacrifice.[8]

This tribute was likely written by the *Herald and Advertiser*'s editor, James E. Brown, who would run the paper for over forty years. On the cusp of a new century, he looked back longingly at a time when blacks could be seen as docile and faithful retainers. "Only a few of those old darkies are left, and they are fast descending the hill of life and nearing the last mile-post, and when they pass the familiar figures of the 'olden days' will have vanished like a sweet dream,"

Brown wrote. But whatever yearnings he and others had for a return to the racial simplicities of this old world, whatever wistful hopes they might hold that the worst had now occurred, they were about to be terribly disabused. A "new Negro," a "nocturnal marauder" of the most horrific sort, was about to shatter their complacency.

"ASSASSINATION NEAR PALMETTO; MR. CRANFORD BRAINED WITH AXE" read the headline of a special bulletin in the *Atlanta Journal* on April 13, six days after "The Ante-Bellum Darkey" was published. Datelined Palmetto, the report briefly recounted that Alfred Cranford, a prominent farmer and landowner whose plantation was located some four miles south of Palmetto, had been killed around 7:00 p.m. the previous evening while having supper with his wife and family. The murderer was "a negro, armed with an ax, [who] stepped into the house and behind Mr. Cranford and dealt him a blow on the back of his head which crushed his skull and caused the brains to ooze out." The murderer then dragged Mrs. Cranford into an adjoining room and there "assaulted her." After he left, Mrs. Cranford "ran from the house and went to that of her father-in-law about half a mile distant, and gave the alarm." She identified the assailant, and although his name was not given in this initial report, the description was: "The assassin is described as being of ginger-cake color, has a black moustache, and has the habit of shaking his head while talking."[9]

The April 14 editions of the Atlanta papers and the *Newnan Herald and Advertiser* began to fill in the details. "Murder and Rape" read the Newnan headline; "Awful Tragedy near Cranford's Mill Wednesday Night—Work of a Devil." The *Journal* ran its story on page 4: "Cranford Murdered; His Wife Assaulted." "Brutal Crime near Palmetto Last Night Will Almost Certainly Result in a Lynching This Afternoon," the paper predicted. The *Constitution* went even further in determining the murderer's fate in its front-page article: "Determined Mob after Hose; He Will Be Lynched If Caught," continuing "Assailant of Mrs. Cranford May Be Brought to Palmetto and Burned at the Stake." This headline now identified the "Devil" as one "Sam Hose" and made primary his assault of Mrs. Cranford rather than the killing of her husband. It also recorded the intentions of the men in pursuit: to bring him back to the scene of the crime, make him stand before the Cranford family, and then consign him to the fire for public immolation.

The *Newnan Herald and Advertiser* offered a lengthy prologue before giving the details of the murder and rape, both as preparation for its description of what had occurred and as an explanation of what was surely to come:

> The most brutal and revolting crime ever perpetrated in Coweta county was committed by a negro fiend Wednesday night near Cranford's mill in the Seventh district.

When the full enormity of the devilish deed became known a storm of indignation swept over the community, and the excitement produced by the shocking details is yet at fever heat. The peaceful, law-abiding people of Coweta never experienced a more bitter sense of outrage, nor were ever more determined in any purpose than that the black brute, whose carnival of blood and lust has brought death and desolation to the home of one of our best and most worthy citizens, shall be run down and made to suffer the torments of the damned in expiation of his hellish crime. That he will be caught there is scarcely any doubt, and the prediction may be made with reasonable assurance that before the sun goes down to-day the career of this monster in human form will have been brought to a timely end.[10]

The Atlanta papers were less extravagant in their prose but much of the same mind as to the inevitability of the punishment. Connecting the Palmetto shootings with this more recent murder, the *Journal* reported, "The crime was a terrible one and it has embittered the feeling against the negroes in this community and it would take only the slightest disturbance to start serious trouble. The Palmetto lynching of several negroes several weeks ago is still fresh in the minds of the people, and there is a determination among the citizens to avenge such crimes as have been committed by negroes recently, notably the burning of Palmetto and the crime of last night."[11] The *Constitution* noted, "Mrs. Cranford has signified a wish to see the negro lynched, and the understanding seems to be that he will be brought here. There have been whisperings of burning at the stake and of torturing the fellow, and so great is the excitement and so high the indignation that this is among the possibilities. Whether the negro is burned or hanged, it now seems certain that he will face his victim before paying the penalty of his crime and that she will see the execution."[12] The *Griffin Daily News and Sun* added its own bit of macabre humor to the proceedings: "The Hose Will Not Put Out This Fire," its headline punned wickedly.[13] Both the *Washington Post* ("Tracked by Bloodhounds") and the *New York Times* ("Hunt for a Georgia Negro") also reported the story, and the *Post* repeated Mrs. Cranford's alleged desire to witness the execution.[14]

The first detailed account of the crime was published in the *Constitution* on Friday, April 14. The source was E. D. Sharkey, who was married to Alfred Cranford's sister and had gotten his information from talking to Mattie Cranford herself. Sharkey told the paper that Sam Hose had been employed on the Cranford farm for some time and had been considered a "steady workman." Recently, however, he had "made threats against Cranford" to other black workers, and they had informed their employer. Cranford had then talked to his father, G. E. Cranford, and the night before the murder, his father had loaned him a pistol for protection. On the evening of the twelfth, Cranford was eating supper with his wife and four children. He saw Hose in the yard through the window and called to him. Hose did not answer the first time, so Cranford called again from the table. Hose then responded, and while the Cranfords continued to eat, he entered the house "not by the regular door, but through Mrs. Cranford's room." He had removed his shoes and was carrying an ax used to chop wood. He came quietly into the dining area and was already standing behind Cranford with the ax raised and ready to strike when Mattie Cranford looked up to see him. According to Sharkey's report, "Before she could scream he had brought the blade down upon Mr. Cranford's head, splitting his skull to his eyes. Cranford fell over sideways to the floor. The negro then struck him on both temples with the handle of the ax, driving in the skull. He then kicked his victim on the left side of his face and in the left side. Black bruises on the body corroborate this. Cranford lived three hours after the blows had been struck."

It got worse, according to Sharkey. After braining Alfred Cranford, Hose forced Mattie to take him through the house, a baby held in one of her arms and a lantern in the other hand, as he looked for things to steal. They then returned to the dining area where Cranford lay dying in a pool of his blood and brains. At this point one of the other children, Mary Estelle, hysterically asked her mother, "What is Sam doing?" Infuriated, Hose "struck the child on the side of her head, knocking the little girl about six or eight feet." Next, he "snatched the eight-months-old baby from the arms of its mother and dashed it to the floor." At this point in the telling, Sharkey reached the final outrage:

> Then with renewed threats of death in case she made the slightest outcry, Sam Hose assaulted Mrs. Cranford literally within arm-reach of where the brains were oozing from her husband's head. After committing the assault the negro said, "Now I am through with my work, let them kill me if they can." And left the house.

Mrs. Cranford waited to be sure Hose was gone; she then gathered her children, cradling the injured infant, and herded them through the dark to the home of her husband's father. When the group reached the gate to the house, she called for help and collapsed in a faint. Her father-in-law rushed to the gate and found her and the children. Once she was revived, she told her awful story, and Grippia Cranford immediately "raised the alarm throughout the county for miles around." Sharkey ended his retelling by noting, "When those people catch that negro there is going to be a lynching sure, and they will be right."[15]

Sharkey's account was guaranteed to enrage its audience. His portrait of Sam Hose fed the fears and hatreds of a white community that was already on guard against black terrorism. This portrait fits every stereotype. Hose is devious, making his threats in secret to his fellow blacks and then creeping, shoeless, into the house literally through Mrs. Cranford's room, thus violating both the family's and specifically the wife's domain before any actual assault takes place. His manner of murder is horrendous, splitting his employer's head to the level of the eyes with an ax blade as the wife looks on helplessly, her voice literally paralyzed by terror. The subsequent unnecessary and insulting blows to the head and body indicate his utter disdain for the white man. Having committed this act, Hose then turns to robbery, delaying the actual attack on the wife but showing his mastery by forcing her to accompany him and hold the light while he plunders. The rape itself is possibly set off by the wailings of the small children, whose cries enrage him. His heartlessness in viciously cuffing the little girl and then "snatch[ing]"— an ugly, brutal, malicious word—the baby from the mother confirms that this is a monster capable of any deed. Finally, he assaults Mrs. Cranford on the floor of the dining area in the presence of her children, takes her lubricated in her husband's blood, "literally within arm's reach" of his dying body. And then Sam Hose makes his departure with a melodramatic verbal flourish worthy of any stage villain—"Now I am through with my work, let them kill me if they can." It can be heard as a boast—"I am beyond your ability to control me"—or as an acknowledgment that the white community would be justified, even in the devil's own eyes, if awful death were the outcome. Or possibly it is simply a stoic acceptance of the inevitable.

Although the first reports centered on Alfred Cranford's murder, the rape of Mrs. Cranford quickly become the focus of local outrage. Jacquelyn Dowd Hall has noted that the role of a "violated" white woman in southern society was "subtle, contradictory, and demeaning." The humiliation and degradation that came from being identified as a victim of black rape was "mingled with heightened worth as she played for a moment the role of the Fair Maiden violated and avenged. For this privilege—if the alleged assault had taken place—she might pay with physical and psychological suffering in the extreme." Indeed, she would likely become the subject, again in Hall's words, of "acceptable folk pornography."[16] This was certainly the case with Mattie Cranford, who told her story to, and then had her story controlled by, white males, most prominently her brother-in-law Sharkey, the *Atlanta Journal* reporter Royal Daniel, and finally the northern correspondent George Hepworth. Others would later embellish the details even further, adding extra layers of lewdness on the story. As the *Constitution* hinted to its readers, "The crime of the negro, Sam Hose, who is charged with these deeds, is more horrible and brutal than was at first supposed, and as the details have developed the anger of the people has increased until they have determined to wreak summary vengeance upon the negro as soon as he is apprehended. These details are of such a revolting nature as to sicken the heart of the most hardened person."[17]

After Sharkey related the first public account of the crimes, Mattie Cranford again told her story, this time to Royal Daniel, the *Atlanta Journal* reporter who had covered the Palmetto massacre. Daniel set the scene for his readers. "Refined, intellectual and beautiful and happy three days ago, the woman is but a shadow of herself today. Deep lines of sorrow and unutterable grief trace her pale face and the pain in her heart has robbed her of health and happiness probably forever." In this version, Mrs. Cranford elaborated on and apparently corrected parts of the earlier story. She now explained that she and her husband had for a time been suspicious of Sam Hose, who lived near the house in a "shed room." They were also aware of the threats he had made against Alfred. On the eleventh, after they had gone to bed, Hose had knocked at the bedroom door. Mrs. Cranford "struck a light" and warned her husband to take care. When Alfred opened the door, he quickly "stepped behind it," she told Daniel. "This is all that saved him Tuesday night," she felt. Alfred Cranford "sat up" until morning, expecting an assault. The next day, Hose "was glum and didn't have much to say." That evening he came to the house, barefoot, and Mrs. Cranford gave him his supper while the family went into the dining room for their meal. Her husband sat with his back to the inside door so that he could face the outside entrance and "keep an eye on Sam." But as they ate, Hose "darted" or "sprang into the dining room" from behind her husband. Mrs. Cranford continued:

> I saw the ax uplifted above his head, and before I could scream down came the ax with terrific force, splitting Alfred's head wide open, the ax sinking to the eye.
>
> Alfred threw up his hands and looked at me for a second and then fell forward and pitched out of the chair to the floor.
>
> The sight was so awful, the black demon standing over him that I screamed.
>
> "If you just breathe again I'll kill you," cried the negro, raising the ax and holding it over my head.

Hose then hit Cranford again with the sharpened blade on the right side of his head and with the blunt back of the blade on the left. "Not content, the negro, now a fiendish beast, enraged at the sight of blood, kicked and cuffed the dying victim as he lay upon the floor," Daniel reported. Hose then "rushed" to Mrs. Cranford, "tore [her] little baby from [her] breast and threw it across the room." Her daughter Mary Estelle cried, "Oh, don't hurt my poor papa, Sam!" Hose "slapped her full in the face a fearful blow, and the child fell several feet away, unconscious." "If you don't behave . . . I'll kill you too," he addressed the little girl. He then turned to Mrs. Cranford. "I ain't er going to kill you," he told her. "He dragged me into the room, across the body of my husband," Mrs. Cranford explained, but then could not continue. "Oh, it is all so horrible. It'll drive me mad," she cried, unable to describe the rape itself. Daniel now discreetly elided

Chapter Four

these details by infantilizing this adult mother of four in an astonishingly bathetic scene: "Then Mrs. Cranford broke down and wept as a little child whose heart is almost breaking over its first real disappointment or angry reproval," he wrote. At another point in the article, however, Daniel did note that, in the presence of the children, Hose "assaulted, tortured and victimized" Mrs. Cranford "at the negro's pleasure," the blade of the ax held threateningly against her head as he did so.

According to Mrs. Cranford's account, after the rape Hose pulled her "around the room." "He said he wanted my money and I told him he could have anything in the house, just so he didn't kill my children." He opened a trunk and found Confederate bills given her by her grandfather. "He thought it was good money," she explained. Then he dragged her back into the dining room, let her go, "caught up his supper in both hands and ran out of the door," his final defiant words now recorded as "I have done now what I have always wanted to do and they can catch me if they can."

But what was it that he had "always wanted to do"? According to Alfred Cranford's father, Capt. Grippia Cranford, the answer was clear. "The negro killed Alfred to better give him the opportunity to outrage his wife," he told Daniel. "That is why the murder was committed." The captain then described his own reaction:

"I tell you, sir, I have read horrible stories in the newspapers and always thought they were exaggerated, but it has come home to me now.

When I got to Alfred's house his blood and brains were scattered all over the dining room—even brain in the plate from which he was eating when the blow was struck."

Daniel again intervened in the telling:

The old father is broken under the great strain and it is impossible for him to control his emotions when he attempts to talk of the crime that, too, has wrecked his life and bowed his head in sorrow.

Captain Cranford then rallied:

"I thank God that in my great affliction I have the support and co-operation of every man who knows the facts. There is consolation in all of this, but there is no reparation—never."[18]

––––––––––

"Feeling Is Aroused," the *Atlanta Journal* observed the next day in a remarkable understatement. Indeed, from the moment Captain Cranford heard of his son's death, the hunt was on. The *Newnan Herald and Advertiser* reported that "various members of the family were at once sent in all directions to arouse the community. By 1 o'clock in the morning bloodhounds had been brought from Atlanta and put on the trail of the fugitive, and every able-bodied white man for miles around had joined in the chase."[19] "Plowshares rested in half-furrowed fields," the *Constitution* reported on the fifteenth. "Farmers stopped their tilling and merchants suspended business to join in the chase for the negro who murdered Alfred Cranford Wednesday night and made the deed more horrible by an assault upon the wife of the dead man within a few feet of where his bleeding body lay."[20] The day before, Governor Allen Candler had offered a reward of $250 for "the apprehension and delivery of said Sam Hose to either the sheriff of Coweta county, at Newnan, or to the sheriff of Fulton county, in the city of Atlanta." The proclamation noted only the murder, not the rape, as the crime for which Hose was wanted, but it further observed, "The malignity of the crime and the promotion of justice require that the said Sam Hose be brought to trial for the crime with which he stands charged."[21]

Despite the governor's fine words, the papers made it clear that what justice required was not a courtroom trial but one performed by the people themselves, especially those most immediately affected by the crimes. As noted earlier, Mrs. Cranford was reported as wanting to witness the execution, indeed, to "dictate the mode of death and the manner of torture." Royal Daniel related that a "magnificent bloodhound" had been quickly conveyed by railroad handcar from nearby College Park, propelled by "willing volunteers turn[ing] the crank with energetic determination to get on the trail before it was too cold for the dog to follow." Daniel also forwarded the rumor that one of Alfred's brothers "had expressed a desire to decapitate the negro with the same ax which was the instrument of death used by the negro," although this mode of revenge was denied by the family. What Daniel, who had joined one of the parties searching for Hose, strove to explain and justify to the readers of the *Atlanta Journal* was the moral rightness of the family's intentions, and he drew an explicit contrast to the Palmetto vigilantes in doing so:

> There are no mobs chasing Hose. The parties in pursuit are composed of the best people in this section of the state. Lawyers, doctors, merchants, farmers, and every class and creed of men have joined together with but one purpose in view—the avenging of the crime.
>
> There is no attempt on the part of any one to conceal their identity or to defend their action. They do not hesitate to say what they want with the negro:
>
> "We want to make an example of him," said one of the most prominent citizens of the place to me last night. "Whatever death is most torturous, most horrifying to a brute shall be meted out to him when he is caught.

"He should be given a trial by a court of twenty citizens, his guilt proved beyond question, and then apply a slow torch and let him slowly burn for hours."[22]

Daniel, like others in pursuit, assumed that Sam Hose would be quickly apprehended. "Dogs Are at Full Cry at the Heels of Hose" the *Journal* headline read on Friday, the fourteenth, and with hundreds of men scattered throughout Coweta and surrounding counties, it seemed reasonable to think his capture would be imminent. But Hose eluded his pursuers, and within days this region of the state was in the grip of rampant fear and suspicion, fed by rumor and misinformation. It was said, for example, that after leaving the Cranford house Hose had gone to the home of one John Smith, a black preacher, who fed and "harbored" him and gave him a pistol. This "John Smith" was likely the preacher Elijah Strickland, who would himself become a victim of white rage, tortured and hanged, although not many believed the story that he had actually aided Hose. Another report was that Hose had encountered a black woman, Lizzie Arnold, who often washed clothes for him. She reportedly said that Hose intended to escape to Savannah and there "board a steamship" and leave the country. "And I would like to see them catch me then," she reported his boasting, repeating his flourish as recounted by Mattie Cranford.[23]

Similar to the pursuit narrative laid out in the search for "Bill Holt" after the Maruney home invasion several months earlier, bloodhounds now traced Hose to a swamp near the small towns of Turin and Sharpsburg, some twelve miles distant from the Cranford property, and there, according to members of the posse, Hose was spotted and shots were said to have been exchanged. The posse then surrounded the swamp and waited, without success, for Hose to reveal himself.[24] Meanwhile, the alarms and rumors continued to spread. Hose was reported captured near Newnan. He was seen in Griffin. By Saturday, Daniel reported, stories had it that he was "under arrest in Moreland, Zebulon and Barnesville," adding, "but it is not believed here that he has been captured in any of those places and is still at large." A telegram notified authorities that Hose was seen passing through Hogansville on his way to Mountville, and a party of horsemen immediately set out in pursuit. Witnesses reported that "the negro was covered with mud, as well as dust, that he was barefoot and hatless and was breathing so as to be heard a hundred yards away."[25]

On Saturday, April 15, a posse made up of men from Palmetto and Griffin followed Hose's trail to a location just outside Concord, Georgia, where Hose was said to have left bloodstained clothes with a black woman to be washed. He was to call for them the next day. Although this story seemed to be a variation of the one previously told about Lizzie Arnold, the posse staked out the cabin. As they waited, word came by telegraph that Hose was "beyond all doubt under arrest in Palmetto" and that plans were under way to execute him. Not wanting to miss the lynching, the posse abandoned its stakeout and returned to that village. Abe Rogowski, a member of the Griffin party, later told reporters that they "were indignant" when they learned the report was false.[26] He claimed that Hose had been within their grasp, and the false rumor had ruined their chances of an early capture. Rogowski would later participate in returning Hose to Newnan and would share in the rewards offered for his apprehension.

An important convention in newspaper lynching narratives was the dramatic description of the chase or hunt. The fugitive was portrayed as prey, as a fearsome thing to be tracked and killed. "The Monster Still Free: The Beast from Palmetto Not Caught," the *Macon Telegraph* at one point reported. As Mason Stokes has discussed in his book *The Color of Sex*, such "beast" imagery was a staple of the rhetoric of white supremacists, but at the turn of the twentieth century this belief was also being touted as scientific fact. Stokes observes that the theory of polygenesis—the belief that there were different origins among the races—was accepted as truth by many. Frederick Douglass spoke of this theory as an attempt "to read the Negro out of the human family," and, indeed, this was the central thesis of many of the pseudoscientific studies and writings that considered questions of race in the late nineteenth and early twentieth centuries.[27]

Among the most prominent spokesmen for this view was Charles Carroll, who, in 1900, published *"The Negro a Beast,"* a lengthy work that maintained, according to its subtitle, "The Negro [is] a beast, but created with articulate speech, and hands, that he may be of service to his master—the White man."[28] Carroll's proof that "the Negro is not an Offspring of the Adamic Family" was partly anatomical—laborious contrasts between predominant physical characteristics of the white and the black races—and partly theological—"proofs" from the Bible that showed the falsity of evolution and the impossibility that blacks were descended from the original (white) human tribe. The black man was identified, at best, as "a Biped Animal." At the heart of this thesis was the horror of race mixing—amalgamation—which resulted in the various skin hues: reds, yellows, and browns. Carroll thus argued that sex between white and black was a form of bestiality, and that, like any animal offspring, progeny of the black race could not aspire to spiritual understanding or salvation. "They lack the spiritual creation, which forms the link of kinship between God and man, and is only transmitable [*sic*] to his offspring through pure Adamic channels," Carroll wrote.[29] Acceptance of such beliefs allowed southern newspapers a shorthand vocabulary. If Sam Hose or Oscar Williams or Cupid Redding could be labeled "Beast" and be understood literally in that way, then the lurid horrors described would carry an even greater shock. Mattie Cranford had indeed been raped by an animal, and as an animal it must suffer and die.

Alfred Cranford was buried on Saturday, April 15, in the family burial grounds near the home. He was laid next to the grave of his uncle, Z. T. (Zack) Cranford, who also "was murdered by a negro about ten years ago [on Christmas Day, 1889] in a manner somewhat similar to that in which the young man met his death last Wednesday night." Mrs. Cranford attended the funeral "but did not appear to realize either what was then in progress or what had happened: she appeared dazed."[30] According to the *Macon Telegraph*, "His wife stood by his grave but showed no sign of emotion. It is feared that her mind has become unbalanced as a result of the terrible ordeal she has just passed through, and that she will collapse completely when she hears that her negro assailant has been caught and lynched."[31] Concern over Mattie Cranford's sanity became a constant in the daily reports. Sam Hose would soon be described as Caliban, the semihuman monster that had turned on his master, while Mattie Cranford would be portrayed as a mixture of Miranda and Ophelia, an innocent despoiled and driven mad by unsuspected evil. As the Macon paper suggested, some felt that Mrs. Cranford's mental health ultimately depended on her presence at Sam Hose's execution. Otherwise, she might well be completely lost.

Meanwhile, the town of Palmetto, many of its men having left in pursuit of Hose, had once again set armed guards on its streets for protection. On April 16, the *Macon Telegraph* declared, "Palmetto is an ill-fated spot." The paper feared even worse. "The inevitable result of further estrangement between the races, the kindling into fierce fire of smouldering local animosities, and the crime and bloodshed that always follow, constitute the real causes for alarm."[32] Many blacks had already left the region after the massacre in March. Of those who remained, some were now ordered to leave town. A John Floyd, for example, was told he had ten minutes "in which to say goodbye to his family," or he would be shot in the heart. Floyd left with his hat but not his coat, exclaiming in exaggerated, humorous dialect, as represented by *Atlanta Constitution* correspondent Daniel Carey, "Fo' Gawd sake. Yo' ain't neber gwine ter see me round dis here place no more." Four other men with their families were also ordered to leave, including a "Professor Kelly," who ran a school for black children. Two survivors of the Palmetto massacre, George Tatum and John Jameson, were also publicly told to vacate, but they were already incarcerated in the county jail in Fairburn and could not do so. Carey noted that remaining black families were living in fear and that some had joined together, residing and sleeping in groups for protection.[33]

Still the search for Sam Hose continued. In Hogansville, a posse was reported "to have taken drastic measures . . . to extract knowledge from a negro." They put a noose around the man's neck, led him to a tree, and gave him "two minutes" to tell in which direction Hose had gone. "With his knees trembling and with his entire body quaking with fear, the negro swore that he knew nothing," and the party eventually set him free.[34] Headlines in the Sunday and Monday papers stressed both the exasperation of the search parties and the waning expectation of immediate success. "Hose Is a Will O' the Wisp to His Determined Pursuers," one headline in the *Constitution* read, with the subheading "Negro Has Cleverly Evaded All Efforts of the Searchers to Effect His Capture." On the same page were smaller bulletins with headlines such as "Hot on the Trail of Hose" and "Hose Almost in Their Grasp." "Dogs Are at Full Cry at the Heels of Hose," the *Journal* reported on Monday. "They Think His Escape Is Now Impossible." "Circle of Vengeance Slowly Closing on Fleeing Sam Hose" the Tuesday *Constitution* read, adding, "He Cannot Escape, They Say."

Search parties were cheered and applauded wherever they appeared. Local farmers provided plough horses and mules, and families offered their buggies and wagons to the pursuers, who devised a kind of pony-express system, riding or driving until the animals gave out, then exchanging them for fresh teams and sending the worn ones back to their owners.[35] Occasionally, however, the posses caused as much consternation as they gave comfort. The owner of a country store at St. Mark's, Georgia, was badly frightened when the same posse that had threatened the black man near Hogansville approached his place of business. The leader, filthy and exhausted after several days of pursuit, entered the store and asked the merchant to step outside because "the members of the party would like to speak with him privately for a few moments." As Daniel Carey reported the incident,

> The merchant stood still for a moment, his jaw dropping and then like a flash he darted through a rear door, leaving the party in possession of his store. He was seen running toward the woods as fast as his legs could carry him, and could not be induced to stop by friendly shouts.

He was later coaxed back, still shaken by the fear that this was a band of robbers rather than men determined to bring a scoundrel to justice.[36]

The humor implicit in this report gives a sense of how the search for Sam Hose was being reported. Clearly, there was an element of sport to the pursuit, and Hose's ability to elude his trackers, while exasperating and frightening, was at this point still thrilling. Nevertheless, as days passed without capture and Hose was being spotted farther south, this hunt took on a more disturbing aspect. Any black man could be seized and threatened at will. In the towns of Greenville, Fort Valley, and Milner, blacks were arrested on the possibility that they were the fugitive Hose. Some were simply victims of bad luck, deemed suspicious for any number of minor reasons. In LaGrange, thirty miles southwest of Newnan, the sighting of a "very suspicious character" by "two or three different parties" caused searchers to scour the region. As the *LaGrange Graphic* explained, "It is not known that the negro that the LaGrange posse is after is the negro Hose, but however, he is . . . undoubtedly some outlaw fleeing from justice."[37] The *Macon Telegraph* reported in its Tuesday, April 18, edition, first that Hose had been shot to death "on the banks of Cane creek," followed immediately by another report that he had been spotted at a store near Fort Valley and had later forced a farmer at gunpoint to give him food.[38] On the same day, the *Constitution* reported, "Several negroes answering the description of the fleeing brute have been seen at various points in the section through which it was expected that Hose was attempting to make his escape, but upon being captured by armed posses they proved not to be the man wanted and were released."[39]

One unfortunate man, identified as having the strikingly similar name of "Dan Holt" and of bearing strong resemblance to the fugitive, was seized by a "large party of determined men," escorted to the Cranford home, and put forward for identification by one of Alfred's brothers. Set free on the brother's say-so, the man was again arrested by another group before he could leave the area, returned to the Cranford farm, and again set free upon identification. "He is still at Fairburn and is afraid of leaving the town for fear that he will be caught and violently dealt with before he can establish his identity," the paper noted.[40]

Hose's ability simply to disappear encouraged whites to think that a massive black conspiracy was at work. Indeed, there were now rumors that Hose had been aligned with the "gang" that had attempted to burn down Palmetto. These accounts suggested that Alfred Cranford had been a member or even the leader of the vigilantes who had performed the Palmetto massacre, and that Sam Hose's killing of Cranford was both revenge and the opening salvo in an outright race war. Despite earlier condemnation of the Palmetto shooting, many now proclaimed it to have been entirely justified. "If the Palmetto lynching was so bad, and if [anti-lynchers] really want the law to take its course, is there not enough in the murder of Cranford and the ten times worse than murder of his helpless wife to elicit from them at least their disapproval of the crimes committed by Sam Hose, and at least an expression of that great desire to see the law enforced they so eagerly evinced in the former case?" one correspondent from Fairburn wrote to the *Constitution*.[41] The *LaGrange Graphic*, discussing "The Trouble at Palmetto," made direct the connection between the January fires and the Cranford tragedy. There may have been "some innocent negroes" among those shot down in Dr. Johnston's stone warehouse, the paper conceded, but posed the question, "What would you do, you who sit off and judge such things? . . . The thought of it is fearful, but human nature is the same every where and there is a limit to human endurance." After discussing Hose's crimes, the paper concluded in frustration, "It is sacrilege to even try to weigh these things in the scale against the lives of the black brutes whose extermination is made necessary through the defense of these things."[42]

Villages and towns continued to fortify themselves, to set up patrols at night, to believe every rumor that passed by word of mouth, by telegraph, or by newly installed telephones in some parts of the region. The papers filled their pages with bulletins so that their readers were caught in a maelstrom of gossip and growing paranoia. But these accounts were also self-congratulatory, filled with incidents of brave men, applauded by their communities, putting aside their everyday lives to take on the challenge of this moment in history. This was a sanctified mission and, as the papers constantly asserted, not the mindless barbarism of a rampaging mob. The *Atlanta Journal* spelled out this view in its Tuesday edition:

> While the men are pursuing the negro through swamps and over hills, spending sleepless nights, not resting for food nor stopping to change clothing, the women are praying for success to crown their efforts and bring the negro to a swift punishment. . . .
>
> Failure to capture Hose has not interfered in any way with the determination and eagerness of the men in pursuit. The delay and failure, on the other hand, [have] been tantalizing, and now every effort is being put forth to effect his capture. There is no probability of the chase being given up. Men who have been on the track since Wednesday night have not grown weary, although physical endurance has been passed and human laws almost overcome.[43]

White spokesmen also called on the "better negroes" to step up at this dangerous time. The *Telegraph* challenged black leaders like Booker Washington and Bishop Henry McNeal Turner of the Georgia African Methodist Episcopal Church to do more than speak out against black rape; they must also encourage their followers to turn in black criminals, participate in the enforcement of racial order. These black leaders "should bestir themselves earnestly, honestly, untiringly, yea desperately, for momentous issues depend upon it, to stay this devilish tendency so rampant among the viler elements of their race. Let them recognize their responsibility; let them face it resolutely. To shirk it is suicidal. Let them do their duty if they would forestall a reign of terror in this fair land in comparison with which the present is mild and merciful."[44]

Some blacks did take part in the search. "The negroes in and about Milner are aiding the whites as much as possible in the pursuit of Hose and have given it out that they will make every effort to catch him if he remains in that vicinity," one report explained.[45] Still, white communities were convinced that Hose was benefiting from black collusion: in their minds, the secretive race was without question abetting him in his flight, feeding or hiding him, misleading the posses, spiriting him farther away from the place of his awful deeds to some distant bourn of safety.

Despite these public displays of determination, by the eighteenth, almost a week after the reported assassination and assault, there were signs of growing disappointment and desperation. Although papers continued to claim that Hose was on his last legs, "nearly exhausted from hunger and fatigue" or even already arrested and in jail in another part of the state awaiting transportation back to Newnan, the fact that some of these notices directly contradicted each other as they appeared in competing newspaper columns made it clear to readers that no one really knew anything. Hose was now attributed almost supernatural abilities.[46] Just as he had manifested himself phantomlike in the Cranfords' dining room, ax raised and ready to split Alfred Cranford's skull, so was he now eluding the best bloodhounds, the most experienced trackers, the multitude of resolute men who had committed themselves to his capture. It was enough to exasperate and terrify even the most reasonable of men. At the same time, Hose was accorded a certain amount of admiration for his skills. He was proving himself to be a worthy foe.

Seven days and nights Sam Hose has been flying through the swamps, dodging bloodhounds with shrewdness beyond imagination, doubling back on his tracks and making daring dashes for life, with hundreds of pursuers following swiftly after.

How long this unparalleled case will continue is a matter of speculation. It has now passed beyond human endurance, the laws of nature have been overcome and gone beyond and the physical energy displayed by the frenzied negro in his wild flight for life is equaled only by the dogged determination of his pursuers to run him down to death.[47]

The town of Griffin, which had led the search for Oscar Williams, had now committed itself to finding Sam Hose. But even Griffin was growing "somewhat tired" of "rumors" and "fakes." "Griffin is always ready to lend any assistance to any section, but the reports from these sections have reminded them of the cry of 'wolf,' and such things should not be in matters so serious," the *Macon Telegraph* reported.[48] An eight-man posse from the town returned on the eighteenth in a heavy rain, having ended a four-day search that had taken them on a journey of over two hundred miles. According to the *Telegraph*, these men had gone to Thomaston in Talbot County, and there had questioned "two brothers" of Sam Hose, whom they "treated kindly under the circumstances." Although they were "completely fagged out" upon their return, the posse expressed a readiness to start again the next day. Closer to home, in Barnesville, where Oscar Williams had been captured, the Griffin searchers had found little cooperation from black residents. A Mrs. P. S. Parmelee was quoted as saying, "The people in Barnesville and in that section are cool enough to freeze without any ice cream; . . . they are never in a position to give any information or show courtesies to people that will try to assist them, and . . . this last experience . . . will not make the people forget a similar occasion," apparently referring to the manhunt for Williams. Nevertheless, Griffin men were "Determined [to] Follow Hose's Trail Forever" and would always answer calls for help in tracking down black rogues and rapists.[49] Special prayer services were held in Spalding and Coweta counties to ask God that Hose be found and that "the infliction of a penalty which [was] to be in keeping as far as possible with his heinous crime" be accomplished. Dr. Hal Johnston, the leader of the "Palmetto crowd," expressed confidence to the *Telegraph* that they were hot on the trail and made assurances that "no efforts [were] being spared to capture him." Still, the paper noted that this party, like the Griffin one, was "pretty well worn out."[50]

On the eighteenth, Governor Candler increased the reward for Hose's capture from $250 to $500, the most he was by law allowed to offer, and he urged by proclamation that every lawman in the state concentrate on finding Hose. In an apparent effort to encourage the searchers, on that same day the *Atlanta Journal* ran five "photographs"—actually drawings based on photographs "Especially Taken for the Journal"—of Mattie Cranford and three of her children—"Her Interesting Family," as the description put it—sitting and standing in front of the Cranford home. The first showed the house from the front as a simple shotgun building, steps leading up to the main entrance, which was flanked on either side by a window. A covered portico runs along the face of the house. Next to this drawing was one of Mattie Cranford herself, sketched from the waist up, standing beside the porch. Dressed in a black cape, her hair pulled back severely from her head, she stares accusingly at the reader. Even more disturbing is the almost psychotic background of the illustration. From the upper left corner, the porch roof juts and hangs heavily above her head, and just behind her a tree reaches out with its bare limbs reduced to stark black lines streaking violently around her. Below these pictures was a portrait of Mary Estelle, the little girl whom Sam was said to have cuffed across the room. Like her mother, she peers soberly from the page, and again the background is a tangle of trees, limbs, brush, rendered in such a way that the lines of her dress become almost indistinguishable from the thicket beyond. She, too, seems ensnared in a jungle of psychic horror. The last two pictures show Mattie sitting on the porch, holding baby Clifford, his eyes closed so that there is a funereal aspect to the drawing; and Clessie, the three-year-old, dressed in white, standing again against the stark, grasping woods.

These are eerie, powerful pictures, almost fairy-tale illustrations of innocents lost in the malevolent forest, clearly meant to restore the public's waning purpose and stoke their indignation, to remind the paper's readers of the outrages committed against their community by the villain Hose. But if they were taken especially for the *Journal*, they also call into question the daily reports issued on Mrs. Cranford's and the baby's conditions. If the survivors could pose for these photographs, were they actually near madness or death, as was constantly stated? The pictures certainly portray a devastated, mournful sense of loss, but this was also a stoic, indomitable family, one coping with its tragedy even as it demanded rightful retribution. If Mattie Cranford was publicly labeled a "ruined" woman, one who had been sexually humiliated by a ravenous black animal and who would forever carry that stigma, she at this point had the tenacity and courage to put herself forward, to insert herself deliberately into the public's consciousness, and to insist on justice for herself, her children, and her dead husband.

As the searchers' continued failure to find Hose fed the white public's fear of the amorphous blackness into which he had seemingly vanished, trepidation grew into outright paranoia throughout Georgia. "Thousands Impatiently Wait," a headline read. "Every train is met in the rural stations, the telegraph offices are besieged by impatient people who have grown weary of waiting to hear the news, and even in Atlanta there is little discussed save the revolting crime and the great hope that punishment will follow Hose."[51] Black men were still being threatened, chased, arrested, as the reports duly announced. In Griffin, a black man named either Henry or Jim Harris was badly whipped and beaten by a mob of white men who took offense at his comments on Hose and his crimes. Harris had been offered ten dollars by white searchers to tell where Hose might be hiding. Instead, he had declared that "if he did [know], he would be d——d if he would tell them, or anyone else, but would help to conceal him. He was tired of hearing of negroes being lynched by d——d poor white people, and if they ever attempted to harm him, he would show them something."[52] In response, Harris was taken to the spot where Henry Milner and Oscar Williams had been hanged—now known locally as "Lynchberg"—and there "given a flogging to the queen's taste." By the time the police arrived, the crowd had dispersed, "and there was nothing to indicate who had done the work."[53] The next day, a second black man, identified as Dan Franklin, was also publicly whipped in Griffin. The *Columbus Enquirer-Sun* reported that "the same leather strap" used on Harris was employed on Franklin, who had called the Cranfords "poor white trash" and claimed that Sam Hose "was far better than the white woman." The *Atlanta Constitution* was a bit more discreet in this regard, noting that Franklin's comments about white women, and about Mrs. Cranford in particular, were "too horrible to think of, much less to publish in a paper." However, the *Constitution* described Franklin as "one of the meanest scoundrels that ha[d] ever lived in a decent community" and applauded that "a buggy trace [was] almost worn out on his worthless hide." The report concluded, "Nowhere in this country is the negro treated better than in Griffin so long as he knows his place and keeps it, but they must learn, through bitter experience if needs be, that the name and chastity of women must never be sullied by them."[54]

A third man, this one white, would also be arrested in Atlanta for comments he made about Mrs. Cranford. W. E. Pharr, a sixty-three-year-old night watchman who worked for Southern Railways, commented publicly after Hose's death "that he didn't believe Holt was as guilty as he was represented to be, and that Mrs. Cranford aided and abetted the negro in the commission of the crime." Pharr's statement illustrated the suspicion sometimes held but rarely spoken about black rape: that the white woman might have been a willing partner. Pharr suggested that Mattie had a hand in her husband's death, the implication being that she and Hose were lovers who conspired in Alfred's murder. Pharr later defended himself, stating that while "there were some things in the reports about the murder that looked unreasonable," he never meant to impugn Mrs. Cranford herself. He added that if he had been in Newnan, he would have helped in Hose's execution.[55]

The unofficial leader of the search for Sam Hose was now Palmetto dentist Dr. Hal Johnston. Johnston had been elected captain of the Palmetto posse, numbering almost one hundred men, and, as with the Palmetto massacre, he received most of the publicity from the Atlanta papers. As the *Journal* described him, Johnston seemed obsessed with capturing Hose: "Without halting, without a moment's sleep, without food most of the time, Dr. Hal L. Johnston, one of the most prominent citizens in Palmetto, has been pursuing the fleeing negro, followed through swamps almost impenetrable and dashing through treacherous streams, with but one purpose in view, bending every energy [,] straining every muscle."[56] It was hard not to connect this horrible murder, occurring so close to Palmetto, with the incidents that had aroused the town earlier, and whites quickly assumed that Hose was somehow involved with the black gang that had been so brutally obliterated. Over a century later, a Palmetto resident would explain, "Palmetto was still so outraged with the blacks who had tried to burn down the town that when Sam Hose killed Mr. Cranford, they just went berserk."[57]

By Friday the twenty-first, Johnston was in his ninth day of chasing Hose. The *Journal* interviewed him on its front page. "I have not slept, rested nor changed my clothing since the night of the crime," Johnston stated. He described for the paper how he and his men had followed Hose "from the body of Alfred Cranford to a point west of Roberta on the Flint river, known as the Agency." He again claimed that Hose had gone to the house of "an acquaintance" soon after leaving the Cranford home.[58] The posse had then followed him to nearby Turin, then to Sharpsburg, where they temporarily lost his trail at a large religious gathering presided over by Bishop Henry Turner, among the most prominent black leaders of the day. Turner had served in the Union Army as a chaplain during the Civil War and later worked in the Georgia Freedman's Bureau during Reconstruction, but he believed in separation of the black and white races and was a leading proponent of the "Back to Africa" movement.[59] Turner had also been outspoken in his opposition to the Spanish-American War, arguing that blacks, especially, should not participate. "As the Filipinos belong to the darker human variety, the Negro is fighting against himself," he had argued. "Any Negro soldier that will cross the ocean to help subjugate the Filipinos is a fool or a villain."[60] At this meeting, Turner was speaking on the Palmetto massacre and encouraging his black audience to band together against further white violence. Although Turner had earlier cautioned that "to talk about physical resistance [was] madness," by 1897, in the words of his biographer Stephen Ward Angell, he had "changed his mind. Violence in self-defense against mobs no longer seemed like madness to him. It was essential for their self-respect that blacks be able to use whatever means were available to combat lynchers."[61] Thus, the appearance of Johnston and his men so soon after the Palmetto shootings, now hot on the trail of Sam Hose with intentions to lynch him, caused considerable consternation among the crowd. Johnston later claimed that the bloodhounds lost their scent at the meeting. "That wiped out [Hose's] tracks," he stated. His insulting meaning was that the mass smell of so many black people obliterated the individual odor of one black man, but his implied suggestion was that Hose's fellow blacks were aiding him in his escape, and that once Hose succeeded in disappearing into the black underground, he might never be found.[62] "I am not after the reward but the negro," Johnston insisted. "I will take up the trail again tonight and will follow it till the negro is caught."[63]

The next day Johnston, despite his avowed disinterest in any reward, made a public appeal for financial help. "Owing to heavy losses from fire and the expense of our citizens in their efforts to capture the incendiaries, we find that it will be impossible to continue the chase after Sam Hose or Holt unless we can secure financial assistance," he stated. The reward for Hose's capture was now $1,250: $500 from the governor, $500 from the *Atlanta Constitution*, and $250 from the Coweta County commissioners "and others." Johnston included a detailed description of the fugitive, provided him directly by Mattie Cranford:

Name, Sam Hose, alias Holt.
Color, ginger cake.

Height, 5 feet, 8 inches.

Age, 23 to 25 years.

Small head and face, nervous movement of the head when talking; holds it stiff and to left when talking and looks down when walking. One little finger crooked and stiff. Hair cut short with a patch on top not cut.

Has slim appearance and narrow hips. Dress: Spotted or leopard or pole cat hat, gray jeans pants, new shoes, about No. 8; brown coat, with red checks. He has Confederate money which he attempts to pass.

Last seen in swamps of Flint river, between Crawford or Taylor county, going south.

His route must be down Flint river or Southwestern railroad or across from Taylor to Chattahoochee river, or may take back track to Macon or to Savannah, making to Florida.[64]

In the same edition of the *Atlanta Journal*, the front page warned, "Negroes Vow to Revenge," explaining, "Six negroes of Palmetto have registered a vow to kill six citizens of the town, each negro selecting his victim and swearing to execute their threats at the first opportunity." Alfred Cranford, "who was chopped to pieces ten days ago," had been one of the six selected victims. Among the other intended victims was, most prominently, Dr. Hal Johnston, "who was active in securing evidence against the negro incendiaries" and who had received a letter "a few days ago" indicating that he "would be killed at the first favorable opportunity. 'Prepare for death,' said the letter of warning, 'for you are a marked man.'" "I know that I will be assassinated at the very first possible opportunity and I know there are other citizens of the town who will be killed by the negroes when the opportunity presents itself," Johnston stated. Another potential victim, Henry Beckman, also linked his place on the death list with his pursuit of Hose. "I have been working night and day without rest to catch Hose and have done everything possible to locate him," he said, "and my efforts may cost me my life, but we are determined to capture Hose if it requires every penny we have and the combined efforts of every citizen of the place."[65]

Chapter Five

The Wild Ride

According to later reports, Sam Hose had quickly fled from Cranford's Mill after killing Alfred Cranford and by Friday, the fourteenth, had arrived at the home of his mother near the Jones plantation outside Marshallville, Georgia, located some one hundred miles away between Macon and Columbus. While posses threatened, arrested, and sometimes tortured innocent men, Sam Hose apparently hid in plain sight at his former home. The Jones brothers, J. B. and J. L., who finally seized him and received most of the reward for his capture, related their story to the papers on the day of Hose's execution. J. B. Jones told the *Constitution* that he had read an account of the "terrible crime" and the description of the fugitive. His "suspicions were at once aroused" when he heard that a "strange negro" had recently showed up on his plantation. Upon investigation, he recognized the man as "Tom Wilkes," who had worked for him previously but had left after "he had been indicted by the grand jury for attempting to assault an old negro woman in Macon county." J. B. claimed that he and his brother kept surreptitious watch on Wilkes until Wilkes, aware that he was being observed, dropped out of sight for a few days. Jones finally located him again at the mother's home, and then he and J. L. arranged with a black man who was "intimate with Holt" to "deliver him" into their hands. Wilkes was "enticed to a certain place," J. B. related, "and, as he was passing through a dense grove of woods my brother and myself sprang upon him and secured him before he had time to offer any resistance." The capture occurred at 9:00 p.m. on Saturday, the twenty-second. Wilkes's face, the *Constitution* reported, "had been blackened with soot in an attempt at a disguise."[1]

The *Atlanta Journal*, whose correspondent also talked to J. B. Jones on the train bringing Hose to Newnan, offered some variations in the story of the capture. In this version, Jones first recognized Wilkes on Wednesday, the nineteenth; "but as his name had been printed as Hose and Holt," Jones explained, "I did not think he was the man the people were after until I thought of the description, and then I was certain that it was Wilkes and that he had changed his name." Jones "watched him continually, day and night," until he and his brother were able to set their trap with the assistance of their hired man, who invited Wilkes to a "cakewalk" Saturday night. As Wilkes and his companion headed to the social, the brothers followed quietly, one on each side of the road, and then "ran in and caught him before he knew what [they] were doing." Wilkes at first denied being the fugitive Hose but soon "confessed, saying he was guilty." It was the brothers, in this account, who disguised him with lamp black "all over his face and hands so as to conceal his copper color." They then drove him by buggy for twenty-six miles to Powersville, near Macon, to board the train that would take them to Atlanta, where they could turn him over to the Fulton County sheriff and collect the reward.[2]

A third version of the capture was reported by the *Macon Telegraph*. A reporter talked with J. L.—identified incorrectly as J. R. Jones—in Macon as Jones was returning from Newnan. He had left shortly before the lynching because he was "tired and broken down" with the excitement of the past two days. His brother, J. B., had remained behind to collect the reward. J. L. repeated that Wilkes (as they had known him) had previously worked on their farm. "I knew the negro from infancy. His brother and his mother both live at my plantation and his brother is my foreman." Jones claimed that Wilkes had been a good worker, but that "four weeks ago" (he probably said "four years") he had raped a woman and fled before he could be arrested. When Jones heard about the Cranford murder and rape and then read a description of the fugitive, he immediately suspected that the man identified as Sam Hose in fact might be the Tom Wilkes he once knew. Jones said, "[I] at once began to keep a lookout for him, as I thought he might come back to my place where his mother lived." Once J. L. got word that Wilkes had indeed returned, he paid the hired man fifty dollars, as he put it, "to get [Wilkes] where I wanted him." On that Saturday night, as the man and Wilkes walked down the road, the accomplice gave a prearranged signal, at which point J. L. and his brother rushed in and took Wilkes "after a short struggle." "He knew that we knew him and made no denial of the fact that he was the right man and laughed at us saying that we would find out that he had committed no crime." Later Jones would recollect, "I always thought the negro a very quiet man until he raped the woman on my place, and when I read in the Telegraph that he had committed the horrible crime at Palmetto I was astounded. I thought he would finally drift back home."

Once taken, Hose (as the Jones brothers now called him) cooperated fully with his captors as they drove him by carriage to board the early-morning train

Chapter Five

to Atlanta. "At Fort Valley I got a doctor to paint Hose's face, so as not to be recognized," J. L. Jones told the Macon reporter, but when they reached that town, he "knew the identity of Hose had been discovered."[3] In a separate article, the *Telegraph* gave further details of just how Hose was "discovered" at the depot. Word had preceded them to Macon that a black man was being escorted as a prisoner on the train from Albany. When confronted, the Jones brothers initially refused to identify themselves and denied that their captive was the fugitive being sought so intently throughout this part of the state. This man, they insisted, was guilty only of larceny, and they were taking him from Albany to Chattanooga, not Atlanta. They then called attention to his deep black color and reminded the Macon group that Sam Hose was light skinned. Their insistence, however, further aroused the suspicion of the group. One of the railroad men stepped forward to inspect the captive more closely. He first rubbed the man's face and came away with "burnt cork." He next looked in Hose's mouth, lifting his upper lip to see if the front teeth were missing, "one of the chief marks of identification of the man wanted." Subsequent inspection convinced the Macon men that this was, indeed, the murderer/rapist so long pursued. He wore "badly torn" clothes under a "slicker" or raincoat, and they could hear the jingle of chains underneath as he moved. Despite their conviction, they made no attempt to prevent the Jones brothers from continuing on their journey with their prisoner.[4]

Sam Hose's skin color is one of the more macabre aspects of this already bizarre narrative. Whether Hose had attempted to disguise himself or, more likely, the Jones brothers had had it done to throw off suspicion, the detail added one more absurdity to this series of events. Sam Hose's identity was always in question, from his name—Hose, Holt, Wilkes—to his background. Once in flight, he seemed to disappear *into* the black world, generating the prevalent suspicions that he was being aided in his escape by his fellow blacks, but in his invisibility *any* black man could then be suspected or identified as "Sam Hose." It was as if white fear of black violence found Hose's face nowhere and everywhere. Once captured, in order to preserve the "black beast" long enough for proper punishment and the monetary reward that it would bring, the beast literally had to be made blacker than he was for his temporary safety. He must once again dissolve into the anonymous background of dark nothingness, one more black felon in a world of general black iniquity.

There is, undeniably, a horrifyingly weird aspect to this disguise. Grace Elizabeth Hale has described the incident as a humiliating performance of exaggerated "blackface," a form of minstrelsy: "In this early spectacle lynching, it seemed, the minstrel act bridged the distance between the faithful, laughing slave and the 'black beast rapist.' Before he could be the beast, Hose played a more familiar role, the joking black fool."[5] In truth, Hose was perceived as a frightening monster, one of the "new blacks" who refused to play exactly that traditional part of the fool. Nevertheless, Hale's point is a provocative one, and the blacking of Sam Hose offers intriguing opportunities for interpretation. As Eric Lott explains in *Love and Theft: Blackface Minstrelsy and the American Working Class*, "the material capacity of burnt cork or greasepaint, mixed with paint and smearing under the flickering gaslights, to invoke coal, dirt, or their excremental analogues was often acknowledged," and this disguise was another humiliating effort to erase identity, another abasement of a man whose self was already so much in flux.[6] The accounts of Hose's capture further emphasize the slow revelation of the man beneath the blackface, as the generic "darkey" prisoner is gradually revealed as the man "Sam Hose." In addition to the white man's suspicious yet audacious investigation of the captive's body—lifting his lip to inspect his teeth as one might an animal or a slave on the auction block, a wet finger or piece of cloth making the first cut through the corked layer of false epidermis—Hose's very real "Sweat of Terror" would also undermine and dissolve the public disguise to reveal the terrified face underneath. Thus, in the first news of his capture, we are presented with

> Sam Hose, fiend of many aliases, with features painted to inky blackness, which sweat of terror removed in streaks, revealing the copper-colored skin beneath, appearing ghastly.

which reads almost like a poem. And later, on his way to the stake, we are told, "perspiration poured down his face, which had been painted black before the journey to Newnan was taken up, washing away the burnt cork in streaks, which in contrast made him seem almost livid."[7]

Hose's face at this point must indeed have been horrifying, his mask in shreds, the "livid" slices of copper flesh showing through the black coat as though his face were flayed. This appearance may in fact have been the source of later claims that skin was cut and peeled from his face by the crowds before his burning. Knives would indeed soon penetrate his flesh, and his blood would then further sluice through that cork, replacing it with another color altogether. And then the flesh and the cork and the blood would be burned, crisped, rendered black yet again, another, though not yet final, mockery imposed on this tortured body.

Thus, despite these almost comical efforts at disguise, Hose was recognized and identified in Macon. A telegram was consequently sent early that Sunday morning from Milner, a stop on the train route, to Griffin, fourteen miles to the north, alerting the citizens there that Hose had been captured and would soon be in their city. Once again, stalwart Griffin was ready.[8] "How in the world the people in Griffin learned of the affair I will never be able to know," J. L. Jones later said, "but they seem to have a faculty for getting on to such things as this, and I guess they were on the lookout." Given Griffin's recent history, this was at best an understatement. Many members of this crowd had very likely waited in a similar manner on the train carrying Oscar Williams, and on those ferrying companies of the Tenth Immunes, but Sam Hose was a far greater catch than any of these. Thus, armed and determined, they watched the clock, and, according to the *Constitution*, when the train arrived at 10:00 a.m., "hundreds of people gathered at the depot and parties were selected to board the engine and prevent the train from leaving until it had been thoroughly searched and the negro secured." As the locomotive pulled into the station, "the crowd gave a cheer and rushed into the second coach in which it was understood Holt was confined." Their first search failed to find him, but he was then discovered, like Oscar Williams, locked in a toilet room for his temporary safety. The door was beaten in "under the blows from the butt of a Winchester rifle," and Hose was revealed "heavily chained and locked to the car." The men took him off the train and presented him to the still cheering crowd. Some now argued that Hose should be burned to death on Hill Street in downtown Griffin, but one of the Jones brothers "begged them to let [him] take [Hose] on" to Newnan so that they could collect the rewards. After some consultation, "cooler heads prevailed," and it was agreed that Hose should be transported to Newnan, turned over to the Coweta County sheriff for the necessary signed receipt, and presented to Mrs. Cranford for final identification.[9] Authorities in Newnan were notified by telephone that Hose had been found and would be delivered to them later in the day. However, the Griffin crowd insisted that representatives from their city should now accompany the party. Because there was no scheduled run from Griffin to Newnan, the crowd duti-fully collected thirty-five dollars, and a special train was ordered from Macon.[10] It consisted only of an engine and one coach, but when it left Griffin at 11:40 that Sunday morning, "in this coach and on it and on the engine and in it 269 persons found room for their feet."[11]

Despite the circus appearance of the train, festooned by men hanging all about the engine and the coach, the reports stressed the strange formality and even courtesy displayed during the journey: it was as if the Griffin contingent wished to draw an implied comparison between themselves and the supposedly unruly black soldiers they had so recently confronted in their town. As the *Journal* noted,

> Probably a more orderly crowd never left Griffin, not even on a Sunday school picnic excursion.
>
> Everybody was cautioned not to shout, and all guns were taken and placed under the seats so they would not show through the car windows.

At every road crossing, at every farm house and in every village passed, the people were out en masse to cheer the train, telegrams having been sent ahead, but not a word came from the train in answer to the public demonstration of the populace.

Under this fire the men rode in silence, such self-control never before seen.[12]

The *Telegraph* gave more detail:

> The run from Griffin on a special train was made quickly, and at the depot there was no excitement. The necessary $35 was soon made up and the train, under the headway gained with that careful and veteran engineer, Charles O. Bradbury, passed along smoothly, as Monroe M. Emmerson and O. Y. Ross heaped in coal. They had orders at 11:38 to leave Griffin, and at 1:01 they were in Newnan without a mishap, in spite of the fact that from every conceivable place there was some person hanging on. The engineer, Bradbury, and all of his assistants, were vigilant, and the squeak of the whistle and the ringing of the bell [were] heard almost continually. Mr. Ed Lovelace, the manager of the Western Union Telegraph Company [in Griffin], went along by request, and to him is due largely that no excitement prevailed along the line, and that only cheers met the train.

Among the other Griffin representatives were R. A. Gordon, P. F. Phelps, Wilson B. Mathews, and Abe Rogowski, who assisted the Jones brothers in guarding the prisoner.[13]

Although the Jones brothers had prevented Hose from speaking when he was first unmasked in Macon, once he was identified and nothing was to be gained by his silence they allowed several reporters to talk to him. The papers would later disagree over just what Hose said during this "wild ride" to his death. Some reported that he was so terrified he could barely speak, but correspondents from the major papers approached him with questions. The *Constitution* quoted Hose as saying, "I killed Cranford but did not assault his wife. My reason for killing Cranford was that he had threatened to kill me."[14] But the *Journal*'s correspondent gave another account. He explained, "When I first saw the negro I was sure another mistake had been made, for he was a jet black negro." Told by one of the Jones brothers about the disguise, the correspondent watched as one of the party "dampened his finger and rubbed it across the forehead of the negro and the coppery color came back to life." Then the correspondent questioned Hose while Joseph H. Drewry, a special correspondent from Griffin, took notes:

> Hose talked of his crime wildly.
>
> "Yes, captain, I killed Mr. Alfred Cranford," said the negro.
>
> And he paused and looked up as if he thought I should say something.
>
> "What made you kill him, Sam?" I asked, looking full in the half upturned, anxious face, with staring eyes.

Chapter Five

"Lige Strickland told me he would give me $20 to kill him and I dun it. When I went back to get the money, Lige said he didn't have it.

"I assaulted Mrs. Cranford and that's what I'm sorry about. I don't mind killing the man."

The reporter further maintained that Hose repeated this confession to Sheriff J. L. Brown at the Newnan depot and then again at the stake: "The negro stuck to his same story all the way through the crucible."[15] The *Macon Telegraph* also reported that Hose admitted to a telegraph operator at Brooks Station, where the train stopped for a short time, that he was "guilty of all he [was] accused."[16]

The accounts agreed that the prisoner was well treated on the train. "He was not crowded by the curious neither was he tortured with questions." The *Journal* observed that Hose "talked in a low voice" when responding to queries, but that he "stopped at frequent intervals to catch a glimpse of the flying panorama of country out of the window, knowing that his life was running out with each revolution of the car wheels."[17] The *Constitution*'s view was that Hose "was badly frightened and it was a difficult matter to induce him to talk at length."[18]

As the train made its slow procession from Griffin to Newnan on that Sunday midday, the news was being announced throughout the city. Most of Newnan's upstanding citizens were in church when the first telephone call came through, but word rapidly made its way into these houses of worship and through the congregations. Some pastors were reported to have announced the capture from the pulpit, and services ended abruptly as worshippers hastily made their way to the downtown train station. By the time the engine and coach had made its thirty-five-mile run, the "best people of Newnan were out" waiting, and church bells rang in celebration as the "Griffin special" first came into sight.[19] A crowd numbered in the thousands blocked the track so that the engine had to stop before reaching the depot. Although described as "orderly" while they waited for the arrival, the multitude now began to shout, "Bring him out!" "Take him off!" "and other remarks calculated to jar upon the nerves," as the Newnan paper described the scene.[20]

Surrounded by this rapidly growing and increasingly unruly throng, the men holding Sam Hose inside the coach car found themselves in a difficult situation. How were they to negotiate the crowd in order to deliver the prisoner safely to the Coweta County authorities? As an effort at appeasement, Hose was made to appear twice at a window of the coach, chains around his hands and neck. The crowd cheered at the sight. Then the doors and windows of the car were locked and closed, and Coweta County sheriff Brown was brought through the anxious horde and onto the train to receive the prisoner. Brown reportedly hesitated to take possession of Hose, as was required for the reward, and the captors called on Hose to confess to the murder and rape for the sheriff. Hose at this point admitted only the murder, saying, "I am Sam Hose, and I killed Mr. Cranford." The sheriff still hesitated. "I will have to get him identified in addition to his confession," he said. A man who had once farmed near Palmetto and knew Hose was then "pulled over the heads of the crowd" and brought into the car. "Howdy, Mr. John," Hose said, acknowledging the man. Sheriff Brown still refused to sign the receipt for delivery, explaining, "My county commissioners have instructed me not to receive the negro unless he is delivered to me in the county jail." The frustrated captors once again agreed, but everyone recognized that getting Hose from the train through the waiting spectators and to the jail would prove difficult. As the *Journal* reported, "The Griffin crowd was afraid that if Hose was taken from the train the people of Newnan would lynch him and the people of Newnan were afraid that the party from Griffin would do the same thing."[21] After a further parlay, during which representatives from both groups promised to control their members— "Griffin people are not hoodlums . . . and we give you our word of honor we will not harm the negro until he is delivered to you as the sheriff of Coweta county in your jail," Brown was assured (although the promise made clear the crowd's eventual intentions)—the sheriff spoke directly to his fellow Newnan citizens, asking for safe passage. The *Journal* recorded Brown's appeal as follows:

> "Boys," cried the sheriff, waving his hand for silence. "Listen to me a minute. Hose is in this car. He is to be delivered to me at the jail. I have given these people my word of honor to stand for the negro's safety. Will you have me violate my solemn word of honor, citizens of Newnan, or will you be quiet and promise me on your oath not to do a violent act or lay hands on the negro until he is receipted for in the jail of Coweta county?"
>
> "We will, sheriff," came a shouted reply. "Tell 'em Hose is safe until he is delivered and signed for."[22]

To ensure further Hose's temporary safety, twenty men were deputized as guards to accompany the prisoner to the jail. Five of them surrounded Hose, their heads held next to his in a protective circle, while the rest of the group formed a "hollow square" around them and pointed their rifles "in all directions" in warning as they made the journey from the depot. As they passed residences, men left their homes to join the procession. Some churches were still letting out their congregations, and many joined in the march. When they reached the middle of town, "a mighty shout came up. . . . Everybody was shouting and waving their hats. Hose was almost choking from the binding of the chain about his throat and the anguish of soul and body," the *Journal* reported.[23] The Newnan paper later explained:

The procession which wended its way through the streets to the jail had more the appearance of a triumphal march than a demonstration of mob violence. There was much suppressed excitement, of course, but no disorder—a sense of supreme gratification at the sight of the negro in chains, but no unseemly exultation.[24]

Once safely at the jail, the parties recommenced their negotiations as outside the crowd again grew anxious. Sheriff Brown seemed determined to follow the letter of the law, although he surely knew what the final outcome would be. After all, no one had promised to respect his authority once Hose had reached the jail and had been officially received. Hose had been hustled through the back door of the building; Brown and his officers had then tried to prevent others from entering. The *Journal* pictured the sheriff heroically facing this surging mob, grasping his rifle and shouting, "Men, stand back for God's sake. You are my friends, but friend or foe, I will lose the last drop of my blood before another man enters this jail. I give you fair warning." Other members of the mob tore out a window to enter the building, but they too were pushed back by officers, "with guns pressed against their bodies." Brown was again urged to sign the receipt for the Jones brothers since Hose was now physically in his custody, as required, but still the sheriff refused, arguing that as long as the mob essentially had control of the jail, he could not legally claim responsibility for the prisoner.[25]

The *Macon Telegraph* reported that at this point, at Sheriff Brown's request, former Georgia governor W. Y. Atkinson, who had returned to Newnan to practice law after his two terms as chief executive, was brought into the negotiations. Like the man who identified Hose in the train coach, Atkinson was lifted above the crowd and passed overhead by hands to the entrance. Once inside, he advised the sheriff not to sign until Hose was safely placed in a cell, had been properly identified, and the crowd had dispersed. Atkinson then offered to address the crowd himself. "He was promptly given an exit through a window, the only mode of voluntary egress, and in a few moments he bobbed up serenely in front of a door and made a speech," according to the *Telegraph*.[26]

While Atkinson spoke to the crowd, Sheriff Brown signed the necessary receipt, which read:

Received of J. B. Jones, R. A. Gordon, Wilson Mathews, P. F. Phelps, Charles Thomas and A. Rogowski, one Sam Holt or Hose (alias) or Tom Wilks [sic] in a live condition and unharmed. Delivered as the murderer of Alfred Cransford [sic] of near Palmetto, also a rapist. April 23/1899.[27]

With the sheriff's signature, the legalities were complete, the reward was assured, and the charade ended.

Chapter Six

A Holocaust of Human Flesh

While the quasi-legalistic proceedings were taking place inside the jail, the crowd surrounding the building, now composed of people from Newnan, Griffin, and the surrounding countryside, continued to grow, both in size and impatience. "There were all kinds of inciting cries, people mad almost with excitement and frenzy, begging for men to lead them in storming the jail," the *Journal* reported. At nearby homes and city buildings, people climbed on roofs for a better view, and women stood at windows waving handkerchiefs in support before they "gradually were overcome by horror and simply stood in silence and awe, not knowing what moment there might be a frightful riot. They had friends and relatives, fathers and brothers and loved ones in the crowd, and they hesitated in making any further demonstration, as they knew their cheering was driving men to madness never before known."[1]

In the jail, after Sheriff Brown finally put his name on paper assuring that the reward would be paid, he told his jailer, a man named Alsabrook, to place Hose in a cell. However, before the jailer could do this, "ten or fifteen men suddenly entered the corridor from the stairway and swooped down upon the negro." Brown "protested," but Sam Hose was now in the hands of the mob.

It is impossible to know if these proceedings in the jail were sincere efforts to safeguard the prisoner. Most accounts of prisoners taken from authorities stressed similar heroics of the lawmen, if only to give them legal cover. Brown surely knew from the beginning that Sam Hose would never reach trial, at least not a legally sanctioned one. Nevertheless, at this point two men made apparently sincere efforts to control the mob and to prevent the lynching that now seemed inevitable. One of these was William Yeates Atkinson.

Atkinson was born in Oakland (Meriwether County), Georgia, in 1854, the son of a slave owner. After his father's death in 1873, he worked to put himself through school. One of his jobs was that of teamster, an experience that later earned him the handy political sobriquet the "Wagon Boy of Coweta," which he used in his campaigns. Upon earning his law degree, Atkinson established his practice in Newnan in 1877 and soon became one of the town's leading citizens, serving first as solicitor of the Coweta County court and then, in 1885, being elected as representative from Coweta County to the state General Assembly. In 1890, he was named president of the state Democratic Convention, and in 1892, he became speaker of the state House of Representatives.

Atkinson was only thirty-nine years old when he declared in the race for governor, and at first he seemed a long shot at best. His opponent for the Democratic nomination was Gen. Clement Evans, a Civil War veteran who had served under John B. Gordon and had led the final southern attack at Appomattox. Moreover, after the war, Evans had been ordained a Methodist minister and had gained great respect as a religious leader. As Barton Shaw has written in *The Wool-Hat Boys*, his study of the Populist movement in Georgia, "Evans's friends never tired of delivering teary-eyed tributes to his valor and to the five wounds he had suffered in defense of the Confederacy. . . . Although he had little political experience, Evans seemed an ideal candidate for governor. He embraced no unorthodox views, he favored free silver, and he would shroud the campaign in the Stars and Bars and the cloth of the clergy."[2] Both the *Constitution* and the *Journal* supported him for the nomination. Atkinson, on the other hand, was seen by many as a callow, unprincipled, but well-connected opportunist who had no respect for the old southern traditions and beliefs. Nevertheless, the young man soon pulled ahead of Evans in their race, and Evans eventually withdrew, much to the disgust of "old veterans" in the state.

Atkinson then faced the Populist candidate James K. Hines, and despite a contentious and ugly campaign, during which Atkinson was accused of advocating "social equality" for blacks and charged with general corruption and acts of chicanery, he was declared winner. His victory was marred by charges of voter fraud, and he had alienated many old-time Democrat loyalists during the campaign. As Shaw notes, "Atkinson's coup d'etat had left Bourbons and old Confederates sullen and resentful. Allen Candler, Atkinson's secretary of state [who would succeed him as governor in 1898], later said that 'the Wagon Boy of Coweta' had raped the party to gain the gubernatorial nomination."[3]

Once in office, Atkinson quickly proved that he was, indeed, not of the old school. Among his reforms, he was especially vehement in his opposition to the practice of lynching. Although the Democratic Party in Georgia was by no means an avid defender of racial justice, Democrats had sponsored numerous anti-lynching bills in the General Assembly. During Atkinson's first term as governor, the state was "alive with mobs"—there were twenty-two lynchings recorded, including that of Oscar Williams, which he had tried to prevent—and Atkinson was determined to assert control over this lawlessness. He proposed a combination of stern and liberal "solutions," including public executions and the imposition of the death penalty even for attempted rape. But he also insisted that local authorities fulfill their legal duties or face punishment themselves. If a sheriff failed to protect his prisoner against a mob, that sheriff could be fired. If the sheriff were in danger of being overwhelmed by the mob, he should both free and arm his prisoner so that the prisoner might defend himself. Atkinson also proposed that if a lynching did occur, the relatives of the victim(s) could sue the county for the loss of their family member, even if the guilt of the accused was certain.[4]

Although he had been unable to get any of his antilynching proposals through the General Assembly, Atkinson's attempts to do so and to reform the convict-lease system gained him strong support from black voters. During his first term, Atkinson had pardoned a black man named Adolphus Duncan, who had twice been convicted of the rape of a white woman and sentenced to hang even though he was almost certainly innocent. While campaigning for reelection, Atkinson was savaged by his Populist opponent for this pardon, which Atkinson himself highlighted in his efforts to gain black and Republican support. His political enemies charged that Atkinson so disapproved of lynching that he would pardon any black rapist. They also claimed that such leniency would encourage other blacks to assault white women. The racial fearmongering proved especially disruptive in the last days of the race, but the governor stood by his decision. "I pardoned Adolphus Duncan because he was innocent," he told the *Constitution*. "If you want a governor to allow an innocent man to be hanged just because a heinous crime is charged against him, then you should elect another man. So help me God, I will hold the place with that understanding."[5]

In a speech to the Georgia legislature at the beginning of his second term, Atkinson directly addressed the practice of lynching, stating forthrightly:

> There is . . . no justification or excuse for a resort to lynching, even in this class of cases [black rape of white women], where the defendant is charged with the most dastardly and horrible of crimes. No man doubts in these cases that the law will punish the guilty, and if he did he could not find a remedy by making a murderer of himself. The remarkable fact exists that in a majority of instances the party lynched is taken from the custody of officers. I can understand how a near relative of the victim of the lust of a human brute who sees before him the man whom he believes has committed the outrage, and in the heat of passion, slays him, can enlist the interest and sympathy

of the community; but how any one can fail to condemn those who are guilty of the cowardly act of taking from the officers of the law a man who is disarmed and helpless, and hanging him without trial, surpasses my imagination. . . . This barbarous practice does not decrease, but increases crime. . . . I condemn it and will not apologize for such lawlessness. To exterminate the practice it must be made odious and dangerous. The penalty should be the scorn of the people and the punishment of the law.[6]

Given this background, one can only imagine Atkinson's feelings as he now stood outside the jail on this Sunday afternoon in his adopted town, watching his outraged fellow citizens, agitated by the crowd from Griffin, grow wilder and more furious and hysterical with each passing minute. Passed through the window of the jail and into the mob—for a mob it now was—Atkinson ascended the steps of the jail and called out to the people. He appealed to their civic virtue and good sense. At first he asked that they allow Hose to be tried—and executed, for he had no doubt that such would be the verdict—by the court, which could be immediately convened. The *Macon Telegraph* recorded his plea:

My Fellow Citizens and Friends: I beseech you to let this affair go no further. You are hurrying this negro on to death without an identification. Mrs. Cranford, whom he is said to have assaulted and whose husband he is said to have killed, is sick in bed and unable to be here to say whether this is her assailant. Let the negro be returned to the jail. The law will take its course, and I promise you that it will do so quickly and effectually. Do not stain the honor of the state with a crime such as you are about to perform.[7]

When this proposal was rejected by loud cries and derisive shouts, he next asked that Hose be taken out of town to the Cranford farm and there be positively identified one last time before any such lynching should occur, perhaps hoping that the distance—some twelve miles—and the time it would take might wear down the mob's vehement passion or allow authorities to send in militia to halt the proceedings. Or perhaps Atkinson simply wanted the deed to take place outside the city limits of his beloved city. He later explained that, if the lynching had to occur, he did not want it "enacted on [the] courthouse square . . . to the terror and horror of the women and children."[8] Whatever his mix of reasons, Atkinson did not hesitate to challenge the mob. Shouting above the uproar, he gave a final warning: "Some of you are known to me, and when this affair is finally settled in the courts, you may depend upon it that I will testify against you."[9] The Newnan paper reported that while Atkinson attempted to control the crowd, "some drunken lout—a stranger to the people of Newnan—pointed a pistol at the speaker," but Atkinson "did not even pause in his speech," and the man did not go beyond his initial threatening gesture.[10]

Newnan judge Alvan D. Freeman followed Atkinson in calling for order, but he, too, was shouted down. "We are your friends, judge," one man reportedly called out, "but this is a wrong time to talk to people who have been outraged by one of the most revolting crimes the mind can conceive of."[11] Both men knew there was little else they could do. Atkinson himself would write the next day, "[Given] the high character of the people on whom this man committed a crime more brutal and villainous than can be found in the criminal annals of the state, I do not believe there is a section of the state where the feelings of an outraged people could have been suppressed or controlled."[12]

With Hose now in its possession and cries of "On to Palmetto!" "Think of his crime!" and "Burn him!" the mob, a "whirlpool" of bodies, began a procession through the streets of Newnan, a parade that gathered its own momentum, "up and down and back and forth, the people in a dog trot and getting faster at every step."[13] The *Newnan Herald and Advertiser* carefully noted the winding of the procession:

> Leaving the jail at 2:15, the mob turned up the street to the left and passed in front of the Hotel Pinson, taking a straight course thence down Spring street. When nearly in front of Mr. J. E. Robinson's residence the mob turned and retraced the distance to the corner where Capt. J. A. Hunter resides. It then passed along by the Central Baptist church, across Washington street, straight through to Brown, then into Jefferson, out Jefferson to the cemetery, and thence across to the corner of Mr. E. M. Hudson's lot, at the intersection of the streets which cross each other at this point.[14]

Although this described route is somewhat at odds with Newnan's present street plan, one could still walk it today. The impressive Central Baptist Church was newly built, the cornerstone laid only in July of the previous year, and some members who had attended the Sunday-morning service now stood on its steps watching or joined the procession as it passed by. The entire route would normally have taken some twenty or thirty minutes to walk, but at every corner the crowd halted and hoisted Hose above their heads so that the prisoner could be seen. "Ladies waved their handkerchiefs and applauded," the Newnan paper reported.[15] One man carrying a rope was told to get rid of it—there would be no hanging, certainly not in downtown Newnan—and when a man appeared with a buggy, the crowd "shouted in unison," "Don't let that negro get in that hack. . . . Make him walk. We are walking. Drag him if he won't walk."[16]

One final rite had to be enacted before the mob left town with its victim. Their march had now brought them to the McLeroy home, where Mattie Cranford was in seclusion, recovering under her parents' care. Mrs. McLeroy (the family name was usually cited in newspaper accounts, incorrectly, as "McElroy," the name of another prominent Newnan family) and a sister of Mattie were waiting in the yard at the gate of the fence. Although her daughter remained inside—"She Is in a Pitiable Plight, and May Lose Her Mind—Baby May Die," the *Macon Telegraph* still insisted in its headlines—Hose was brought forward to meet "the accusing gaze of the good woman whose daughter he had defiled," for one last identification.[17] Both she and Hose were described as "trembling"—he "cower[ing] like a dog"—as they faced each other. "Mastering her feelings," Mrs. McLeroy spoke to the prisoner.

"You know that you must die, Sam, and I want you to tell the truth. Why did you kill Mr. Cranford? Who put you up to it?" The trembling wretch hesitated a moment, and then answered, "I killed Mr. Cranford because Lige Strickland promised me $20 to do it." He would not talk further, and with a shout the mob then turned into the road leading to Palmetto and was soon out of sight.[18]

The *Journal* recounted the scene with greater drama:

"What made you do it, Sam?" cried Mrs. McElroy [*sic*], the mother, now hysterical, her body trembling from head to foot.

"Oh, Sam, tell the truth. Don't go to your death with a lie on your lips. Confess it all, and may God have mercy on your poor soul."

"Yes, mam," was the half reply Hose made.

He was trembling like a leaf.

"Oh, God have mercy on us all; oh God, have mercy, have mercy," was the soul harrowing scream of the poor woman. . . .

"Burn him," said a man who was standing close to Mrs. McElroy. "Mercy is not for him. Burn him like a dog." . . .

Hose again confessed, eyes bulging and nostrils distended, quaking and trembling like the wretch he was.[19]

"To the stake!" voices again cried, and some proposed to burn Hose there before the McLeroy house, but Mrs. McLeroy "objected strenuously," and the mob, respecting her wishes, resumed its march out of town.[20]

On the road to Palmetto, the order of the crowd began to break down. The procession moved, "thousands strong now," with increasing speed. At the front formed a long line of buggies, wagons, and other conveyances, their drivers "fighting for position in line." Behind them came the men on foot with Sam Hose, propelled ever faster forward by the chain around his neck. As they left the city, word came that a train from Atlanta, loaded with people, was nearing Palmetto. Some interpreted this to mean that Governor Candler had sent militia to stop the execution. The crowd immediately abandoned its plans to march to the Cranford place: "The mob at once decided to burn the prisoner at the first favorable place, rather than be compelled to shoot him when the militia put in sight."[21]

Two miles outside town, the marchers passed a woodpile, "several cords of dry split pine."[22] "That's my wood," a man identified as Joe Featherstone called out. "Take it, boys, and welcome." "Every man made a break for this pile. The wood disappeared as by magic and with the passing of the crowd there came the complete removal of the wood." At about the same time other members of the mob broke into a country store, closed for Sunday, and brought out two cans of kerosene. One of these was carried by a man identified only as the "Pennsylvanian," who would soon soak Hose and the wood for burning.[23] Local papers made much of this point: it was important to stress that a northerner, who might well have been expected to condemn the burning, was, in fact, a main participant in it, providing the fuel that fed the fire that burned the man to death. Readers outside the region needed to realize that one of their own, having once come to understand the realities of race and justice in the South, would willingly join in the act. The unnamed Pennsylvanian, identified by Mary Louise Ellis as Benjamin Frankfort, a Philadelphia journalist, would stand as proof that most northern critics spoke either from hypocrisy or from ignorance.[24]

Despite their original intentions to take Hose to the Cranford home, by now the mob had grown both weary and anxious. They "were straining" under the weight of wood and kerosene, with the difficulty of prodding and pushing the chained Hose along the road, and by the increasing speed of the forced march. And now they feared the imminent arrival of the militia. Thus, when they reached the place where the roads divided on the outskirts of the city, a site known as the Old Troutman Field, they halted and made their final preparations. It was deemed "a place . . . favorable for the burning."[25]

Death by burning was common in the world of 1899. Many houses still had open fires in their kitchens for cooking and in other rooms for heating. Since houses were most often constructed of wood, the chance that a home might go up in flame was great. Another danger was accidental scorching when clothes caught ablaze from open fires or when children fell into the fireplace. Wood stoves and heaters had reduced the possibility of such accidents, but with a careless touch or misstep, anyone could be severely seared in a second's time. Also, a cracked chimney or a bad draft or an overheated stove could engulf a house in fire with almost no warning, and if other buildings were nearby, a raging inferno could easily ensue. There was very little to be done for anyone who suffered extensive burns, and death was often a relief for these victims after their final struggles.

Newspapers at this time regularly carried accounts of such burnings and deaths, and their descriptions recognized the fact that what was being consumed was flesh, and that death by fire involved, among other things, the roasting of that flesh. Thus, such images as "Children Baked Alive: Three of Them Cooked in Their Father's House," "Whole Family Burned: All Five Are in Ashes," "Young Man Is Burned to Death While Ill and Helpless in Bed: Charred Body Found in Burning Building by the Firemen," "Children Were Cremated: Two Youngsters . . . Meet an Awful Fate," or "Pinned to Earth; Roasted to Death" provided newspaper readers with graphic reminders, if any were needed, that human bodies were made of meat and would fry in flames just like any other animal fat. This last headline underscored just how easily, and awfully, a human body might be reduced to something unrecognizable. On March 10, 1899, a teamster named John Holland, a "respectable wagon driver" from Dublin, Georgia, on a journey in the early morning hours, had stopped to build a fire against the stump of a tree in order to warm himself. Another tree had blown down across the stump, and when the fire burned away this support, the trunk of the second tree rolled off and pinned Holland to the ground on top of the coals and fire, which then slowly cooked his body. As one account told its readers:

> It was evident that he had made a fearful and pitiful fight for life. All around the exact location of the tragedy the earth had been plowed up by the fingers of the desperate man, who had flung the turf on his back and on the tree with the hope of extinguishing the fire. He had also grasped at the grass, weeds, rocks, anything that promised a leverage, and frantically worked to free himself from the blazing load which was torturing him beyond description, and rapidly reaching his vitals. It is certain that death came to him only after some hours, and after the flames had bitten into his body and maddened him into straining every scorched nerve and muscle to despairing effort. When his cousin, at 11 o'clock this morning, dug out the body, it was a charred and indiscriminate mass, only recognized by shreds of the clothing which the man had worn. Bones had been broken in some parts of the body by the force of his awful struggle and a harrow seemed to have been run over the ground within a few feet of the smoldering embers.[26]

There is a goodly amount of unseemly relish in this description, to be sure; it is a horror story meant to frighten but also to titillate the paper's readers, and it does so in part because death by fire loomed high among the awful dooms that might await any innocent wayfarer on this earth at this time. (A close second in newspaper stories was, in this pre-automotive world, sudden mangling by trains.) Tales of being burned alive, therefore, not only excited perverse fascination but also carried primitive terrors that imbued their hearers or readers with a fundamental sense of horror and awe. The terrible drama of the burning of the Windsor Hotel in New York, for example, gained much of its power from this horror of fire, mixed with that of falling or leaping from great heights.[27]

For these reasons, the choice to burn a man at the stake, auto-da-fé, was a profound one. On the one hand, it was the act of heathens, of savages, an inhuman torture that only a barbaric people would inflict. After Sam Hose's death, comparisons between his lynch mob and tribes of cannibals or wild Indians appeared in newspapers throughout the country. However, death by fire did have historical precedent in America, where it had been practiced during colonial times. Some crimes were determined to be of such magnitude that a concomitant punishment was required. The greater the torment, the greater the fear it would instill in other potential criminals. In his study *The Death Penalty: An American History*, Stuart Banner notes that although in medieval Europe burning was the accepted mode of execution for heresy and witchcraft, the American colonies generally hanged these offenders and reserved burning for slaves who murdered their owners or plotted rebellion and for women who killed their husbands. Because burning was *always* horrible, unlike hanging, which could be quick and relatively painless, it was seen as "a form of super-capital punishment, worse than death itself." Banner writes that death by burning was thus rarely employed, and that sometimes criminals condemned to this fate were first hanged and then burned after death, a mercy in the wider scheme of things.[28]

Nevertheless, southern lynch mobs could argue that when they burned criminals at the stake, they were continuing a practice established by the first settlers, and that the fearsome, ordinarily inexcusable magnitude of the punishment was simply demanded by the need to preserve the greater social order. Besides, by the time Sam Hose was burned alive by fire, criminals in northern states like New York were being cooked by electrical currents that sometimes caused their bodies to smoke and their veins to burst and their hair to go up in flames. What, in truth, they could say, was the difference?

But of course there was always a difference, for burning was usually only part of the exercise, and by the time it occurred, the victim might yearn for the death it would finally bring. One of the first spectacle burnings, one that would provide a protocol for Sam Hose's execution, took place in Paris, Texas, on February 1, 1893. The man executed was an African American named Henry Smith, who was accused of raping and murdering "Little Myrtle Vance," a white child, a "babe," of three years, eight months. Smith was said by some to be mentally feeble, but not all accounts agree on this. He had earlier been arrested by Deputy Sheriff Henry Vance, Myrtle's father. According to later constructions of the story, Henry Smith wanted revenge—Vance had cuffed and mistreated him during the arrest—and had decided to accomplish it through the child. He abducted Myrtle as she played in her front yard and carried her to a nearby pasture and woods, where he first raped and then, after sleeping through the night with the unconscious, dying girl next to him, strangled her the next morning. Hastily burying the body—but neatly placing her stockings in her shoes, along with her folded clothes, at a little distance—Smith fled town. He was caught after six days at Clow, near Hope, Arkansas, and returned to Paris, where plans were already under way for his torture and death. Indeed, the Paris newspaper, *The Republic*, had notified its readers, "The Negro, Henry Smith, who assaulted and murdered little Myrtle Vance has been caught and will be brought here tomorrow. He will be burned alive at the scene of his crime tomorrow evening. All the preparations are being made."[29]

Some ten thousand spectators had gathered by the time the train bringing Smith from Arkansas arrived at the Paris depot. The town had closed the public schools, local saloons, and other business establishments, so that everyone could attend the execution. Smith was described as in a state of "complete collapse" when he was taken off the train, but the town had orchestrated a procession, a "float" complete with a cardboard "throne" on which the man was seated and then handed a "scepter" to hold, "in mockery of a king," as the *Fitchburg (Massachusetts) Daily Sentinel* put it.[30] He was paraded through the streets as this idiot king while onlookers chunked rocks and clods of dirt or worse at him or ran forward to punch him.[31] Just outside town a platform had been constructed with the word "JUSTICE" painted across it. There Henry Vance, his teenage son, and his two brothers-in-law waited to take their own revenge.[32]

A photograph by local photographer J. L. Mertins shows Henry Smith tied to a pole on the platform that rises some ten feet off the ground. His shirt has been removed. Next to his feet is a small oven in which iron pokers are being heated red-hot. Also on the platform are the representatives of the Vance family. Other men are crowding the steps leading up to their level, and filling the foreground of the picture are scores of behatted men, and perhaps some women, straining for a better view. Some have somehow lifted themselves above the crowd, found something to stand on to afford them height and a superior perspective. An ominous smoke rises against the white sky behind the scaffold.

The photograph presents a stark, frightening, and astonishing image: the balance is perfect, the picture bisected horizontally by the human masses in the foreground and the empty void beyond. In the exact middle of the picture is the platform, its supports forming a V that inserts itself into the crowd below. Above the vector of this V and above the *T* in "JUSTICE," which proclaims itself in white paint on the platform face, stands Henry Smith, gazing, it seems, with placid curiosity at Henry Vance, who is kneeling at his feet. Henry Vance is about to push one of the searing iron rods into Henry Smith's flesh. He hasn't started yet, because Henry Smith's body is loose, his shoulders sagging, and when Vance does start Henry Smith will contort and moan and will continue to moan as Henry Vance and his son and his dead daughter Myrtle's uncles methodically work their way up his body, poking and rolling an endless round of hot irons into his legs and against his genitals and at the base of his spine and into his chest and arms until they reach his head, at which point they will burn out his tongue by forcing an iron into his mouth and throat and sear out his eyes, one at a time, so that what they then will consign to the fire is no longer all that human, if ever it was to them or to the crowd, but more a groaning, stinking, smoking thing.

It is a horrible picture, all the more so because, at this point, it seems so matter-of-fact. The kneeling figures could be searching for coins dropped on the floor, with Henry Smith telling them where to look. Or if Henry Vance were given to forgiveness, he might be washing Henry Smith's feet while his son, leaning against the scaffold railing to the right of Smith, observes a moment of humility and grace. There were additional photographs of Henry Smith's death ceremony, but none is more terrifying than this one.[33]

After the Vances were done torturing, after some forty to fifty minutes of careful attention to Henry Smith's poor body, they poured oil over him and over the platform, stacked combustibles under the scaffold, and set it ablaze. After some time, many thought Smith was dead, but once the flames had burned away what was left of his feet, he lifted his head and began to wail from his seared and scarred mouth and throat, causing some in the crowd to wail involuntarily along with him in shock or possibly terror. When the fire burned through his ropes, he "raised the crisp and blackened stumps to wipe the sightless sockets of his eyes"; and when the weakened ropes further released him from the stake, he fell forward and crawled to the edge of the platform where, for another moment, he sat, teetering, all balance lost, and then toppled off the scaffold into the crowd itself, which, packed as it was, could not avoid him as he fell. So, back into the fire they shoved him, and still again when he once more rolled away, until finally whatever was left of Henry Smith stopped moving and simply rested and smoked. Later the relic hunters found teeth, found bones, in the ashes.

So how can a people possibly justify or defend such actions? This was the task J. M. Early, self-identified as "An Eye-Witness," set for himself. "Let us try what virtue there is in fire," he wrote in the first chapter of his treatise, *"An Eye for An Eye" or The Fiend and the Fagot*, subtitled, *An Unvarnished Account of the Burning of Henry Smith at Paris, Texas, February 1, 1893, and the Reason He Was Tortured*. For seventy pages, Early describes, explains, and rationalizes the actions of the mob, of which he was himself one. He does not avoid the horror of the act. On the first page he states:

> A being had better never be born than in just punishment for a deed so dark and diabolical, so terrible that it outraged and enraged all the world into justifying a moiety of the earth to execute him by the extremest engine of execution known to savage or civilized man—fire.[34]

Furthermore, he admits,

> Since the bigotry of priests, and the diabolism of misconceived ritual rights have been restrained by law, born of reason, which makes man akin to Deity, there has been a renunciation of the fire ordeal, and scarce a being in a hundred years becomes a martyr at the stake. None by process of law.[35]

How, then, can there be "virtue" in "fire"? Not to mention the "few strokes of the refinement of torture" that were added?

Early's answer is to point to the monstrousness of the crime committed by the offender, "heinous" enough to "enrage a people of letters, of undisputed morality, or social refinements, to go in the very shadows of the churches to which they belonged, stake the offender and burn him as did the people of Paris, who executed Henry Smith by fire." Although Early concedes that the "American Sambo," since emancipation, has "transcended all expectations," a creature like Henry Smith is such a fiend that "Divinity" itself calls for actions beyond those allowed by law.[36] People reach to God by employing faith and reason, but some deeds are so fundamentally evil that reason, and law, stand helpless before them. In these cases, Early declares, man must courageously put the law aside, put compassion and mercy and even humanity aside, in order to confront the base malevolence before him. Thus, the dedication of his "little Book":

> To every Father and Mother, in all the Earth, who
> can say to Those who Executed the Mur-
> derer of Little Myrtle Vance,
> "WELL DONE, THOU GOOD AND FAITHFUL SERVANT!"
> The Author dedicates this little Book.

Early accomplishes his defense of Henry Smith's agonizing death in several ways. First, he emphasizes the "little girl babe or tot" as victim, even to the point of including her portrait ("The Baby for the Murder of Which Henry Smith Was Burned at the Stake") on the front page of the book. He appeals shamelessly to parental love, asking his readers to consider their own children and then to place themselves in the Vances' position:

> During the day you hear it sing the little baby songs which you have taught it, and speak its simple monosylabic [sic] vocabulary. You kiss it, you fondle it, you love it; yes, you are an idolatress—you adore it. When it gets sick your heart sinks within you, down, down, until you pray God to spare it to you yet a while longer. Then, when it gets well, your heart comes up, and all that seemed dark and desolate now ripples in a halo of light. That is just the way it is.[37]

Then comes the monster, a "fiend in human shape":

He is a tall, dark, ragged, lusty demon. The evil in his eye gleaming in the dark. In his ragged rundown shoes, he comes noiselessly, as the thief that he is. So expert in skulking that even the dogs are unaware of his whereabouts. He finds my child at the gate. He looks here, there, everywhere in the dunn [*sic*] of the fast falling night, and there are no eyes that see him. He stoops and winds a long sinewy arm about its little waist, the skin of which was as black as the designs of the heart, and the covering of the skin dirty and tattered as crime's rags. Quick he draws it up to his calous [*sic*] trunk while he places the hand of the other arm over the mouth of my child to prevent its giving alarm to me—to anyone. Then he glides away, away.[38]

In this description, Myrtle Vance becomes "my child," any reader's child. The lascivious suggestions in Early's description now must appall and outrage even more—the long, sinewy black arm around the babe's waist, the black hand over her mouth, the "nude limbs of the growth" in the woods where he takes her.[39] But Early can shock in other, more graphic, ways as well. He relates a jailhouse interview with the prisoner.

> Captors, "Well then, tell us Smith, what did you do? How did you kill the child?"
> Prisoner, "Well, when I reached the woods where you say the child was found, I sat down by a tree and I drew it to me like I would a boot."
> Captors, "Did it cry?"
> Prisoner, "Yes, a little, but I put my hand over its mouth so it could not cry much."
> Captors, "Well, go on."
> Prisoner, "Well, when I found I could not draw it on me, I took my hands and tore it open, and then I drew it on me."

Like a boot. On a foot. And the next morning, finding that "it was kinder moving and groaning . . . I then choked it to death and covered it up with leaves, and set out to make my escape."[40]

"The lizards of the brain of the most infernal had perhaps never stung to such infamous crime," Early writes later in his booklet, but although a rape very likely did take place (Early includes a coroner's report describing the injuries, which seems authentic, although one would be foolish to accept Smith's guilt based on this source alone), it is most unlikely that Smith, described elsewhere as an "imbecile," spoke the words attributed to him.[41] And though Early spares no epitaphs in portraying Smith—"more damnable than all the damned: foul, letcherous, leperous [*sic*] with the festered scabs of leprosy clotted about his heart, whose very tread cankered the earth, whose touch poisoned, and whose breathe contaminated every thing with which it came in contact"—he is more restrained in describing the execution itself than were the newspapers.[42] If the "spirit of Lodi" caused the "uprising of the people" and the "drawing of fire across the trail of the monster of retributive justice," it is nevertheless time that "Heaven approve[d] of the action" since the "figments of law" were clearly inadequate to address the horror of the crime. By no means a "mob," the people who undertook this duty were "the salt of the earth," worthy of praise rather than condemnation.[43]

It is necessary to consider at such length the Henry Smith torture and burning in order to understand the fate of Sam Hose, six years later. We might wonder to what extent Early's booklet provided a blueprint for the process of the Sam Hose execution. Although Hose does not rape or kill a child, he does strike one little girl and throws a baby boy to the floor before raping Mrs. Cranford beside her husband's dying body, in front of her stunned children. His escape and flight enrage the community, as did Henry Smith's, and the procession through the town once Hose is caught fulfills the civic ceremony enacted in Paris, Texas, the need to afford the citizens an opportunity to vent their fury and to console them that order is being restored. In both cases, the pyre is set up just outside town, removed enough to suggest some degree of decorum but close enough for the town's citizens to attend. The "refinement" of Smith's tortures surely exceed those Hose endured, although it seems moot and even indecent to weigh these horrors against one another. At heart, what is significant is that J. M. Early and Paris, Texas (and other places as well by 1899), had given these Georgians leave to do the things they did, had, in effect, challenged them to do them. The headlines had predicted it from the first moment, the family had requested it, the citizens had expected it, and according to Early, the Bible pretty much demanded it. Governor Atkinson could talk all he wished about the law and the deleterious effect this act would have on Newnan's good name. *Not* to do it: that was what had become inconceivable.

At the same time, it is curious to note how the various newspaper accounts of Hose's capture, torture, and execution cautiously begin to humanize the man. The "brute," the "demon," the "monster" now is accorded a degree of dignity, even of courage. Although there is never any doubt that he deserves his punishment, no matter how extreme, there is also the very real sense that he is playing out his role in this ritual, and that he is doing it well. On the other hand, the need for a relatively composed victim was essential if the execution was to have any pretend dignity at all and not degenerate into mere butchery.[44]

Thus, the *Newnan Herald and Advertiser* described the scene:

> To have offered resistance to this delirious, tumultuous mass would have been madness. Swept off on the turbulent tide of human passion, uncomforted by a single pitying glance from the hundreds of fellow-creatures who looked on as he was being dragged along by the avenging mob, the miserable wretch realized that his doom was

sealed. A recollection of his own dark deeds probably nerved him to stoicism; perhaps he had become reconciled to the fate which he knew awaited him. However this may be, he did not whimper; did not ask for mercy at the hands of his tormentors. Terrified he must have been, but sheep never went to the shambles more unresistingly than did this negro to the stake.[45]

Daniel and other reporters describe Sam Hose as stoic, prepared for his death and the horrors that preceded it. "He made very few outcries and in the whole proceedings acted as coolly as the warmth of the fire would permit," the *Griffin Daily News and Sun* commented archly.

> Self confessed and almost defiant, without a plea for mercy and no expectation of it, Hose went to the stake with as much courage as any one could possibly have possessed on such an occasion, and the only murmur that issued from his lips was when angry knives plunged into his flesh and his life's blood sizzled in the fire before his eyes.
> Then he cried, "Oh, my God! Oh, Jesus!"[46]

Not all accounts agreed on this point. The Associated Press report, which was published throughout the nation, made much of Sam Hose's initial screams of terror and pain. It would later be suggested that his subsequent silence was caused by the removal of his tongue during the preliminary mutilations. The local accounts, however, omitted these details, if they occurred. Daniel especially insisted on Hose's fortitude, perhaps to draw a starker comparison between the subject and the mob.

The *Atlanta Journal* placed on its front page, in the middle of the accounts of his capture and death, "The First Picture of the Negro Yet Printed—Made from a Photograph Taken Yesterday for The Journal." It is a head shot, including the chest and shoulders. The man is dressed in a coat and a shirt buttoned at the collar. His head is shaved, his mouth is slightly open, and he stares above and to the right of the camera lens. He wears no chains, he shows no fear. But neither is he threatening, terrifying. The picture portrays him as dignified, self-possessed, hardly the brute described so often in previous descriptions. One need only compare it to the cartoonish illustration published in the May 13 issue of the *National Police Gazette*, in which a grotesque Hose, his Negroid features exaggerated, prepares to strike Alfred Cranford while Mattie, clasping her child to her breast, recoils in horror. Other, smaller, illustrations in the *Journal* show Hose at the train window and then being removed from the train, but we can hardly see him in these drawings. There are also sketches of the march to the stake and "The Smouldering Funeral Pyre" that remains once the deed is done, but Hose, alive or dead, is not visible in them. Thus, this is the physical image readers of the *Journal* would have in mind as they learned about the lynching. He

Chapter Six

does not look like an ax murderer, a child beater, or a ravenous rapist. The man, instead, is a martyr, determined and prepared, as the accounts indicate, for the horror to follow. Indeed, in these accounts, both written and illustrated, it is the crowd, the "howling mob," that becomes the focus of revulsion, of apology, and of shame. This is shown in yet another illustration, a "Halftone Supplement" ("Well Worth Framing"), also published by the *Police Gazette* in its May 13 issue. A full two-page illustration presents "Sam Hose, the Brutal Negro Who Killed Mr. Cranford at Palmetto, Ga., Drenched with Oil and Cremated at the Stake," with the shouting mob on verso and the burning man on recto facing each other. The men hold knives and cheer, while two women in the crowd also watch, one pointing at the victim in celebration. In the foreground is a kerosene can. The muscular Hose, in the midst of the flames, his eyes wide and his mouth agape in agony but also in protest, strains wildly against his chains. The picture, for all its tastelessness, nevertheless places the viewer in a difficult position. The joy of the crowd at the suffering of the man is appalling. The *National Police Gazette* was a northern publication and infamous for its tabloid reporting, but its images of Hose's "cremation" drew on reports written by southern journalists. Thus, for all the initial efforts to explain or to justify the mob's actions, for all the talk of selfless men diligently enacting their civic responsibilities, for all the pontificating about righteous revenge and higher justice, the newspaper accounts make it clear that, at bottom, this is a disgraceful deed. Necessary, they might argue, but ultimately reprehensible.

And so here, in this "favorable place," the Old Troutman Field, at a little past two on a warm Sunday afternoon, a crowd numbered in later accounts at two thousand but probably smaller pushed and elbowed as spectators found their places in a huge semicircle around the site of Sam Hose's ritualistic death, a pine tree in the middle of the field.[47] Men lifted and waved their hats in salute, nodded and smiled and shook hands with their neighbors in congratulations as the fire was being prepared. The *Constitution*, as always, stressed the orderliness of the crowd. In contrast to the disguised shooters of the Palmetto vigilante gang, these participants made no effort to conceal themselves. "Masks played no part in this lynching. There was no secrecy, no effort to prevent any one seeing who lighted the fire, who cut off the ears or who took the lead. The whole male community seemed to be a unit, and while the majority of those present knew each other, it is doubtful if a man can be found who will say he saw any one he knew."[48]

Royal Daniel of the *Journal*, however, described a different, less-organized scene. Daniel was a Newnan native, and he seemed disturbed by what he was witnessing in his hometown. He wrote, "Hundreds of infuriated and frenzied men, delirious with delight at his capture, cheered Sam Hose to death yesterday afternoon at the stake, their only regret being that human minds could not conceive of torture more agonizing."[49] Daniel examined the event in excruciating detail for the *Journal*'s readers. Hose, in his account, was first chained to the sturdy pine tree by the men leading the mob. "The men about the stake were calm, the orders were given in low voice, and there was absolute order and decorum, if such may be said, when the final crisis came." The other members of the crowd, sweating and weary after the exertion of the forced march, caught their breath while preparations continued. Once the chains were made tight and the wood was stacked around the prisoner's feet, a man spoke to the crowd. "'Don't shoot, boys,' cried one of the ringleaders. 'He's ready, but let him die by inches.'"

The leaders then turned to Sam Hose himself and asked for his confession, which Hose is reported to have made as follows: "I am Sam Hose. I killed Alfred Cranford, but I was paid to do it. Lige Strickland, the negro preacher at Palmetto, gave me $12 to kill him." The crowd roared at this admission but was again quieted. "Let him go on. Tell all you know about it!" someone shouted. Hose, "shivering like a leaf," continued: "I did not outrage Mrs. Cranford. Somebody else did that. I can identify them. Give me time for that!"

But now the crowd had had enough, and despite protests that Hose be allowed to name others who might have been involved, an extra chain was placed around his neck and fastened to the tree, its links tied by string. At this point, the knives came out, and at this sight, which "seemed to forecast the terrible ordeal he was about to be put to," Hose, according to the Associated Press report, finally lost the remarkable composure he had maintained thus far. He shrieked, giving forth a yell "which could heard for a mile."[50] Someone stepped forward and cut off an ear; another man did the same. "The blood gushed in a nauseating, spouting stream. A cheer went up from the mob." Someone else then "plunged a knife in the fleshy part of his side." At this point, "Hose pled pitifully for mercy and begged his tormentors to let him die." When warned by one of the ringleaders that Hose might, indeed, die before he could be burned, a voice from the crowd responded, "Oh, well, we are just playing with him; we ain't going to kill him." But other men now began to stab and mutilate Hose's body. His fingers were severed, joint by joint, and passed through the boisterous crowd.[51] "The shrieking wretch was then deprived of other portions of his anatomy," the *Macon Telegraph* reported with arch circumspection, but the *Journal* stated in bold print that Hose was "emasculated" before the fire was started. Daniel noted that "many [white] hands [were] cut in the delirious frenzy of the men to perform the bloody task."[52]

At approximately 2:30, someone shouted, "Come on with the oil," and four men, the Pennsylvanian among them, staggered forward with a large can of kerosene, which they lifted with much difficulty above the head of the bleeding,

Chapter Six

mutilated man, who struggled against his chains and cried out against the coming agony. "Willing hands struck matches and a hundred little flames flashed into the rich pine and blazed like lightning through the kerosene," Daniel reported. "The sound of frying, sizzling human flesh, and the smell of the charred and slowly baking body was nauseating and revolting beyond all description."[53] For the next fifteen minutes, Sam Hose, in the words of the *Savannah Morning News*, "tusselled with life and death."[54]

Royal Daniel again turned his attention to the crowd:

> "Don't make it too hot," was the warning.
>
> "Glory to God," screamed an old white haired man, who was jumping up and down in unison with the wretch's contortions. "God bless every man who had a hand in this. Thank God for vengeance."
>
> The fire crackled and flamed.
>
> Then the fire, with a roar, darted up the man's clothing and ran up his back, burning away every rag, burning his hair away, singeing off his eyebrows.
>
> When the clothing was burned away, the flames fell back and began eating away with gnawing hunger at his feet.
>
> Slowly the fire crawled upward, men pulling the brands away to keep the flames from burning too fast.[55]

After his initial shouts of horror and pain, Sam Hose endured the rest of his death largely in silence. With his hands reduced to charred stumps, he desperately pawed at his chains. As Daniel described it in ever more horrific detail,

> With the strength of a demon Hose tugged at his chain, threw himself against the tree and jerked backward, beat his head against the tree, tried to climb away from the flames, but not a word did he utter, but stood, stoical, grim, defiant, not even breaking his silence to breathe a prayer for the welfare of his soul.
>
> Then Hose began to beat against the chain that held him in his agony.
>
> With ponderous blows he beat with his right hand upon the links.
>
> Piece by piece he beat the flesh off his hand, the fingers were stripped of flesh and sinews until the bones, protruding, were snapped by the blows.
>
> The odor of burning flesh was indescribably nauseating.
>
> Around and around the tree the negro swung in his agony and his contortions, so fearful, brought cheers from the crowd.
>
> "Down in front," cried those who were on the outer edges of the circle straining, tip-toeing people.
>
> "Oh, don't jump so, Sam; it don't hurt you," came a tantalizing shout, followed by jeers.
>
> "What did you do it for, Sam, if you didn't want to get warmed up a little?"

But these mocking cries fell upon deaf ears.

The negro was battling in the flames with wildest and superhuman energy. Now he was twisting around the tree; now biting at the bark of the pine, jumping and springing and twisting and fighting for every inch of life, kicking the embers with his dangling legs, blood vessels bursting, eyes protruding, but not a word, not a tear, but, oh God, the horror of his face, the agonizing look, the hellish expression![56]

The *Griffin Evening Call* added yet more terrible observations about the burning, likely obtained from some of the Griffin men who attended the lynching. The paper reported that Hose attempted to pull himself with his "fingerless hands" up the tree away from the flames. When he fell, the chain around his neck snapped, and he tumbled forward into the fire and coals. A member of the crowd then pulled him out of the flames "that death might not come to end his sufferings too quickly." At this point, the paper narrated, others surrounded the blistered body and began to hack at it with knives for souvenirs. Finally, one man "in mercy to the negro, cast him back into the flames, and began to pile on pine wood. A cord at least must have been thrown on him, and nothing could be seen but his head." It was now that Hose, in his final agonies, caught one piece of wood in his mouth and bit down on it "as if it had been an apple," the Newnan paper reported. "It was a horrible, sickening spectacle, and many were forced to turn away from the ghastly figure," the *Call* observed.[57]

Royal Daniel's account, which had carefully described the hysterical, carnivalesque celebrations of the crowd as well as the frantic struggles of the victim, now took on an unusually personal quality. He examined himself as an observer, one near enough to see the absolute pain and terror Sam Hose was suffering and the equally absolute indifference to both exhibited by most of the men surrounding him. "Hose was conscious for exactly twenty minutes. Each minute seemed an hour to me, and each hour to him must have been a century of torture and terrible agony, such agony impossible to imagine."

I stood as close to the flames and the writhing figure in their midst as the heat would permit. Men crowded around, pulling out the burning wood when the fire became too hot.

I became sick and faint, as did everybody who was within reach of the odor of frying flesh. . . .

After ten minutes of untold agony Hose snapped his chain and fell into the embers and flame.

He would probably have run, but his feet were burned away. He simply fell helpless in the flames, bouncing and beating himself in the red hot embers.

This was exactly at 2:40 o'clock.

The negro was picked up, thrown against the tree and the chain wrapped tightly.

An Ohio man rushed through the group, grasped a can of kerosene oil and dashed it on the wretch.

His deed was applauded.

For another ten minutes the negro was conscious, his writhings increasing as the fire blazed higher.

At 2:50 o'clock he swooned and fainted and consciousness was gone.

The figure hung limp and apparently lifeless, held only by the chain to the tree.

"Oh, he died too quick," came a regretful comment from the crowd.[58]

Like all these accounts, Royal Daniel's narrative makes for difficult reading, but his first-person witnessing of the torture and execution gives his article an authority missing from most of the other reports. The Newnan paper, whose reporter (likely the editor James Brown) also seems to have observed the burning, described the scene more circumspectly than did Daniel. "We have given the whole story," the paper explained in its Friday edition (April 28), "without varnish or embellishment. It is bad enough, we will not deny."[59] This is possibly a rebuke of Daniel's personal interjections, his excessive morbidity, and certainly the reporter was open to charges of sensationalism. Nevertheless, although Daniel had written with less sympathy for the victims of the Palmetto massacre and their families than had Frank Fleming of the *Constitution*, here his reporting is more complex because he had experienced the sights and sounds and smells of the execution. If his account of Hose's death seems intentionally lurid, it also forced his readers to confront themselves in the reading. His attention to the crowd, his refusal to construct them simply as dutiful citizens, and his insistence on detailing their barbaric behavior underscore the revulsion he felt and insisted his readers feel also.[60] The Newnan paper editorialized in its account: "We have no apologies to make to our Northern critics. We owe nothing to that section. Our civilization is distinctively Southern, and we thank God for it."[61] But Daniel was far more appalled by than thankful for the behavior he witnessed.

As with the tradition of burning criminals found guilty of extraordinary offenses, dismemberment of the body also had its roots in earlier forms of justice. In colonial times, bodies of the executed might be left on public display for weeks to be eaten by birds, insects, microbes. Stuart Banner writes that sometimes the corpse would be slathered in tallow or pitch to retard decomposition and then hung in chains or placed in a gibbet, an iron cage that could be raised into the air to allow better viewing. A variation of this procedure was to dismember the felon's body, usually by decapitating and then quartering, which allowed the sections to be shown at various places at once. The head, usually affixed to a pole, would be the primary display, but sections of the quartered corpse could be taken to other parts of the city or surrounding area. As Banner notes, "We may surmise that further dismemberment, although allowing for a greater number of display sites, was thought to reduce the visual impact of each one. A severed head must have been considered a better deterrent than an ear, an arm better than a finger." A further refinement reserved for the very worst offenders was disembowelment while the criminal was still alive, which, in effect, allowed the victim to watch himself die as the bowels spilled, sometimes into fire, thus combining the two most exquisitely excruciating torments.[62] This may, indeed, have been done to Sam Hose, as Ida Wells-Barnett would later claim. Emasculation and disembowelment both involve cutting on the lower torso, and by accident or intention Hose might well have suffered this most rarified punishment, although it is never directly mentioned in any of the contemporary accounts.

Nevertheless, one of the more disquieting horrors of Sam Hose's execution is the public vying for body parts and surviving bone fragments and, lacking that, other items associated with his death—splinters from the tree, burnt wood, links of chain, any parcel of clothing not consumed by the fire. "Men scrambled and fell over each other in their mad haste to secure something that would be a memento of the horrible tragedy," Daniel wrote. "Men shouted with joy as they showed these nauseating relics to their friends and fabulous sums of money were refused with contempt by many who were happy in the possession of their trophies and spoils."[63]

Clearly these things were being taken as memorials, as items that could be shown to others or publicly displayed, as his knuckles would be the next day in the store window of an Atlanta shop. These remains conveyed status on the owner, whether he had himself severed the digit or dug through the ashes or had bought the prize from someone who did. A correspondent to the Newnan paper, while defending the tortures inflicted on Sam Hose—"why should it be considered a thing incredible to burn a sinner who seems to have forgotten humanity and civilization, when most of the first preachers of the Gospel which has done so much to refine and civilize this country were killed—some by stoning, others by beheading, one by burning with his head downward, and still another by being skinned alive?"—did object to the taking of relics of Hose's "carcass," explaining, "We want to forget him and his crimes as soon as we can."[64]

But perhaps for some it was more than that. Local papers would later make jokes about superstitious blacks who skirted the site of Sam Hose's death, fearful of what spirit might linger at that awful place, but these jokes likely reflected a similar sense of repressed awe felt by the whites themselves inspired by these relics. The kind of public questioning, of denial, of blame shifting, that would take place over the next months, and the organized but ultimately unsuccessful effort to remove the memory of this event from the community in the years to come, would indicate a conflict in the communal consciousness. These corporal remains, whether cooked by fire or mummified by time, must have taken on a kind of juju for their owners, must have become mute but potent signifiers of an unexplainable mystery, not only that of Sam Hose but of themselves as well. Certainly for some these *objects* would carry no more moral weight than a rabbit's foot, but even a rabbit's foot suggests a way the world works that is beyond rational thinking. And for many, with the smell of Sam Hose still high in their noses and the echoes of his terrified screams in their ears and the carousing of the crowd still sharp in their minds' eyes, surely some of these people studied, touched, felt the weight of these remains in their palms and found themselves suddenly wondering how it all could have happened.

What the crowd had accomplished, in its crude, dumb, but ultimately needy way, was a public dissection and study of Sam Hose's corpse. As Banner notes, such investigations of the criminal body became a "formal arm" of British penal policy in 1752, when Parliament passed an act calling for the performing of anatomies on the corpses of certain felons "that some further terror and peculiar mark of infamy be added to the punishment of death." He explains that in America, although laws allowing anatomization were regularly passed, "Like burning, gibbeting, or dismemberment, dissection was an enhancement to a murder sentence, not a standard part of one."[65] But dissection had an economic as well as a scientific aspect to it. Sam Hose's body parts were sold on the spot as keepsakes, obviously without his consent, but condemned criminals sometimes negotiated with doctors or medical schools before execution to sell their bodies for medical study. Still others, who may have been without family or were so poor that no one could afford even the most humble burial, fretted that their corpses would go directly from the gallows not to potter's field but to the morgue, where they would be left to the macabre machinations of physicians or students, who could manipulate the body at will. This was the case with poor Robert Lewis, whose wife shrieked in hysterics when she feared his body was being transported to a medical school in Atlanta after his hanging and who was, indeed, later autopsied in an effort to determine the source of his depravity.[66]

To what degree were these good Georgia citizens seeking such knowledge of themselves as they took Sam Hose apart? And to what degree did these remains weigh on their minds as they later displayed them in public or studied them in solitary? These are not questions directly confronted by a reporter like Royal Daniel, but they are there in his report, embedded in the details he provides, not only of the crowd and its actions but of Sam Hose himself as he faced his death.

Whether Sam Hose in fact faced his end stoically by choice, in keeping with some personal sense of dignity and propriety, or whether in his final minutes he screamed in blind, agonizing protest at the impossible cruelty of the crowd that was doing him to death with such relish, it apparently was necessary that the local reports accord him—formerly the monster, the fiend—a modicum of admiration as he stood his torture. It helped to restore order to the universe. Daniel thus ended his report by stepping back from the scene and turning his attention to the community at large and then to the world itself:

> All night the fire was burned and great flames painted the sky crimson, as though a mighty conflagration was in progress.
>
> Farmers and their wives and daughters watched the grimly painted sky and there was rejoicing throughout all the counties where the apparent phenomena of the heavens was visible.
>
> Negroes gathered about their doorsteps and looked aghast at the weird scene and kept silent vigil, realizing beyond all doubt the horrible lesson that had been taught on the Sabbath day.
>
> The sky beamed down upon the dark woods this beacon light, flashed it from hill to hill and dale to dale, carrying with it for many miles the announcement that a mighty wrong had been avenged.
>
> It was the handwriting on the clouds, the lights throwing weird shadows across the country, streaming through the dense forests and reflected in the sluggish streams that wound through the valleys.
>
> A piece of wood was thrown upon the fire. Sparks danced upward to the sky, fanned by the artificial breeze of the flames. The sparks were as a myriad stars jetting, bursting and falling through space.[67]

That night, a reporter from the *Macon Telegraph* (most likely Goode M. Guerry, who also investigated the Lige Strickland hanging) visited the scene of Sam Hose's immolation. Earlier he had gone to the McLeroy home to see if Mattie Cranford would grant him an interview. Her mother had refused him, saying that her daughter was in "a most pitiable condition" and that doctors still feared for her sanity. The baby Sam Hose had snatched from her arms was still in "critical condition." The reporter had also talked to Sheriff Brown, who now claimed that the crowd had dynamite and had threatened to blow up the jail if Hose were not handed over, an explanation that had also been used to compel the transportation of Oscar Williams, and later the turning over of the three Leesburg men to the mobs that lynched them. Now the reporter stood in Troutman Field, surveying the scene. In only a few short hours, the "leading citizens" of Newnan had removed all remaining signs of the proceedings, had sought to erase all evidence that the spectacle had occurred. "The tree to which Hose was tied was cut down and divided as souvenirs. Even ashes were taken up, and when I visited the scene the pale moonlight showed no traces of the terrible death that had been suffered there a few hours before," the reporter related.[68]

On the following morning, April 24, Dr. Hal Johnston, "weary of the chase but [still] determined," returned to Palmetto. He claimed to have been "within eight miles of the negro" when Hose was captured by the Jones brothers. "I would have caught him as surely as you live," he assured the *Atlanta Journal*. He had also missed the execution, but he felt "satisfaction" that he had been on the "right trail" and had done his duty.[69]

On the same day, U.S. attorney general John W. Griggs remarked in Washington on the Hose lynching, saying that the incident "had no Federal aspect [to it] and that therefore the government would take no action whatever in regard to it."[70]

Chapter Seven

Beware, All Darkies!

Sam Hose's death on that Sabbath afternoon in April set loose a frenzy in this part of west Georgia, and it is unclear how many others became collateral victims. There were immediate rumors of other killings in Coweta and Campbell counties, men supposedly implicated by Hose as connected to the black gang that had terrorized the region through arson and threats of death. The *Macon Telegraph* noted that as many as five suspects were being pursued by mobs determined to put an end, once and for all, to the "negro outlawry" that plagued their communities. The white posses were "determined to protect their families and property at all hazards."[1] The *Griffin Daily News and Sun* reported that an Albert Sewell had been hanged by a group from Palmetto, and that it was now searching for two other suspects.[2]

Although other names would be given in subsequent reports, only one man would be confirmed as a secondary sacrifice in the Hose spectacle. That was Elijah Strickland, the man Hose had identified as the instigator of his attack on Alfred Cranford, even though many openly questioned the truth of Hose's accusation. The prevalent view of Strickland was that he was a "good negro," a man in his sixties who was born in slavery and thus knew how to behave, unlike younger, undisciplined blacks like Sam Hose, who were adrift in the world and thus more likely to revert to their innate savagery. Strickland also was a preacher, a man with a family, one who was known to urge caution to his people and who had the respect and the partiality of many prominent whites in the community. After his death, darker views would circulate, and he would be named by some as a villain in disguise, the secret leader of the

Palmetto arsonists and assassins, a criminal mastermind pretending to be a worthy and dutiful man of God.

When word first spread throughout the region that Sam Hose had been captured and would in all likelihood be lynched at the Cranford plantation, the Atlanta and West Point railroad was besieged by customers hoping to witness the deed. In LaGrange, a group of some 150 men gathered and requested that the railroad make a special run of the "Goober," as the local train was known, from West Point to Palmetto. The railway agreed, but just as the train was leaving West Point, word came from Newnan that Hose had already been burned to death. "The crowd then dispersed from the depot," the *LaGrange Graphic* reported, "but all day they hung around in squads discussing the affair and eagerly catching every scrap of news in regard to it."[3]

In Atlanta, the afternoon paper, the *Journal*, had already sent its correspondent Royal Daniel to Newnan to report on Hose's capture and staff artist William Larned to Palmetto, where it was assumed the lynching would take place. The paper put out an extra at 2:30 that Sunday afternoon giving the most recent details, and crowds gathered in front of the *Journal* office awaiting the latest news. "The demand for it was something tremendous," the *Journal* reported.

> The vast crowd . . . surged toward the door and hundreds of papers were gobbled up before the boys could turn the corner. In ten minutes the thousands in Broad street were reading the details of the capture. On rushed the newsboys and in less than half an hour the great crowds around the central corners, the hotels and the thousands surging in and about the union trains bound for the scene of action were all reading the extra Journal. Every train carried hundreds of extra Journals, which were greedily bought along the route, the people getting the very first news of the capture and eagerly devouring it.[4]

The paper put out a second extra containing the details of Hose's death at 4:30, and again the response was "simply phenomenal." Newsboys tunneled into the crowd hawking this latest edition, while men shoved their money at them and grabbed at what they offered, waving the papers over their heads and sometimes shouting out details of the public burning to the crowd at large.

At first reports of Sam Hose's capture, many Atlantans rushed to Union Station to take the regularly scheduled 1:00 p.m. train to Palmetto. When that run, made up of six coaches, sold out, the Atlanta and West Point railway was able to arrange a second special train at 3:20, to supplement the next scheduled run at 4:20. This special train was made up of ten passenger coaches and two baggage cars, with one engine at the head and another pushing from behind. The company reported having sold 1,127 tickets, not including those who rode for free or paid on the trains. All cars were "crowded to their utmost capacity, and many were compelled to stand throughout the trip." Tickets were sold at reduced rates as a kind of public service to allow as many as possible to attend the event. "The railroad, while not encouraging a lynching special, nevertheless acceded to the demands for such a train, and made it possible for the people who desired to go."[5] The *Constitution* observed, "No time was lost on the way down as the trainsmen were as anxious to be in time to see the lynching as were the people on the train."[6]

It was assumed that, in keeping with lynching protocol, Hose's death would take place near the site of the Cranford plantation, where the murder and rape were said to have occurred. At the community of Cross Ankle, several miles outside Palmetto and within view of the Cranford home, men had already prepared a bonfire for Hose's burning, and a group of passengers, estimated at 250, disembarked from the first Atlanta train at this place. When word subsequently came that the execution was taking place outside Newnan, "a more disappointed crowd could hardly be imagined than this one," and many either began making arrangements for hacks or wagons to carry them to Newnan or began walking or trotting down the railroad track in hopes of arriving before the spectacle was over.[7] Many stayed, however, and early on the morning of Monday the twenty-fourth, a train conductor would report seeing the bonfire ablaze at Cross Ankle, with men surrounding the fire and shooting into it. This is apparently the event William Larned illustrated on the front page of Monday's *Atlanta Journal* captioned "Scene near the Cranford Home," which shows a large, armed crowd gathered near the railroad tracks, a small fire ablaze in the distance, with stacks of wood nearby ready to feed it when the victim appeared. There were false reports that, having missed out on Sam Hose's lynching, the crowd at Cross Ankle had consigned Elijah Strickland to this fire as a substitute victim. But it is even now unclear whether some other unknown sacrifice was in fact burned in those flames or whether the disappointed crowd had simply set the fire and shot their weapons in frustration or drunken celebration.

Among those who had set out from Palmetto to Newnan was a group of especially anxious men who hurried to the scene of Hose's execution. "Oh, my God, have they burned him before we could get here?" one was quoted as saying, "and there was genuine pathos and regret in his voice that was almost choking with emotion," a *Journal* correspondent reported.[8] Many in this bunch had been drinking, and in their disappointment they now turned their attention to Elijah Strickland. Strickland and his family lived on a plantation, located near the Cranford farm, owned by Maj. Wesley W. Thomas, "an ex-Representative, and one of the most distinguished citizens of Coweta county," according to the *Newnan Herald and Advertiser*.[9] These men, numbered between twenty-five and fifty, set off in search of the preacher just as night began to fall. They retraced their journey back toward Palmetto and arrived at Strickland's cabin around 9:00 p.m. The family had gone to bed, and the cabin was dark. The men surrounded it and called out to Strickland to dress himself and come outside, which he did. As the mob took him, his wife and children ran screaming from the cabin and quickly alerted Major Thomas of what was occurring. The major and his son W. M. Thomas immediately went in pursuit of the men in an attempt to save Strickland's life.

The mob first intended to take Strickland to the Cranford farm and hang him there, but they were overtaken by the Thomases before they could reach this destination. Thomas spoke earnestly to the crowd, his words recorded in later accounts:

> Gentlemen, this negro is innocent. Holt said Lige had promised to give him $20 to kill Cranford, and I believe Lige has not had $20 since he has been on my place. This is a lawabiding negro you are about to hang. He has never done any of you any harm, and now I want you to promise me that you will turn him over to the bailiff of this town or to someone who is entitled to receipt for him in order that he may be given a hearing on his case. I do not ask that you liberate him. Hold him, and if the courts adjudge him guilty, hang him.[10]

Thomas and the men continued to debate Strickland's guilt. Strickland apparently had freely admitted having talked with Sam Hose on the night of the murder, but some members of the mob felt that he "had [admitted] this in the cunningness of his guilt to establish his own innocence."[11] Nevertheless, Major Thomas was able to convince the men that they should wait for a proper trial, and after a vote, the crowd agreed to this request and turned to escort Strickland to the Palmetto jail, where he could be kept until his guilt or innocence was determined. On the outskirts of the town, one in the crowd even suggested that Strickland be handed over to Major Thomas, but just as Thomas was about to leave with Strickland, a second gathering of men, some of them also described as inebriated, arrived. "We have him here; let's keep him," one from this group shouted, and the rest of the men quickly agreed. When Thomas again protested, a member of the mob drew a pistol on the major as they led Strickland away. The infuriated major went off in search of Palmetto mayor T. P. Arnold to ask for "his official assistance." When he returned without help, the "newcomers" sent word by a messenger that Thomas "had better leave town before they returned." Newspapers reported his response to this insult with much admiration. Infuriated, the major "drew himself up and said emphatically":

> "I have never before been ordered to leave a town, and I am not going to leave this one."

And then the Major, uplifting his hand to give the words force, said to the messenger:

> "Tell them that the muscles in my legs are not trained to running; tell them that I have stood the fire and heard the minies from a thousand Yankee rifles, and I am not frightened by this crowd."[12]

In the meantime, this second group of men had taken Strickland into Palmetto, and there, in front of the post office, they held a "mock trial." According to the *Columbus Enquirer-Sun*, both blacks and whites informally testified for Strickland, while other whites spoke against him.[13] Goode M. Guerry, the reporter from the *Macon Telegraph*, seems to have been present during these events, and his account purports to be a firsthand witnessing of what followed. According to Guerry, "after much wrangling," the men determined that Strickland "must either confess or be lynched." The mob then marched through the little town on their way to a grove of trees on the outskirts. As they did, some Palmetto citizens approached them, asking that they not go through with the lynching, but the men "hooted at" these pleas.[14]

At the first likely tree, a little over a mile from the center of town, the mob stopped and placed a rope around the preacher's neck. The leader demanded that Strickland confess. The *Constitution* quoted Strickland as replying, "I have told you all I know. You can kill me if you wish, gentlemen, but I have nothing more to tell."[15] Guerry recorded his statement in dialect: "I's got nothing to confess, boss. If you kill me you'll kill er innercent man. I can't say no mo." The men then hauled Strickland into the air, allowed him to strangle for a time, and then lowered him to the ground to give his confession. Again he refused, and again he was pulled off the ground to swing about and choke until he would "grow stiff in agony." This was repeated, according to Guerry, at least six times, but Strickland through it all maintained his innocence.[16]

The grove where Strickland was being hanged was located near the home of J. J. Givens, the Palmetto town marshal, and at some point during these proceedings, the Newnan paper reported, the marshal's son approached the mob and requested "that the lynching not occur so near his father's house." Recognizing Givens's dilemma, the men obliged, removing Strickland a final time to a field near the home of Dr. W. S. Zellars, where he was "led up to a persimmon tree and there hanged."[17] Guerry noted that the tree was not more than fifteen feet high, and the limb from which Strickland dangled was only some nine feet off the ground so that the earth's foundation was just tantalizing inches beyond the old man's toe reach. Before he died, at approximately 2:30 Monday morning, Strickland's ears and one or more of his fingers were severed, but these men were weary and growing sober after a long afternoon and night, and the torture seems more perfunctory than inspired, as it was with Sam Hose. Guerry reported that by the end the group had grown smaller, numbering as few as eight men, and that "only four took active part." "Not a single shot was fired, and the negro was not fully dead before the crowd disbanded, all seeming to be anxious to leave the scene," Guerry noted.[18] Strickland's refusal to confess, in addition to his resolve in facing his death, must have disappointed the men. It was, in any case, a poor substitute for Sam Hose's extravagant demise.

The next morning Guerry returned to the scene of the lynching, which he described as a mile and a half from Palmetto on the Fairburn road and about "twenty paces" from the Atlanta and West Point railroad. Strickland still hung by his neck, and another group of curious onlookers watched his corpse quietly sway from the limb. "The crowd was made up entirely of white people," Guerry noted, "negroes shunning the place as if it were bewitched. There were several women and children, all standing curiously noting all surroundings and traces left by the mob." In the morning light, Guerry made several new observations. Strickland's hands were bound behind his back, "but his legs hung loose, in such close proximity to the tree that the remark was made that he could easily have relieved the strain on his neck by locking his legs around the tree had no one prevented him." He had clearly strangled to death, indicated by his protruding tongue and the fact that "there was no room for a drop to break his neck, even had the small cotton rope been strong enough." Someone had pinned a "scrap of bloodstained paper" to Strickland's coat. On one side it read, "N.Y. Journal. We must protect our Ladies. 23–99." The other side of the paper held a warning: "Beware, all darkies! You will be treated the same way." The body was left hanging until nine o'clock that morning, and many in the crowd, gaping though they did, proclaimed the hanging an "outrage."[19] When Strickland was finally taken down and his pockets searched, a "rare collection of articles" was discovered, including two buckeyes, an "odd-shaped bone," a hair ball, and a conjure bag containing "pebbles" and "some kind of brown powdered substance." These were identified as "his instruments of mystification to the ignorant blacks" of his neighborhood and congregation. Like the relics taken from the Sam Hose execution, these items were highly sought after by collectors.[20]

Guerry, who did the most thorough follow-up of this lynching, offered several possible reasons why Sam Hose implicated Lige Strickland in the murder of Alfred Cranford. Rumor had it that Strickland had disapproved of Hose and had "ordered him away from his house" because of Hose's interest in one of his daughters. Guerry also reported for the first time that Hose had come to Strickland's cabin soon after leaving the Cranford home on the night of Alfred Cranford's death and had asked the preacher to lend him clothes and help him escape. Strickland apparently refused and later informed some of the searchers that Hose had visited him and that his intentions were to make his way to Marshallville and there hide out with his family. If this was true, then much of the drama surrounding Hose's flight is called into question, and the heroics of the chase seem inflated. Strickland had been fearful that Hose "would come back some time at night and kill him," and some now interpreted Hose's accusations as a final attempt to get even with the man who had given him away. Guerry reported that an anonymous member of the group guarding Hose had quoted the prisoner as saying, "that d———d old Lige Strickland got me into this," which was taken as proof not of Strickland's guilt but of Hose's desire to take revenge.[21]

Guerry also interviewed Major Thomas on the Monday of Strickland's hanging. Thomas again made the point that "Strickland was 'a white man's darkey.' He was old and had all the respect for white people that all ante-bellum negroes have." Thomas threatened to identify participants in the lynching. "I know who most of the members of the first party were, and will give them out if demanded by the proper authority. I am sure that if a thorough investigation is made that the offenders can be found out, for the men that I recognized in the first party could probably give the names of the men who took Strickland away from me."[22]

Despite Thomas's willingness to testify, when the coroner's inquest was held on Monday morning, no one asked for this information. Indeed, it soon became clear that no one wanted to know. Palmetto's Justice of the Peace Cummings presided over the inquiry in the very warehouse room where the Palmetto shootings had occurred weeks earlier. Guerry attended the inquest and noted that the room had only recently been painted to cover bloodstains from that event. Strickland's body remained outside the building in a wagon and was never officially examined by the coroner's jury. When Major Thomas was called to testify, the judge left the room saying that he needed his "form book" and remained absent during the whole of the major's testimony. No other witnesses were called, and once Thomas had completed his testimony, the judge returned with the book and asked the six-man jury for its decision. It "rendered the usual verdict—death at the hands of parties unknown," according to the Newnan paper.[23] At the coroner's prodding, reporter Guerry began asking questions of the major, at which point two members of the jury "hastily" exited the building. Guerry then requested that the foreman ask Major Thomas to identify the men he had recognized, but the foreman refused, and Guerry was told that "this was not [his] affair."[24] Although Strickland's death had been an awful one, it was not as horrific as Sam Hose's more extensive torture and burning, and there had been at least a pretense of justice in the mock trials and efforts at obtaining confessions. This inquest was clearly intended to paint over Strickland's unfortunate hanging as effectively as Johnston had painted over the blood of the men killed and wounded in his warehouse.

Moreover, not all were willing to concede that Strickland's lynching had been a miscarriage of justice. J. M. Quigley (misspelled as Quigby in the report), "one of the most prominent planters of Meriwether county," was quoted in the *Constitution* (the article was reprinted in the *Newnan Herald and Advertiser*) as saying "that he had known Lige Strickland . . . during slavery, and Major Thomas was the first person, white or black, who had ever found any good in him. The negro belonged to Mr. Quigby's [*sic*] father-in-law, and before his emancipation was strung up two or three times for poisoning a valuable horse belonging to his master." Quigley also asserted that Strickland had been run out of Meriwether some four years earlier because "his conduct became so repulsive to white people and decent negroes." Strickland "was known to have had more than one wife" and "used his ministerial garb as a cloak to shield him in his checkered career, which since childhood had been but a series of crimes."[25] The "Country Philosopher" Bill Arp (Charles Henry Smith), writing about Strickland in his column in the *Atlanta Constitution*, provided further defamatory information.

> Lige was a preacher in Meriwether county, and his father-in-law, Aaron Watson, says he was the meanest nigger in the county, that he beat his wife up scandalously and cut and gashed her with a butcher knife and the members of his own church took him out one night and gave him a hundred lashes and told him to leave the county. Then he settled down in Coweta and turned politician and made himself generally a disturber of public peace and good order, and finally capped the climax by denouncing the white people and defending Sam Hose. The general opinion is that Lige got off pretty well, for they didn't burn him.[26]

Still others suggested that Strickland had been involved in the Palmetto fires and had hired Sam Hose as an assassin to enact revenge on the Palmetto whites who had shot down the men arrested for the crime. Yet another explanation, still accepted by some in Palmetto today, was that Strickland himself had gotten into an argument with Alfred Cranford over a cow. "People said he was a mean black man who pretended to be a preacher because it put him in a better light," one resident explained. "Everything I'd always been told was that Lige Strickland was that way and that he knew Sam Hose was willing to kill somebody for money."[27]

As the crowds began to disperse on that Sunday afternoon and evening, passengers boarded trains to return them to Atlanta, to Griffin, to points south. The

Atlanta–West Point railway cars were filled with "excursionists," who, the *New York Times* reported, were "loaded down with ghastly reminders of the affair in the shape of bones, pieces of flesh, and parts of the wood which [had been] placed at the negro's feet."[28] In three days, on Wednesday the twenty-sixth, many of these same excursionists would celebrate Confederate Memorial Day, and it is likely that some of these relics were passed around at the parades and ceremonies held in Atlanta and other towns throughout Georgia and Alabama. As one train neared Atlanta, passing near Fort McPherson, it was pelted by rocks that broke windows. Two passengers were "painfully injured." The incident was blamed on angry blacks infuriated over Hose's death.[29]

On the following day, after the sham coroner's inquest into Lige Strickland's lynching, reporter Goode Guerry followed up on one final rumor that still another black man had been hanged and "was swinging from a tree at Alfred Cranford's late home." Guerry made the four-mile trip from Palmetto alone to that sad site but found no corpse. Instead, the Cranford farm was deserted: "not a single trace that a human being had been on the place in a week." He described the scene:

> In a wash pot that stood in the yard was potash soap that had been made on the day of the murder but was untouched. Chickens clucked around in the yard, safe from thieving blacks, who dared not go near the place where one of their race had merited his terrible punishment. The place that a few days ago was the happy home of young Alfred Cranford and his family, was the picture of desolation. A slow rain was falling, which only intensified the appearance of desolation.[30]

Guerry also noted that many blacks were continuing to leave the county, including some who were prominent property owners: they were "selling out at almost any price." By the middle of the following week, groups of blacks were still abandoning this part of Georgia. "Well, I tell you, boss," one black man was quoted upon arrival in Atlanta, "t'ings is got too hot down in Coweta county for de darkies. By sundown dare won't be a nigger in Coweta or Carroll counties."[31] In Palmetto, all blacks were warned to be off the streets by dark, and the *Atlanta Constitution* noted, "They have learned that the best policy is to obey." But this removal came at a price. With the resulting shortage of labor, white farmers feared that they would make no more than "half crops" on their holdings.[32]

That Monday night, Palmetto was described, with perhaps unintentional irony, as "quiet as a country burying place." By nine o'clock, all lights were out, and white citizens rested "with a feeling of safety" they had not had in months, "for it [was] not feared that an incendiary, however bold, would venture to commit his dastardly crimes after the events of the past few weeks."[33]

In Newnan, a "party of citizens" had dutifully gone to the place of Hose's death and "obliterated all traces left of the tragedy," the *Macon Telegraph* reported. "The charred remains of wood that had not been carried away by the

Chapter Seven

souvenir hunters yesterday were buried, and also the ashes. The tree trunk left by the parties from Atlanta, who carried off the body of the tree, was cut down level to the ground." The thinking was that "traces of the tragedy might be demoralizing." In contrast to the mob violence of the previous day, Monday was recorded as a day of recovery and thoughtful consideration, the "main topic" of conversation being "the uncalled for lynching of Lige Strickland."[34]

Over the next weeks, newspapers throughout the country and in Great Britain headlined Sam Hose's and, to a lesser degree, Elijah Strickland's deaths. In general, northern papers condemned the acts for their savagery, "Cruel as Anything Recorded in Aboriginal Warfare."[35] The *Chicago Tribune* wrote, "It is almost inconceivable, in these days of enlightenment, that men professing to be civilized can be found practicing cruelties more revolting than those of the Apaches."[36] Some southern publications joined in the outcry. The *Savannah Morning News*, for example, stated plainly the often implied motif of cannibalism that ran just beneath the surface of many of these accounts. The paper quoted an attorney in the city as saying, "The men who mutilated their victim, and, after burning him, cut up and sold pieces of his flesh and bones as souvenirs, have given a lesson in savagery and barbarity to the most savage and barbarous. If they had only eaten some of the cooked flesh, they would have completed the picture and made the lesson perfect."[37] The same paper several days later objected to the "effort of some of the Northern newspapers to make it appear that all of the newspapers of Georgia and of the South condone the offense of the mob which lynched Sam Hose," finding such statements "contemptible."[38]

But other southern papers tried to defend and to explain. On Tuesday, April 25, the *Atlanta Constitution* offered a long editorial titled "Let Us Reason Together." "The condition of life in a country where two races live in common is always one full of peril," the editor, most likely Clark Howell, wrote. "The right of the superior race to rule the ignorance within it, is something which may be argued against, but which can never be removed." Blaming "outsiders" for inciting the southern black race, normally "the most docile of the inferior races," the editorial addressed the concerns of whites, especially in rural areas such as outside Palmetto, where the Cranfords lived. "The small farmer and his wife, needing hired help, engage it. The wife is forced to remain alone in her little cabin while the men are out at work, bravely hiding her fears, but in constant dread. Such a farmer was Alfred Cranford; such a wife he had, and such a fate as she met is what has driven half the men of Georgia mad—but every man of them either the husband of a wife or the brother of a sister!" Although the paper asserted that "95%" of the black race were "law-abiding, or perhaps 'neutral' would be a better word," nevertheless, it criticized blacks for their suspected protection of Hose during his ten days on the run. As to the lynching itself, the paper implicitly condoned it, improbably arguing that "Mrs. Cranford's chastity would be cross-questioned if the case [had been] taken into court" and that there was the possibility that Hose would have been found not guilty due to the vagaries of the law. On the same page, the paper congratulated itself for its role in Hose's capture through its reward of five hundred dollars. "Sam Holt might escape from half a dozen counties of contiguous territory, but he could not wholly escape that territory which is covered by The Constitution." "The Constitution was my inspiration," one of Hose's captors, J. B. Jones, told the paper. "As soon as I read it, I went to work." The paper concluded, "All that The Constitution wanted was to serve the country people of the south to whom the occasion meant so much. Safety for wives and children, security for the hearthstone!"[39] The paper's five-hundred-dollar reward was divided among six men: J. B. Jones, R. A. Gordon, P. F. Phelps, Wilson B. Mathews, C. B. Thomas, and Abe Rogowski.[40]

The *Rome (Georgia) Tribune* loudly proclaimed, "Death to all ravishers!" and offered this proposal:

> Let Georgia's laws be amended. We are against mob law; we must put down mob law; but how? There is one crime which the people of Georgia and the people of the South will not tolerate. No use to mince words. Death is the penalty to the negro or white brute who ravishes a woman. Why not make the killing of such creatures, who are "worse than murderers," justifiable homicide? That would at least put mob violence within the semblance of law.

The editorial continued, "Sunday, April 23, 1899, will be known as 'black and bloody Sunday' in Georgia," and concluded: "When we read of the vengeance of the crowd on the 'brute fiend' and remember that the Book of Books says: 'Vengeance is mine, saith the Lord,' we can only imagine what more excruciating agony is in store for such a creature in the hereafter."[41] Taking up this image of the hereafter, however, the black-owned *Americus (Georgia) Investigator* proclaimed a different view:

> We know of no place on earth we would hate to pass through on our way to heaven but Palmetto, for we would be afraid that we would be taken off the gospel train and lynched and sent by another route to the great eternity beyond. No, we would not attempt to pass through that town if it was the direct route to glory.[42]

In May, the Newnan paper noted that a newspaper editor in Kansas wrote of Sam Hose's burning at the stake that "it was hell." "It sho was, Cap!" the *Herald and Advertiser* happily agreed.[43]

Among the many voices that decried the lynching of Sam Hose and Elijah Strickland was that of the great orator and agnostic Col. Robert Green Ingersoll.

Ingersoll's father had been an abolitionist preacher, and Ingersoll himself had fought on the northern side during the Civil War, most prominently at the Battle of Shiloh. He later served as state attorney general in Illinois, but he was best known for his liberal, often radical stands on race, religion, and politics. Dubbed by his detractors as "the Great Infidel," "Colonel Bob" defended the idea of "Freethought"—"blasphemy is an epithet bestowed by superstition upon common sense" was one of the ways he expressed his views on religion—and he was commonly reviled for his agnosticism.

Ingersoll was nearing the end of his life when the Hose and Strickland lynchings occurred—he would die within three months—but his outrage was undiminished. Indeed, it was so great that the acclaimed orator for once found himself almost speechless. "I know of no words strong enough, bitter enough, to express my indignation and horror," he said. He then scoffed at the pretensions of the South. "The savages who did these things belong to the superior race. They are citizens of the great republic. And yet it does not seem possible that such fiends are human beings. They are a disgrace to our country, our century, and the human race." Ingersoll seemed stunned by the degree of viciousness and barbarity perpetrated in these deaths. "Let me say that what I have said is flattery compared with what I feel. . . . I am utterly at a loss for words. Are the white people insane? Has mercy fled to beasts? Has the United States no power to protect a citizen? A nation that cannot or will not protect its citizens in time of peace has no right to ask its citizens to protect it in time of war."[44]

Ingersoll's incensed remarks naturally outraged defensive southerners. It was bad enough that uninformed northerners were so arrogant as to criticize the South's culture, but what right did this "heathen," this "old reprobate," have to pass moral judgment on them? He should look to the state of his own soul instead of concerning himself with matters beyond his experiences. As the *Augusta (Georgia) Tribune* stated, "Colonel Bob Ingersoll says the men who lynched Sam Holt were fiends and words fail him to anathematize them as he feels. Perhaps if it had been Colonel Bob's son-in-law whose head was split open and Colonel Bob's daughter was the victim of the fiend, Colonel Bob would not be lost for words."[45] The *Atlanta Journal* went further in its denunciation. Ingersoll, it declared, was "a Godless, Christless, Bibleless man, believing in no hereafter." He was "far lower than the lowest savage on the moral scale" since savages believed in *something*, however false, whereas Ingersoll had the advantage of knowing about Christianity and yet still denied the "inspiration of the Bible." In the opinion of the *Journal*, he therefore was "barred from passing upon moral actions of any kind whatever."[46] The Newnan paper sniffed, "Criticism from this godless old wretch is infinitely more grateful to the sensibilities of Christian community than the most fulsome praise that he could bestow. Unless he changes his creed he may yet meet the prowling spirit of Sam Holt in his future rambles along the dark Plutonian shore."[47]

Less easy to dismiss, however, were voices from the pulpit. Methodist ministers met in Atlanta on the day following Sam Hose's execution and decried both the crime and the lynching, noting that such extralegal public events threatened the fabric of southern society.[48] The Reverend Joel T. Daves introduced resolutions that spread the blame. "While it is true that the negro was inhumanly punished yesterday, yet the crime that he committed was so horrible that even the public, even the newspapers, have not made known the details. I heard the whole story from one who knew it all, and the crime that the negro committed in detail is beyond words," he explained. Like Governor Candler, Daves called on black leaders and teachers to instruct their young men in proper moral behavior, and he added that a root cause of these crimes was "liquor, that stirs up all the evil passions of the heart." Nevertheless, after further discussion the ministers took no immediate action on the various resolutions.[49]

Among other religious leaders who took stands on the lynching was the most famous preacher in the South at that time, and one of the best known in the nation, Samuel Porter Jones. Jones presented himself to his public as "plain Sam Jones," and his message was a simple one: "Quit Your Meanness." By that he meant that the true Christian should live a simple, good life by shunning temptations such as drinking, gambling, the theater, baseball, dancing, and other activities that led to bad behavior. Jones wrote a regular column for the *Atlanta Journal*, and on Saturday, April 29, he took on the issue of Sam Hose's lynching and the role of the mob. Under the bizarre title "Burning of Sam Hose, Anti-Spitting Law" (Jones approved of the antispitting law, although he wondered why the city of Atlanta did not put as much effort into correcting other vices), he acknowledged that Sam Hose's deeds demanded swift punishment—"Rape means rope, and diabolical crimes mean mobs," he reiterated—but still he asked, "How can good citizenship, law and order be compensated by such cruelties as this mob wreaked upon its victim?" Jones then proclaimed:

> Every man to his liking, but excuse me, gentlemen, I do not want to join a mob. I am willing to help hunt the criminal down. I am willing to divide my last dollar in his prosecution before the courts. I am willing to stand by the sheriff when he drops the victim through the trap and his neck is broken, but I am not a judge, I am not a jury, I am not a sheriff, and therefore I am not an executioner. I know there are thousands who differ with me on this subject. Gentlemen, you take your course and I will take mine.[50]

Over the next weeks Jones continued to criticize the mob. At the same time, the Reverend Dr. Len G. Broughton, minister of the Atlanta Baptist Tabernacle, inveighed even more forthrightly against the lynching. On the Sunday night

Hose was tortured and burned, Broughton denounced the mob's actions during his evening service and called its members murderers.[51] Later that week, he received two packages in the mail. The first contained, it was reported, flesh cut from Hose's body, "about the size of a hen's egg," laid out on a leaf of lettuce and garnished by several onions. Accompanying the package was a note suggesting that since Broughton "loved" blacks so much, "the enclosed might make for him a palatable dish, or, if he preferred, he might make a 'Brunswick stew.'" The note, signed by the "Committee of the Citizens of Palmetto," also warned that Broughton should leave the state within seven days or face death.[52] Broughton destroyed the package in disgust. Later that week a second package arrived filled with black crepe and another warning, which the *Constitution* described as "obscene," telling him to retract his earlier statements and thenceforth remain silent on the subject of Sam Hose's lynching. Broughton, however, refused to back down, and the following Sunday he again criticized the mob. That night the Baptist Tabernacle was vandalized, a water tank torn from the wall in the lavatory and water and paint splashed over the floor. Placards were also placed outside the Tabernacle with messages such as "Who will join a crowd to whip Broughton, the negro lover?"[53]

Over the next few months, Sam Jones began to equivocate in his condemnation of the lynch mob, as Darren Grem has shown in his examination of Jones's response to the Sam Hose lynching.[54] By August, Jones was writing, "The man, white or black, who commits an outrage on a virtuous woman, deserves death. Sam Hose deserved to be burnt, but I am in favor of the sheriff executing the criminal, except in cases like Sam Hose, then anybody, anything, anyway to get rid of such a brute."[55] Broughton, on the other hand, never wavered in his stance. After the warnings and the attack on his church, he was quoted in the *Constitution* as saying: "No guard will be placed around the church and only the usual precautions of locking the doors will be made to prevent further vandalism. I have not asked for protection for myself and will not do so. I fear nothing from the crowd and will continue to denounce lynching upon every occasion."[56] Outside the state, his sentiments were reported more directly. "I have been threatened with all sorts of vulgar threats," he was quoted in the *Arizona Republican*. "But I want to say that I am not afraid of *every* howling devil in Georgia and in hell. I am minister of my pulpit, and if you don't like it, you may go out. . . . The good people of Georgia shall not, with my help, be slandered by the foul deeds of a howling mob of assassins."[57]

Still other prominent voices weighed in on the Hose execution. Charles Henry Smith, under the pseudonym "Bill Arp, the Country Philosopher," had a weekly column in the *Atlanta Constitution*. Smith had created the character of "Bill Arp" at the beginning of the Civil War, using exaggerated eye dialect in the manner of south and southwest humorists like A. B. Longstreet, Johnson Jones Hooper, and, most remarkably, George Washington Harris in his "Sut Lovingood" sketches. Arp continued writing his public letters through Reconstruction, criticizing the federal government's policies. In 1878, he became a correspondent for the *Constitution* and concentrated largely on "the pleasures of rural life." His feelings on race were strong and unequivocal. Blacks were at best childlike, and emancipated blacks were both offensive and dangerous. "The whole of Afriky have cum to town," he wrote in 1865, "wimmin and childern, and boys and baboons and all. A man can tell how far it ar to the sitty better by the smell than the milepost."[58] In an essay titled "Races and Human Nature," he made clear his, and his community's, view of proper race relationships. Of the white and black people, he wrote, "One loves to command and the other to obey, one to govern and the other to be governed. . . . It is the guardian and the ward, and this relation is as agreeable as it is natural, so long as the one is humane and patriarchal and the other is obedient and industrious."[59] Arp often cited "human nature" as his rule of judgment: there could be no argument in his mind that the world was fixed in specific ways and that to challenge these ways was both absurd and against the teaching of God.

According to Arp scholar David B. Parker, before 1890 Charles Henry Smith advocated lynching only when there was irrefutable proof of rape and it was clear that the justice system would move too slowly to offer a convincing deterrent to other blacks. However, as the century's last decade began, Parker writes, "The black man seemed suddenly to frighten Arp."[60] By 1899, Arp could declare, "Let the good work go on. Lynch em! Hang em! Shoot em! Burn em!" In a column titled "Bill Arp Grows Caustic about the Critics of Lynching," he rejected the argument that the burning of Sam Hose was excessively gruesome or emblematic of a shift in social justice. "The lynching of Sam Holt is over," he declared on April 30, one week after the event. "History is just repeating itself." Arp then reminded his readers of the burning of Henry Smith in Paris, Texas, six years earlier, noting, "The same adjectives were used and the same anathemas hurled at our people." Now it had happened again, and the same people were saying the same things. Arp's question to them was, "What are you going to do about it?" His answer, "Nothing, of course." As a former slave owner, Arp proclaimed, "Our slaves were educated by fear of the lash or the whipping post, and you can pick them out today. It is their children, born here since the war, or their grandchildren who are in the chaingang." But imprisonment had not proved to be the answer; according to Arp, "Confinement in jail nearly crushes the soul of a white man, but a negro is perfectly contented there." New laws might help, but as long as blacks could vote, there was no chance of enacting effective statutes that might better control them. For that reason, Arp argued, black men were largely indifferent to the law, and whites had little recourse but occasionally to rise up and deliver the harsh justice that was normally prohibited. As for himself,

Arp avowed, "I am as good a man as any horror-stricken editor or preacher. I am kind in heart and love my fellow man and fellow woman," but "I rejoiced when the brute was caught and burned." He concluded:

How much [Hose] suffered is of no consequence to me, nor am I afraid of the crowd that did it or that will do it again. It was the unanimous verdict of a very large jury, a jury of men and women, and I am not chicken-hearted about such suspects as Lige Strickland, nor would I take very much sympathetic talk from other negro leaders who raise their bristles. I know and feel that the white people of the south have been kind; yes, overkind to the negro since the war and that yankee emissaries have alienated him from us and we have got no thanks for all we have done. Sooner or later we will have to take away his vote and establish the whipping post and then, and not till then, will we have peace between the races.[61]

Outdoing even Arp in this view was Rebecca Latimer Felton, the women's rights advocate who was progressive on most matters other than race. But here she was unforgiving. One of Felton's most quoted lines, taken from a speech made in 1897 describing white women's fears of black rapists, was, "If it takes lynching to protect women's dearest possession from drunken, ravening beasts, then I say lynch a thousand a week." She found "the premeditated outrage on Mrs. Cransord [sic] infinitely more intolerable than the murder of her husband," averring, "I have even less regard for the apologist of the black fiend than pity for the perpetrator." Although she admitted that slavery was "full of evils," she claimed, "The misguided negroes of the country have been tutored and trained into hellish hate and fiendish cruelty to the white women and girls of the south. . . . I do not forget the white victims who, without warning or excuse, are dragged into an abyss of woe, suffering and despair, compared to which oblivion would be a boon, and murder a present blessing!" She concluded, "Sam Hose needs and deserves no trial. When such a fiend abandons humanity to become a brute, then he shall be dispatched with no more civil [sic] than would prevail with a mad dog's fate after he had bitten your child."[62] In response, a leading black newspaper, the *Salt Lake City Broad Ax*, posted a dire warning to her and to the South:

Ah! Mrs. Felton, there is the rub; the South would have slavery and she must now pay the penalty, and the time will surely come when human blood will flow as freely throughout the South as water, and when that time does come you Mrs. Felton will not be in favor of lynching a thousand Negroes a week for the edification of the Christian white ladies and gentlemen of the South.[63]

Arp, Felton, and Jones were public spokespeople whom one would have expected to comment on such events, but an unusual addition to the dialogue and, ultimately, to the controversy, soon appeared. Mrs. William Y. Atkinson, known as Susie, whose husband had attempted to prevent Hose's lynching, expressed her horror at the killing of Sam Hose in a letter written the day after Hose's death. She spoke as a white southern woman, whose need for protection was, according to defenders of the practice of lynching, the reason the punishment was necessary. On April 25, her letter to a friend in Atlanta concerning the "Newnan occurrence" made its way into print. "I am just recovering from the terrible day of fire and blood in this heretofore law-abiding town," she began. She noted that, since it was a Sunday and not a work day, there had been many idle men on the street, which encouraged the formation of the mob. Then she made a comparison that would enrage defenders of the lynching:

> The occasion reminded me of the Sunday afternoons in Mexico City just before a bull fight, only here it was much more intense in the blood-thirstiness; for in the Sunday amusements in Mexico there is only the doubtful danger of a man losing his life, but here there was a certainty of death the moment the horrible creature's foot rested on Newnan soil, for a crowd of armed men brought him.
>
> Again, this affair varied from Mexican cruelty in that the participants on entering the arena reversed the custom of men torturing to slow death one animal. Had the walls of the coliseum been around that burning stake and its writhing human form, a scene of old Rome would have been perfectly reproduced in this community, and doubtless the spirits of the ancient Caesars would have applauded their apostles of the nineteenth century as "the pyre's thick flame shot a dismal glare."

Mrs. Atkinson then tried to correct a detail that she found especially objectionable: that "the ladies of Newnan" had cheered and waved handkerchiefs in support of the lynching. She maintained that women and children had stood silently as the procession made its way along the streets of the city, and that none of them had attended the actual burning. "While we feel that no punishment could be too severe for that criminal," she continued, "it is generally deplored that one so barbarous was given him in this community. The possible injury to the boys and young men is inconceivable." Having focused on the crowd, and recognizing the event's deleterious effect on the young males, especially, she finally and deftly shifted the blame from the law-abiding town of Newnan to its sister city Griffin, which took open pride in its willingness to enforce extralegal racial justice. "We rejoice to know that the mob, on its arrival, was not strengthened by Newnan people. The prisoner was safely protected by an escort from a neighboring town—Griffin. Their faces were the last into which he looked."[64] With this conclusion, in which she corroborated her husband's contentions that the mob was made up largely of men from out of town, Mrs. Atkinson started a firestorm of her own, one that would pit Newnan and Griffin against each other for weeks to come.

Despite Mrs. Atkinson's insistence that women did not participate in the lynch mob, such was the general portrait (as illustrated in the *National Police Gazette*, for example) that gained credence as the story of Sam Hose's death spread. Several years later, in 1903, a writer in the *Portsmouth (New Hampshire) Herald* inveighed against female observance of these displays, noting that it had begun when "white women and girls of tender years" had witnessed the torture and burning of Henry Smith. "Since that date ladies have often attended such social functions and more than once enjoyed the sensation of applying the torch." The correspondent then used the Newnan lynching as an example and in doing so reversed in the most insulting way an argument often used by southern spokespeople.

> Worst of all, perhaps, young women watched the mob about three years ago cut up the body of Sam Hose and sell his liver and other parts, which modesty keeps out of print, for souvenirs. This is the class of people who would have us believe that the colored people are sueing [*sic*] to be their social equals. God forbid that the negro shall ever look for such society! There is not an intelligent, industrious, common-sense colored man living that would marry a woman whose moral sensibilities and motherly instincts are so deadened that she can behold with joyful enthusiasm the burning and mutilation of a naked man. What white man in the north would want a woman for his wife and to be the mother of his children, who finds happiness in such a social diversion? The very question is repulsive to every decent man.[65]

While this debate was under way on the state and national scene, the local communities began to assess their own responsibilities. Griffin editor Douglas Glessner offered no apologies and strongly criticized the "hypocrisy" of those Georgia papers—including the *Atlanta Constitution*, the *Savannah Press*, the *Savannah Morning News*, the *Macon Telegraph*, and the *Augusta Chronicle*—that had either condemned the execution or had published editorial samples from other papers that did. "What they have reprinted from the Northern press doesn't amount to the life of a Filipino," the irascible editor scoffed.[66] In general, Griffin remained proud of its participation in the Hose episode. Unlike the trains returning to Atlanta that were stoned by angry blacks, when the "committee of Griffin citizens" who had taken Hose to Newnan made its return late that Sunday afternoon, the members were accorded "a triumphal entry into the city." The *Atlanta Journal* reported:

> At every stop on the return the question was "what did they do with him?" and when told that he had been burned at a stake the men would yell, the women would clap their hands, and not a few murmured a fervent "Thank God!" between their tears. If anything the women were more enthusiastic than the men, and certainly they were more thankful that Hose had been made to suffer, as nearly as possible as much as his innocent victim.

"Those who went on the special are more than grateful to the good people of Newnan, who treated them so courteously," the report continued. "Nothing was allowed to be paid for and had it not been for their hospitality many a Griffin man would have gone without his dinner and some without a breakfast also."[67] Glessner had described these men as "some of the best citizens in Griffin and flower of chivalry in this section," a phrase that would soon engender a good bit of mockery.[68]

When the *Newnan Herald and Advertiser* published its lengthy account of Hose's capture and execution, it, like Mrs. Atkinson, cleverly charged the Griffin men with the tortures that had occurred. "The prisoner remained in possession of this party [from Griffin] from the moment that he was wrested from his captors [the Jones brothers] until the final act of immolation in the old Troutman field near Newnan at 3 o'clock in the afternoon," James Brown, the Newnan editor, pointed out.

> The people of Newnan have no disposition to "throw off" on the Griffin party. On the contrary, they were applauded by some of our citizens for the interest and enterprise displayed in chartering a special train and hurrying the negro to the Coweta jail; but it may not be amiss to let the fact be known that the lynching and attendant barbarities was not exclusively a Newnan affair.[69]

These remarks, in addition to the accusations made by Governor Atkinson and his wife about Griffin's participation, exacerbated the feud that now developed between the two towns, conducted largely through the editorials of Glessner and Brown.

Glessner, who was born in Ohio in 1856 and had moved to Griffin in 1882, was an outspoken old-party Democrat and an honorary colonel, named so by Democratic governors he had long supported.[70] He was a political enemy of William Atkinson, Newnan's adopted son, whom he saw as a traitor to the traditional Democratic Party in the state and whom he never lost an opportunity to criticize or mock. The conflict started after the shootings in Palmetto. Glessner had earlier berated Governor Allen Candler, Atkinson's successor in the office, for his failure to send soldiers to Griffin during the town's troubles with the Tenth Immunes in early March. After the Palmetto massacre, Governor Candler had publicly connected these killings to the bad behavior of the black militiamen. In response, Glessner wrote an editorial titled "An Unjust Imputation," in which he quoted at length from James Brown's earlier editorial "The Palmetto 'Affair'" in order to refute Candler's remarks that (as Glessner sarcastically rephrased them) "nine poor innocent negroes were shot down by an intemperate mob because others of their color, but in no wise connected with them, had become riotous."[71] Brown had then replied on March 31 in an editorial also titled "'*An Unjust*

Imputation'": "Editor Glessner's animadversions are unjust to Gov. Candler, and do not correctly represent either what he said or what he meant." Brown wrote that the people of Palmetto had not taken offense at the governor's remarks, and that they would welcome an investigation. He concluded:

> If Editor Glessner finds nothing to criticize in Gov. Candler's official acts and utterances more reprehensible than the course which the latter has pursued in regard to the Palmetto lynching, he will have a sterile field for sensationalism; and we must add, on our own account, that the use which he makes of an emasculated fragment of editorial from the columns of THE HERALD AND ADVERTISER as a pretext for his criticism of Gov. Candler is an exhibition of fictive ingenuity that does not, according to our understanding of the ethics of the profession, come within the limits of reputable journalism. Therefore, to borrow Editor Glessner's own expression, the article in The News and Sun is not only an "unjust imputation" of offensiveness on the part of Gov. Candler in his treatment of the Palmetto affair, but it also seeks to embroil THE HERALD AND ADVERTISER by misinterpreting its motive and meaning in discussing the same incident.[72]

On April 7, Glessner replied with cutting sarcasm in a third editorial titled "AN UNJUST IMPUTATION," his use of capital letters distinguishing it from Brown's previously signifying italics. He first declared Brown's editorial "The Palmetto 'Affair,'" published immediately after the Palmetto shooting, a well-written piece "that reminded [readers] of the Jim Brown of olden days." But Brown's objections to Glessner's use of that article in his attack on Candler now baffled the Griffin editor.

> Well, we do not profess to understand, or always follow even when we do understand, Editor Brown's code of ethics; but it has always been a rule of ours when we do unintentional injustice to others to apologize at the earliest opportunity, and especially do we hasten to do so when we find that we have hurt the feelings of such an old friend as "Jim" Brown, as he is affectionately known by his friends. If we were mistaken in supposing that he honestly meant what he said in his first editorial, no matter who might be governor, or what relation he might occupy to the editor, then we are sorry for it; or if we are the cause of his eating words that were uttered in truthfulness, even if he forgot that he was stepping on the toes of his appointing power, we are still more sorry for that—for we regret to see any man so utterly and abjectly stultify himself.[73]

When the "Palmetto Affair" was overshadowed by the lynching of Sam Hose, Glessner and Brown's quarrel grew even more intemperate. In its coverage of Hose's burning, the *Herald and Advertiser* had reminded its readers that, while perhaps fulfilling a civic duty in bringing Hose to Newnan, members of the Griffin entourage also hoped to earn a share of the rewards offered for Hose.[74] On

April 28, Glessner defended the Griffin men by attacking Governor Candler and former governor Atkinson:

> After some of the best citizens of Griffin and flower of chivalry in this section had chartered a special train to carry Sam Hose, who had made more desolate than hell the home of a citizen of Coweta county whom he had first slain with an axe, to place him in the custody of the sheriff of that county, inside the jail and out of the way of the mob that had assembled, Ex-Governor Atkinson got up and denounced these men and declared with up-raised hand that if the negro was lynched he would hold these citizens of Griffin responsible and prosecute them, pointing out those whom he knew. His words being answered in proper form by the citizens of Griffin and flouted and jeered by those of his own people, who were indignant at the stand he was taking, he became inarticulate with rage and simply shook his fist.

Glessner continued his attack. "That Ex-Governor Atkinson was not making a grand stand play is evidenced by the language of his message two years ago, to the sentiments of which he was known to be deeply wedded."[75] Indeed, as previously noted, Atkinson had proposed that the family of a lynching victim should receive from the county in which he was lynched "the full value of his life, which, in no case, should be less than one thousand dollars." Glessner now exploded: "The idea of giving a thousand dollars to his family for the life of Sam Hose, who had already left his mother's place in Houston county two years ago for a similar crime!" He concluded, "The idea, too, of the recent governor of a great State getting up and defending this known, identified and self-confessed murderer and ravisher. . . . It is a pitiful depth for any man to descend to, as even his own fellow-citizens felt." In Glessner's view, the "Pennsylvania Dutchman" who soaked Sam Hose with kerosene and who "didn't care a d——m" what his northern friends might think "made the best answer so far."[76]

Glessner followed this line of thought again on April 30, when he deftly re-phrased Mrs. Atkinson's comments to quote her as saying that "the last *protecting* faces that Sam Hose looked upon were those of the Griffin crowd" (my emphasis). He hastened to add that this was "no reflection upon the true-hearted Coweta boys who burned the negro despite the protests of Mr. Atkinson that the law's delay would give him a better showing." He then held up Griffin as "An Example to the State" for its willingness to take the law into its own hands, using the town's earlier lynchings, its handling of the black militia, and the recent whippings of insolent black residents as primary examples. Glessner acknowledged that some now saw Griffin as a "bad town," but argued, "So far we can not see that Griffin has overstepped the bounds of moderation and justice, and we hope that it will continue that way."[77]

On May 2, Glessner repeated his attacks against Mrs. Atkinson, again for her assertions that the "last faces" into which Sam Hose looked were from Griffin. If it were true that Newnan citizens did not participate in the lynching, Glessner pointed out, then this was "to assert that ice water instead of red blood runs in the veins of every Newnanite, as it is known to flow in the blue veins of a few of them" (meaning William Atkinson). He further accused James Brown of advising Governor Candler not to pay the state reward to J. B. Jones and the men from Griffin "on the ground that the Griffin parties had not acted in good faith in turning the negro over to the sheriff of the county, although not denying that they held the receipt for him."[78] Candler had indeed delayed the state's payment of the $500 reward until it could be determined whether there was collusion between the captors and the mob. J. B. Jones, the receipt from Sheriff Brown in hand, had come to Atlanta on Monday, the twenty-fourth, to collect the money due him, his brother, and the three men from Griffin: R. A. Gordon, A. Rogowski, and W. B. Mathews. The *Atlanta Constitution* paid its $500, and Jacob Hass, an Atlanta bank president, contributed another $100. Hass had earlier made a pledge to put up $100 if nine other men would do the same as an additional reward for Hose's capture. No one else had joined him in this pledge, but Hass was as good as his word and met Jones at the Capital City bank to see the receipt and write his check.[79] The same five men would also collect $250 from Coweta County. The state eventually paid its $500, but the delay left a bad taste in the public's, and especially Glessner's, mouths. Tossing Brown's words back at him, Glessner concluded, "We have no disposition to 'throw off' on any person in Newnan or Coweta county, but when the manhood of her own people as well as ours is assailed, we are ready to take up a pen in defense of both."[80]

On May 5, Brown, after due consideration, made his own reply in an editorial smartly titled "The 'Flower of Chivalry,' Etc.," in which he repeated Glessner's histrionic phrase six times and further mocked the Ohio editor's high-sounding— and very southern—rhetoric:

> We inferred, of course, that [Glessner] was mightily tickled over the achievement of this gallant contingent of the "flower of chivalry" of Griffin and vicinity; and yet when we sought last week to give credit to these dashing cavaliers for a full part in the ceremonies preceding and attendant upon the cremation of Sam Hose, Editor Glessner affected deep indignation.

Brown did object to the fact that Griffin men were attempting to share in the reward for Hose.

> Willing to divide honors, are they? Good. But what about the reward? So far as we have heard, the "flower of chivalry" of Griffin and vicinity have not yet offered to divide the prize money with the "brave, honest and truthful men" of Coweta who assisted in

guarding the prisoner to the jail, and afterwards followed the pageant headed by the "flower of chivalry" of Griffin and vicinity from the jail to the stake.

Since the Jones brothers had actually captured Hose, and since the Griffinites had taken possession "over a hundred miles from the scene of the capture," Brown had to scratch his head as to why men from Griffin now laid claim to the money. Perhaps, he slyly suggested, it was because they had chipped in for the special train to bring Hose to Newnan for his execution.

As to Glessner's assertion that Brown had attempted to dissuade Governor Candler from presenting the reward to the Griffinites, he declared that charge "absolutely false." The Jones brothers were entitled to the reward, and they would have gotten the full amount if the "flower of chivalry" from Griffin had not taken the prisoner from them. Brown claimed no high ground here. Hose, he admitted, "would have had just as short shrift at the hands of a Coweta mob" as he did from the hands of the men from Griffin. Still, the good citizens of Newnan had no desire to share in the reward, and it was "preposterous" to suggest that Griffin men had somehow tried to protect Hose.[81]

Both papers came to an agreement of sorts when each reprinted an editorial from the *New York Verdict* titled "Fagots and Fiends," which defended the Hose lynching, but Glessner responded on May 9 to Brown in "The Statesman and the Editor," in which he published a statement signed the previous day by Mathews, Gordon, and Rogowski—the three Griffin men who had shared in the reward—according to which Governor Candler "did then and there state openly in our presence, without any request for secrecy, that Mr. Brown . . . had been in to see him that morning" and had asked that the reward be withheld until further investigation proved that "delivery [of Sam Hose] was made in good faith."[82]

On May 12, Brown had the final word. With another inspired title, "Col. Duggy Glessner *Et Al*," Brown recapped the situation.

> According to an old saw, "Who scrubs an ass's head wastes his soap," and we must plead guilty to this folly in an experience recently had with our gifted but gabby contemporary, Col. Duggy Glessner, of The Griffin News and Sun. When pulled up short on a proposition which it is not convenient to meet he has a playful habit of covering his confusion by flying into a rage, only to break out afresh the next moment in some unexpected quarter, and with an entirely new proposition. For example, in our account of the lynching of Sam Holt we made the following amiable references to the "flower of chivalry" of Griffin and vicinity who assisted (?) the Jones brothers in rescuing (?) the unhappy and much-bedraggled darkey from a Griffin mob and conveying him in safety (?) to the Coweta jail.

As Brown put it, after Glessner had "waxed exceedingly wroth" but had failed to disprove Brown's claims, he had thrown in the red herring of the reward.

Brown now presented to his readers statements from both the governor and the state attorney general to the effect that although Brown had indeed spoken with them, he had not attempted to delay the reward for the Jones brothers. The attorney general felt that the Griffin men had "evidently misunderstood" what the governor had said.[83]

Not willing to leave well enough alone, the Newnan paper followed up this report with two other gratuitous "news items": first, that a "Griffin belle" had recently come home in the rain and placed her galoshes in the upper window to dry, which then attracted a crowd who thought a "new awning" had been installed in the building; and second, that "Griffin girls are so pigeon-toed that one can't tell from their footprints whether they are going home or coming to town."[84] With these final insulting salvos, the squabble subsided.

Meanwhile, Governor Candler again found it necessary to comment on the lynchings of Hose and Strickland. Unlike the two governors he succeeded, William Northen and William Atkinson, Candler had done little to combat acts of violence against blacks in the state. A Confederate veteran who had fought in battles in Mississippi and his own state, Candler had been wounded several times and had lost an eye in fighting near Jonesboro, Georgia. He ended the war as a colonel and would be the last native-born Georgia governor to have served in the Confederate army. As governor, his attitude toward lynching was one of public disapproval, but he showed an unwillingness to take effective action against it.

Nevertheless, the events of spring 1899 had challenged the governor, and he found himself having to defend his office against charges of indifference or worse. Unsurprisingly, after the killings of Sam Hose and Elijah Strickland, he blamed such events largely on blacks themselves. "The ballot was thrust into the negro's hand immediately after his emancipation, when he was utterly unprepared for the judicious use of it, and the scallawags and carpet-baggers, who came here and took charge of him, filled his head full of false ideas, characterized him the ward of the nation, and, for partisan purposes, induced him to believe that he would be protected by the general government, whether right or wrong." He again called on "good negroes" like Bishop Turner to speak out against the sort of crimes that "provoke" lynchings in the same way they were condemning the mob actions themselves. Finally, he criticized lawyers who used "technicalities and quibbles to protect their clients, even when guilty," suggesting that this "reprehensible practice" made lynch law necessary, the "mob claiming that if they do not take the administration of justice in their own hands, it will not be administered."[85]

But Candler still had to answer his critics, specifically concerning Hose's execution. After all, word had come hours earlier to both Newnan and Atlanta that Hose had been captured and was being taken to Coweta, where a crowd was gathering. The Atlanta newspapers were putting out their special editions with the latest predictions of the burning, and "excursionists" from the city had had time to find train seats or other methods of hying themselves to the place of execution. What had kept the governor from sending the militia, as he had done so quickly after the Palmetto shootings, to prevent the lynching, as even the mob believed he would?

Candler attempted to address the issue in a statement to the *Atlanta Constitution*. He related that he had learned of Hose's capture from sources in Griffin around 11:00 a.m. that Sunday, when he was told that the Griffin people were taking Hose to Newnan by train. The governor had "immediately called up Newnan by telephone and asked for the sheriff," but Brown was not available. According to the operator, Brown had "gone out in the country, and [the operator] could not tell when he would be back." Candler had then sent the sheriff a telegram instructing him not to receive the prisoner anywhere except at the county jail and not to sign the receipt until Hose was safely in hand. The governor claimed to have heard no more from anyone until 3:00 p.m., when Brown called, acknowledged that he had received the telegram and that he had attempted to follow the governor's instructions, but that a mob of between five hundred and a thousand men had taken Hose from the jail and was even then escorting him to Palmetto for execution. The sheriff, when asked, told the governor that he had not recognized any of the men in the crowd. Candler ordered him to form a posse and go after the mob, but Brown replied that earlier attempts to control the situation by Governor Atkinson, Judge Freeman, and the sheriff himself had been unsuccessful. After another delay of some thirty minutes, Governor Candler was informed by the *Constitution* that Hose was dead, burned at the stake. He again called Sheriff Brown, who confirmed the report.

Candler went on to condemn the event, but he spread the blame widely. Hose's deeds, he proclaimed, were worse than the public yet knew: "The whole thing is deplorable, and Holt's crime, the horrid details of which have not been published, are too horrible for publication, is the most diabolical in the annals of crime." To his mind, the "good and law-abiding negroes" of the community had failed to take this opportunity to stand against such behavior by their people: they were, as Candler put it, "blinded by race prejudice" and could see "only one side of the question." He concluded once again that the black race "must denounce crime and aid in bringing criminals to justice, whether they be black or white. In this way, they [could] do more to protect themselves than all the courts and juries in the state [could] do for them."[86]

Candler's description of the events, which implicitly blamed Sheriff Brown in allowing Hose to be taken by the mob, was not accepted by everyone. The *Augusta Herald* ran a blistering editorial later in the week, titled "Candler Fiddled While Hose Burned," in which the paper accused the governor of having "dilladallied" when he might have prevented the lynching. Candler responded to the charge through the *Atlanta Journal* on Saturday, April 29, calling the editorial "the variest tommyrot" and observing that "life is too short" to become involved in "a newspaper controversy." But he again went over his timeline and asserted, "It was a physical impossibility for me to have prevented the lynching of Hose." He also, this time, insisted that Sheriff Brown had done all he could do as well.[87]

The debate over Hose's execution—Strickland's hanging, which most now saw as an unfortunate mistake, was largely forgotten—was carried out in the papers for weeks afterward. The *Newnan Herald and Advertiser* informed its readers how the community and people were being criticized throughout the country, although it emphasized certain editorials such as "The Negro Question," written by John J. Ingalls in the *New York Journal*, in which Ingalls observed, "The horrible tragedy at Newnan shocks the conscience of mankind, but up to a certain point the action of the mob is intelligible." His argument continued, "History teaches that a superior and an inferior race cannot exist upon terms of equality under the same government. The weaker will go to the wall." Another column titled "Fagots and Fiends," originally published in the *New York Verdict*, appeared on the same page of the May 12 edition and implored the North to "recall the crime" when "this black hell-thing—to call him 'negro' would be to disgrace Africa" outraged the community. "If you must think of this swart Caliban, fire-eaten, tugging at his chain of death, keep also before you the picture of that poor woman, doubly his victim, who must go racked and horror-whipped of memory through every awful day of her existence. . . . Better that a thousand such as Holt burn at the stake, than that one like his victim go shame-lashed and sorrow-haunted to her grave."[88] Such observations from northern papers helped to justify the actions taken. They also supported the idea that the female "victim," Mrs. Cranford, would forever carry the disgrace of the assault imposed on her by Sam Hose, one reason given for avoiding a lengthy, public trial.

Over the next weeks, the communities so racked by both fear and violence began to collect themselves. The towns of Hogansville and Carrollton contributed sixty dollars to Palmetto to help with expenses incurred through the fires, the search for the incendiaries, the massacre, and then the hunt for Sam Hose. Other places in the state made pledges to aid "the once prosperous and happy little village."[89] Wednesday, April 26, was Confederate Memorial Day, and throughout the state, "fresh roses of enduring affection were laid on the bier of the representatives of the sunny Southland's honor, and sacred tears were dropped here and there on the mounds where general and drummer boy lay side by side."[90] At the Georgia State Fair, a special contest was held that week for blacks in which they competed in seven categories: the men in plowing, splitting rails, hammering horseshoes, and making a pair of men's brogans; the women, cutting out and sewing "jeans pants" and cooking the best "farmers' dinner, for three people, six dishes including desert"; and, for both sexes, "picking cotton."[91] On Friday, May 5, two weeks after the lynchings, people from around this section of west Georgia gathered in Grantville, a small community ten miles below Newnan, to celebrate a Confederate veterans' reunion. Mrs. Glenn Arnold was in charge of music and selected "Nearer My God to Thee" as the first song of the occasion, followed by the "best-known and most beloved songs that were used during the civil war." Among the "orators" was Gen. John B. Gordon, who gave his stump talk "The Last Days of the Confederacy." The Atlanta and West Point railway offered half-price fares to veterans and their families on round-trip tickets. The activities included an afternoon baseball game.[92]

During the hunt for Sam Hose, several black men in Griffin had been flogged for "using [their] lip too freely." "It does seem as if the negroes of Griffin would learn to behave themselves in the proper way, after all the lessons that the whites have taken pains to teach them proper manners," Douglas Glessner observed in the *Griffin Daily News and Sun*.[93] But after Hose and Strickland had been put to death, a local black man (as he so identified himself) wrote to the *Newnan Herald and Advertiser* making it clear that he and other "good negroes" were anxious to reaffirm the status quo. He had not expressed any "dissatisfaction at the actions of the mob in dealing with Sam Hose." He had, he admitted, even made a joke at the expense of a fellow black man: "I did hear that Green Brown had one of Sam Holt's ribs, and the next time I met him I asked him about it, being surprised that a colored person should forget his race superstition so far as to handle a dead man's bones." He informed the paper that Captain Cranford, Alfred's father, had always been "especially kind to [him], and has had [his] highest respect and best wishes." He carefully noted, "The respectable part of the colored race here do not uphold such crimes, but try to bring up our youth so that they will not be guilty of such. No punishment is too severe for a criminal of that class, white or black; and I am satisfied that Sam Holt was not lynched because he was a negro, but because he had been guilty of crimes which justified it. I believe that if a white man had been guilty of the same crimes he would have been served the same way."[94]

Meanwhile, Booker T. Washington, speaking in Philadelphia, indicated that he had thoughts on the lynching, but noted, "In view of my position and hopes in the interest of the Tuskegee Institute in Alabama, and the education of our people, I feel constrained to keep silent and not engage in any controversy that might react upon the work to which I am now lending my efforts."[95] From the white people's point of view, these two black responses were more than appropriate.

But other black voices rose in protest. The black-owned newspaper the *Salt*

Lake City Broad Ax, edited and published by Julius F. Taylor, could at first barely bring itself to report Sam Hose's awful death. In a short front-page item, it gave a quick summary and then concluded, "The details of the manner in which they put him to death are too horrible to relate and it only proves to our mind that after all people are nothing more than wild and blood-thirsty hyenas clothed in human skin."[96] A week later, however, the paper attempted to deal with the lynching. At this point, the *Broad Ax* seemed to accept the possibility that Sam Hose had committed these crimes, although it still deplored other aspects of the event.

> The killing of Alfred Cranford, the outrage upon his wife, the terrible fate which befell the negro Sam Hose, who was charged with committing this double crime, the arrest of Lige Strickland the old negro preacher who proved to be innocent and not connected in any manner whatever with the death of farmer Cranford nor with the wrong committed against his wife, his trial and death by the mob composed of the very best Christian (?) gentlemen—these occurrences have and will continue to furnish much material for editorial writers in all sections of the country.

The paper noted that others had argued that the severity of the punishment would serve to dissuade others from committing similar crimes. The *Broad Ax* doubted this reasoning but added, "If this was only true we would heartily say amen."[97] As late as May 30, the paper still allowed Hose's guilt, but now claimed that Strickland, too, had been burned and tortured, and added yet a third victim to the mob's fury, a man named Griggs, whose body "was burned and cut up and sold to the highly (?) cultured whites simply because he expressed his disapproval of the actions of the mob."[98] Taylor continued:

> Admitting that Sam Hose did commit the double crimes which he was charged with committing, still that does not justify the actions of the white criminals or cannibals who lowered themselves in the estimation of the entire civilized world for the purpose of wrecking vengeance upon Sam Hose and to further enable them to cut up the bodies of two innocent negroes and sell pieces of their flesh to the highest bidders.[99]

But the white community had its own response. "From the Ashes of Hose Rises a Terrible Warning," an editorial written by Smith Clayton, proclaimed in the *Atlanta Journal*:

> In the very ashes of this brute of brutes we read the best protection of the mothers, wives, and daughters in their country homes!
>
> In those ashes we see the state safer, the south securer, by the righteous ridding of one more demon. . . .
>
> The conclusion is that the destroyers of the monster, so far from performing an act of savagery, showed themselves the friends of that highest civilization which swoops to avenge the virtue of women, the honor of man, and the sanctity of the home![100]

Beware, All Darkies!

149

Finally, the occasion of that righteous action could be preserved in memory even for those who had failed to obtain a finger or a splinter or a shard of bone. In the April 28 edition of the *Newnan Herald and Advertiser*, tucked between a notice of the death of Mr. and Mrs. J. W. Donaldson's infant child and the announcement of young Alfred Broom's selection as a speaker in the commencement exercises at Emory College was the following advertisement:

> Send 15c to Claude H. Jackson, Newnan, Ga., with name and post-office address, and get a picture of the negro, Sam Holt, while burning at the stake.[101]

Chapter Eight

Lynch Law in Georgia

Shortly after Sam Hose's death, a curious story circulated that his wife and nineteen-year-old son were spotted at the Atlanta depot, preparing to board a train for Washington, D.C., for their own safety. This was the first mention that Hose or Holt had a family, under any name. According to reports, as they waited on the platform, a white man approached them and handed the boy an envelope containing a finger taken from his father and warned that he should "make himself scarce" and never return to Georgia.[1] By May 4, it was reported that the young man, now identified as John Holt, was being "furnished transportation" from Washington to Philadelphia by "the District officials." "He says his mother has gone there and asserts his father's innocence of either murder or rape," the *Constitution* reported.[2] By May 11, John Holt had "mysteriously disappeared" from Philadelphia after having told "conflicting stories."[3] Over the next few months, Sam Hose's "son" would make appearances in several northern cities, tell of his father's death, receive aid from local authorities and sympathetic citizens, and then leave.

It soon became evident that a confidence man or men were passing themselves off in this role, much to the delight of many white Georgians who saw this as further proof of the North's gullibility and willingness to believe the worst about the South. The *Atlanta Constitution* noted with some satisfaction that Sam Hose was twenty-two at the time of his death, and his "son" was but three years younger.[4] On August 19, ages changed and the paper noted that the "son" was "an older man than his father," and editorialized, "It is astonishing how easily some newspapers in the cities of the north become the victims of their own credulity."[5]

Another "fraud" who gained northern attention was Robert McGraw, a black man allegedly known in Cedartown, Georgia, as a local "quack," who was now giving talks in Boston "in which he told of his presence at the lynching of Sam Hose and gave pitiful details of the treatment of colored people in the south." His stories were so powerful that Lillian Clay Jewett of Boston, a philanthropist who led an antilynching campaign in the city (she had brought the widow and surviving children of the murdered Lake City, South Carolina, postmaster Frazier Baker north after the shootings), determined after talking to McGraw that she would come south to Cedartown, "in the very heart of the lynching district," to give lectures there.[6] The *Constitution* concluded,

> As long as northern newspapers will continue to be deceived by self-evident, characterless frauds, they must expect to be the victims of misinformation. It is a queer result of fanaticism that, in discussing the colored question, the views of men whose oaths would not be believed in the courts of any city in the land are readily taken up and spread abroad by the press with all the solemnity of accomplished fact.[7]

Although many southerners laughed at what they considered the North's eagerness to be duped, they sought to confirm in their own minds the justice of the mobs' actions. Just as Lige Strickland's reputation had been sullied in order to mitigate, if not excuse, his hanging, so Sam Hose was now held up for further castigation and calumny. It was again asserted that Hose was one of the six black men in Palmetto who had each sworn to kill one prominent white citizen of the town. This information came from Dr. Hal Johnston, who claimed to have received a threatening letter alerting him that he was still on such a list. The explanation was that Alfred Cranford was the first victim of this plot, which was in retribution for the slaughter of the Palmetto prisoners. It was said that the proposed ambush of H. T. Daniel was also a part of this plan. Rumors circulated about another plot in which blacks would ring the doorbells of potential victims' homes and then hide in the dark, ready to kill the owner when the door was opened. Mattie Cranford had related that her husband feared such a ruse shortly before he was murdered, and in her mind, Sam Hose had, indeed, attempted it the night before the actual murder occurred.[8]

Soon other rumors about Sam Hose's past began to circulate, most shockingly that, in addition to the rape of the woman in Marshallville, he had also murdered an elderly white couple, a Dr. and Mrs. Barrett, living at Creswell, near Griffin. The couple's nephew had been arrested for the killings but acquitted after an "exciting trial," and the murders had remained unsolved. According to the *Constitution*, Hose had confessed the killings to Lige Strickland, who, the paper asserted, had worked with Hose in 1897 in that part of Spalding County. "The negro told Strickland this a year or more ago, but [Strickland] said he did not believe it and did not tell any one about it until [Hose] had killed Alfred Cranford and fled." J. B. Jones supported this story in a letter: "John Wilkes, a brother to

Tom [Hose], says that Tom told him that he killed the old couple of people not far from Newnan, or Palmetto." The *Constitution* assumed this meant the man and woman murdered at Creswell.[9]

Among those who now tried to explain Hose's lynching to people outside the South was former Georgia governor William J. Northen, who had preceded William Atkinson in office (1890–94). Northen was known as a progressive on the question of lynching; after the Atlanta race riots of 1906, he would be active in establishing antilynching leagues to combat the practice. Nevertheless, immediately after the public killing of Sam Hose, Northen offered the following advice:

> My first suggestion is that all homes should be made miniature arsenals, at least to the extent of one good Winchester and one good pistol; that women be allowed to carry weapons upon their persons, concealed, if so desired, and that they be taught the use and handling of firearms, so that they may become their own protectors in the absence of the husband or master of the house. An occasional negro lying dead in the back yard, shot by a brave woman in defense of her honor, will do more to stop this awful crime than all the lynchings that may occur in a year.[10]

In May, Northen took part in an arranged debate in Boston with Bishop Benjamin W. Arnett, a black religious leader, on the topic "The Present Situation as to the Colored People of the South." Despite the proposed debate format, Northen had prepared a speech, and for two hours he held the stage at the Fremont Temple before an audience of fifteen hundred people. Even at that length, he was unable to present more than half his argument, and when he was stopped, the patient Bishop Arnett had little more than twenty minutes in which to respond. In his talk, titled "The White Man's Burden," Northen reviewed the history of race relations in the South before eventually reaching the Sam Hose lynching. He pointed out to his northern audience that publications such as *Harper's Weekly* and the *Boston Herald* had taken what he considered extreme positions on the issue.[11] He quoted the *Herald*, which he claimed had proposed that in the South "every negro should carry a winchester, and, wherever a negro was killed, their brethren should go out on the highways and byways, and the first white man they saw should be shot down." This proposal was not that different from Northen's own, that southern women should be armed, but what about vicious criminals like Sam Hose? he asked. These northern accounts, he noted, contained "not one word about the villainous scoundrel who did the double tragedy—a human fiend . . . not one word of sympathy for the home destroyed, the man murdered, the wife outraged, and the children besmeared with the blood and brains of their murdered father."

Having now finally set the scene, Northen next exhorted his Yankee listeners, repeating the oft-used device of demanding that they put themselves in the place of the Cranfords. He created a stirring *tableau vivant* for them, first asking their forgiveness for what he was about to present: "Will you pardon me if in this presence I tell a part of this horrible tale of woe and misery and loathsome wretchedness that you may somehow understand?" And then he pictured Sam Hose standing in the dining room of the Cranford home, holding the infant boy by the heels in one hand, wielding the ax in the other, hovering over Mattie Cranford as her husband's blood dripped from the hem of her dress. Choose, Hose tells her, your child or your virtue! Northen continued to develop the dramatic, near pornographic moment for these northerners, urging them, "[Picture] the trembling form of your wife—your daughter (can you imagine); curses as only a demon from hell can swear"—before the fiend

> jerks her down—your daughter (can you imagine) and rolls her in the warm blood of the only one she had ever hoped to defend her from such awful, awful, awful cruelty and shame! Hear her piteous cries as she writhes, for two long, long hours, in the embrace of the villain, and then see her as she falls at her father's gate—your gate (can you imagine), half clad and in a death swoon, to tell her horrible, sickening, loathsome, disgusting story (a story I cannot tell here, and which has not yet been told because of the loathsomeness).

Northen employed J. M. Early's rhetorical device of urging identification with the victims—"your wife! your daughter! yourself!"—while also repeating the almost hypnotic refrain "can you imagine" not as a question but as a command. Under these conditions, who among them would not have participated in administering "the punishment of the nethermost hell, whether administered here or hereafter"? Pointing out that the North had its own share of racial outrages to answer for, Northen then offered this advice: "May I say to my friends, the colored people of the north, if they will look after their own business and attend to the lawlessness that occurs in their own bailiwick, they will possibly have quite as much as they can profitably manage." He challenged his listeners: "Do you ask me how these lynchings can be stopped at the south? I answer promptly—just as they can be stopped at the north and in no other way. Stop the outrages and the lynchings will cease. Continue the outrages, and the lynchings will always follow, regardless of threats by the law, whether in Georgia, Minnesota, Illinois, Ohio, or other states."[12]

The response to Northen's speech, the portion of it he was able to give (the entire speech was published in the *Constitution* and other papers), was mixed. To progressive southerners, that the governor had appeared on stage with a black man, had given a "hearty handshake" to Bishop Arnett at the conclusion, and had spoken "reasonably" about the race problem in the nation at large and not in the

South alone, all were seen as evidence of the South's willingness to reach out to the North. Northen had emphasized their shared concerns over race, and many felt that he had proved an effective emissary. However, his audience in Boston was less receptive. They took offense at the lascivious melodrama he created in his talk and were upset by his comments on Harriet Beecher Stowe's *Uncle Tom's Cabin*—he had quoted Dr. Nehemiah Adams, who had written, "If the people, as far as possible from the seaboard, should ask me for a book giving the true picture of a sailor's experience, it would be as fair to give them Robinson Crusoe as to put Uncle Tom's Cabin into the hands of a foreigner who wished to learn what American slavery is." Most felt that, although he had denounced mob violence, he had placed the majority of blame on the blacks of the South rather than acknowledge white responsibility.[13]

Responses to Northen's talk continued through the next months. In June, for example, Joseph W. Henderson, the black editor of the *New England Torchlight*, spoke against the governor's defense of the South. He began by explaining his position:

> Were it not that it was in Georgia that my poor mother was born—that there she trembling obeyed the slave master's whip and felt the slave hound's bite, there that she was sold and deported for life from her blood and kin, I would not stoop to dignify Governor Northen's pro-slavery utterances even with a sneer.

Henderson's main point was that the fear of miscegenation, which he felt was the root of Northen's horror, was primarily caused not by the ravenous black rapist Northen had conjured for his audience but by whites much like the governor himself. "It was the blue vein aristocracy of the south that broke over the fence, defied all law, and the result is that we have black negroes and white negroes— some as white as Governor Northen." To be specific, Henderson noted boldly and pointedly, "Many a southern aristocrat has played the part of the alleged Sam Hose at a black woman's door."[14]

On his return to Georgia, Northen indicated that he was relatively pleased with his reception, despite his inability to present his complete argument to the audience due to time constraints.[15] The columnist Bill Arp, on the other hand, found little to satisfy him in the North's response. "I've sworn off again," he wrote. Picturing Northen as a missionary sent among the heathens, he continued, "I notice that some of their editors are easy on our governor, but none of them have apologized. They have got to repent and apologize before we will be satisfied with their conversion."[16]

Although Northen's attempts to explain southern values to a northern audience had met with limited success, the North did want to know more about these horrific events that had shocked the nation. Even as Sam Hose's wife and child (if they existed) were leaving Georgia, two separate investigations organized by northern forces were under way. By late April or the first of May, the *New York Herald* had sent one of its senior editors, Dr. George H. Hepworth, as a "special commissioner" to explore "not so much . . . the incident itself as . . . the possible causes which led up to it and the possible consequences which might flow from it."[17] Hepworth was a Unitarian minister (inactive) as well as a journalist, had served as a Union chaplain during the Civil War, and had covered events as far away as Armenia for the paper. He spent a week or more in Atlanta interviewing state and city leaders ("judges, lawyers, officials, physicians, business men, college presidents, and professors") and representatives from "the better class of colored men." He also traveled to Newnan to continue his investigation. There he was met at the train station by Mayor Burdett and escorted to the exclusive Virginia House hotel, where he roomed during his stay. He interviewed former governor Atkinson and Judge Freeman, and he spent a half hour with Mattie Cranford at her parents' home and took pictures of her and her children, illustrations of which appeared in the *Herald*. Of Mattie he wrote, "A more pitiful and pathetic spectacle than she presents my eyes never beheld." He went to the site of the lynching, where he "looked on the stump, all that was left, of the pine tree to which the monstrosity was bound, and on the black circle of dead grass and cinders where he was burned." He sat on the piazza of the hotel and debated the morality and efficacy of lynching with "twenty-five of the best citizens of Newnan," some of whom had apparently taken part in or at least witnessed the burning. He also met with "a deputation of colored citizens, who engaged him for about an hour in a general discussion of the conduct and condition of the negro race in this section." The Newnan paper noted that no white person other than Hepworth was present during this last meeting, but that "while his visitors talked freely, their views did not differ materially from those expressed by the white citizens with whom he had previously talked."[18]

In a series of four "letters" to the *Herald* (the first two published on Sunday, May 14, simultaneously in the *Herald* and the *Atlanta Constitution*; the second two on the following Sunday, May 21, in the *Herald*), Hepworth laid out his intentions. "My mission was not one of carping criticism, but it arose from the fact that all states are harmed when one state is either imprudent or unjust or suffers from a great calamity." Although he was "cordially welcomed by the people of Georgia," who, he noted, "take as grave a view of the situation as we of the north do, and as earnestly seek a remedy for existing evils as the spirit of progress could desire," he nonetheless wished to be "entirely independent" and stated, "If as the result of my work I am impelled to criticize some things, and to find fault with certain tendencies which I think are detrimental to the public interest, the people of Georgia may take issue with me as to statement of fact or logical deduction."[19]

Before the first two letters appeared, former governor William Atkinson was interviewed in Atlanta by a reporter from the *Macon Telegraph*. Atkinson, who would be dead before the summer was over, was now described as "looking quite well" and in "excellent" health. He seemed satisfied that the Hose affair was now settled, even though no one had been charged in the killing and he had never been asked to name names. The main topic of the interview was Dr. Hepworth's visit to Newnan, which Atkinson indicated occurred at his suggestion to the Newnan mayor. He had found Hepworth to be "quite a pleasant gentleman." Atkinson described the correspondent's meeting with Newnan's prominent citizens, who had discussed with him "quite freely . . . the recent race trouble in [their] county and the vicinity." He also pointed out that Hepworth had met with twelve or more "of the leading colored men of the city and county, so as to get their version of what had occurred." He added, "What these negroes said we don't know, as none of the white citizens were present, and did not want to be. We wanted Dr. Hepworth to have a full and free talk with these people so that he would have both sides of the question and thereby be informed as to the general status of affairs in Coweta and adjacent counties." The former governor further stated that he had no advance knowledge of what Hepworth's "letters" would say but was certain that the reporter would be fair, explaining, "He is a minister, a man of fine ability and seems to be well informed upon matters of general interest." As to the question of present race relations in Newnan, Atkinson suggested that white employers should consider more carefully the backgrounds of the blacks they hired to work for them, since, in his opinion, most local black crimes were committed by "ex-convicts."[20]

When the *Herald* ran the first of the Hepworth series, it was under the title "Southern Lynchings, Their Causes and the Only Remedy." The two letters were illustrated by sketches, taken from his photographs, of the site of Hose's execution—"Where Sam Hose Was Burned: Stump of Tree Still Standing"— and of "Mrs. Cranford and Children" and "Home of Mrs. Cranford." The illustration of the lynch site is a bucolic scene, Hepworth posing with hat and cane next to a tree, the pine "stump" off to the right in the middle of a burnt circle, a horse grazing quietly in the pasture behind. The family sketch shows a haggard Mattie Cranford dressed in black, sitting on a porch holding the baby Clifford on her lap, the other three children grouped around her. The third illustration is apparently of her parents' home in Newnan, where she was now living and before which Sam Hose was brought for identification by her mother. The wooden picket fence figures prominently in the picture's foreground. The *Constitution*, for its publication, simply provided a dignified illustration of Hepworth himself, seated in profile.

In this first letter, Hepworth showed a deep sympathy with his hosts and treated most of their assumptions with respect. In retelling the story of the

Cranford murder and rape, he accepted the local version of Hose as demon and even added several disturbing, sensationalistic elements. "His crime was unique in its hideousness. Its atrocity was simply unthinkable, and it seems necessary to give its salient points in order that we may understand the inhuman vengeance which was wreaked by a frenzied populace," he wrote. Strongly implied in Hepworth's account was the rumor to which others, including Governor Candler, had alluded: that Hose suffered from syphilis and was possibly deranged by the disease. "This man Hose was a fellow of infinite hatreds. A thousand insanities surged through his nature. Physically corrupt in consequence of nameless immoralities, he did his farm work with a sullen temper, the consequence of his abnormal condition, and excited the terror of the Cranford family whom he served . . . his presence was endured, but under a constant presentiment that harm might result." The unspoken horror, then, was that Mattie Cranford had not only been raped but possibly diseased by Hose during the time he held her sexual prisoner.[21] Second, Hepworth stated that after Hose had "buried" the ax "up to the handle" in Alfred Cranford's brain and then "hewed and hacked him as one hews a piece of timber," he threatened the baby with decapitation if Mattie Cranford failed to submit to him. Like Governor Northen, Hepworth created a *tableau vivant* for his readers:

An active volcano is sublime, though awful in its destructive power; but a man acting under the impulsion of a legion of devils is a sight to freeze the blood in one's veins. Watch such a man at his fiendish work. Holt held the baby by the heels with his left hand—the axe was in his right hand—and threatened to cut off its head unless the mother submitted to his damnable wishes. . . . The woman must decide at once. The uplifted axe was ready to fall. Maternal instinct forgot all else and she cried, "Save my little ones." No martyr ever suffered greater torture than she during the unspeakable hour that followed. She was a woman of refinement, a college graduate, a woman with personal beauty, and at one fell swoop she lost all that makes life dear.

It is unclear if this information came directly from Mattie Cranford, her family, or from other sources he found to be reliable. Nevertheless, Hepworth never doubted that Mrs. Cranford had been raped. Indeed, he accepted completely the argument that white families in the rural South lived under "a mild reign of terror" and that the explanation "we must protect our wives and daughters" was a valid one. Hepworth spoke directly to his northern readers:

If my wife or mother or sister had been outraged by a double-dyed villain, I can't tell you what I would or would not do. When the matter is brought home to yourself you recognize its horror. There are no lengths to which you would not go in the way of punishment. It is easy to condemn a thousand miles away, but hard to condemn when on the spot with a like fate staring you in the face. I neither plead nor excuse. I simply say that I also am human.[22]

In the second letter, given the title "How Lynching May Be Stopped," Hepworth recounted his trip to Newnan and the discussion he engaged in with the town's leading citizens. "They have talked with me frankly and dispassionately. We have thrashed the subject in a generous, but good natured discussion, and I have found them as ready to listen to me as I was eager to listen to them." He made clear his understanding of the crime. "'I have no doubt,' I said, 'that Sam Hose richly deserved all he got.'" Nevertheless, Hepworth attempted to counter the reasons given him for the necessity and severity of Hose's punishment. When the locals explained that in rural areas, law and courts were often inadequate for public safety and "that there [were] some crimes for which the courts afford[ed] no adequate address," Hepworth suggested that there was "abundant evidence to the contrary" and that "courts cannot be practically abolished without serious injury" to the community. One man noted, "The press is on the side of the lynchers," to which Hepworth responded, "It may be the business of the press to represent public opinion nine days out of ten, but on the tenth day, when public opinion is so excited that it cannot see clearly what is right or wrong, it is the business of the press to restrain it." As the discussion continued, Hepworth assured the group that he had come south not as a "hostile critic" but as one seeking to understand.

"Don't apologize," remarked a town official, who sat in front of me. "We want to talk this matter over in a judicial way. You need not be afraid to speak freely. We southerners are just as regretful for some things as you can be, and just as anxious to find a remedy for existing evils as any man on the planet. All we ask is that you shall understand the motives which led to our action and not credit us with a hostility to the negro because he is a negro, for that is not true."

Another, however, made it clear that "the negroes must be impressed with the awfulness of Sam Hose's crime," arguing, "We pursued the course which was most likely to accomplish that end. Exceptional crime, exceptional punishment, was our motto." "The principle will hold," Hepworth answered, "but you did it at too great a cost to yourselves." Violence by whites might well inspire greater violence by blacks. He continued:

Exhibitions of the lynch law spirit produce a reflex action on the community, and it is a very demoralizing influence. The white man can't afford to hang people, for he thereby disintegrates and disorganizes society.

No man is made better by holding a hangman's rope or lighting the fire which burns the worst and most vicious criminal. . . . A score of young men, however chivalrous they may be, do a moral injury to themselves by torturing even a dog. They can't go through a slaughter house without staining their garments with blood, and blood does not fit a man for the duties of citizenship.[23]

Hepworth's last two letters, published in the *Herald* on May 21, were under the title "Dr. Hepworth Discusses the Race Conditions in the South," with the subheading "While the Great Majority of Whites and Blacks Desire to Live in Harmony, a Small Percentage of Each Causes Trouble—Recent Lynchings Have Disturbed Relationships That Were Growing Better." In these writings, Hepworth sought remedies for the social "difficulties" he found in the South. He confidently asserted, "The prejudice of the whites, which is based on the undisputed fact that the negroes, as a race, are inferior, however many or however remarkable the exceptions may be, will give way when the negro proves himself capable of good work in any direction." He also felt that "ninety-five percent" of both races "have no other desire than to get on without friction." But the 5 percent on either side were capable of great trouble, and the antagonism between the races foreshadowed the possibility of outright race war in the near future. He suggested a conference between leading men from both groups as a way "to avert an evil which [was] surely impending." Hose's execution illustrated the growing danger:

> The Sam Hose incident excited the whites, but it excited the blacks still more. The whites will go back to their avocations and to forgetfulness, with nothing more than a disagreeable and probably a regretful memory. Not so the blacks. They are frightened, ignorant, and altogether off their base. They don't know what may happen to-morrow, but they imagine terrible things. If the courts are thrust aside, and the people become executioners, then passion and prejudice will rule instead of justice. The average negro can't reason this out as I am trying to do, but he feels it out without reason, and feeling without reason is the most dangerous element in any civilization.[24]

Dr. Hepworth, in these letters to his fellow northerners, expressed the views of the average white moderate, liberal in theory concerning black rights yet obviously in agreement with southern "leading citizens" who argued that the black race in general was not yet ready for responsible roles in society. The "average negro" was motivated by "feeling without reason," while the southern whites were misguided by their reasoning, but, given the social conditions in which they found themselves, understandably so. Thus, it is not surprising that the *Atlanta Constitution* would applaud Hepworth. Clark Howell, the paper's editor, explained to the *Constitution*'s readers its reasons for publishing the first two letters:

> It is without any prejudice or sectional predisposition that Dr. Hepworth has set about investigating this lynching problem, its characteristics and causes. With a frank

horror of the concrete facts, he is nevertheless curious to see what it is that lies behind them and gives them potency, and anxious to study the actual conditions which, in the closing years of the nineteenth century, and in civilized communities, lead to outrages on defenseless women and the swift and illegal reprisals of mob law.

The lengthy editorial concluded:

> Nevertheless, Dr. Hepworth perceives and asserts that one crime, however atrocious, is no excuse for another, that the whole country is interested in arresting this development of lawlessness, which, if it continues to grow, will finally shake the foundations of society. The excuse of lynching is not an argument in favor of it. Dr. Hepworth's letters . . . will do good in all parts of the country; in the north because he is recognized as a humanitarian and a practical philanthropist; and at the south because his views are permeated with that broad spirit of charity and sympathy which is necessary in the discussion of problems affecting the safety and social existence of the people.[25]

"Ripples," in the *Newnan Herald and Advertiser*, also commented approvingly after reading the first two letters in the *Constitution*:

> We heard most of the conversation in front of the Virginia House, referred to in his article, and don't think he misquoted a single remark. We believe his visit to Newnan will have a good effect, and do much to correct some of the false notions that prevail among the people of the North.[26]

————

Hepworth was not the only investigator to come south to report on the circumstances of the Sam Hose torture death, and the second summary of events would strongly support exactly the sort of "false notions" "Ripples" decried. On Sunday night, April 30, in Chicago, one week after the lynching, Ida B. Wells-Barnett and her husband, L. F. Barnett, held a series of meetings sponsored by the Afro-American Council in black churches throughout the city to protest Hose's execution, which she called the "crime of the century," and Strickland's hanging.[27] Wells-Barnett told the crowd that the Chicago Colored Citizens intended to send their own man to Georgia and publish his findings on not only Hose's death but also the Palmetto massacre and Elijah Strickland's hanging. A white man, Louis P. Le Vin, was engaged for the undertaking, just about the time Hepworth's first letters appeared in the *Herald* and the *Constitution*. There is some question as to Le Vin's professional background—in her study of these events, historian Mary Louise Ellis identifies him as a "traveling salesman" rather than a trained detective—but he went to Georgia in late May posing as "a vendor of hog cholera medicine" and interviewed people "in Griffin, Newman [*sic*], Atlanta and in the vicinity of these places."[28] After a week, he returned to Chicago and on the afternoon of June 4 presented his findings to a mass meeting held at the Bethel Church, led by the Reverend R. C. Ransom, a leading bishop in the African Methodist Episcopal Church, who had raised the money to send Le Vin to Georgia. Ransom and Wells-Barnett then published the subsequent report along with her comments and reproductions of news articles from the *Atlanta Journal* and *Constitution* in order to "give the public the facts, in the belief that there [was] still a sense of justice in the American people, and that it [would] yet assert itself in condemnation of outlawry and in defense of oppressed and persecuted humanity."[29] The pamphlet, "Lynch Law in Georgia," was published by Chicago Colored Citizens in June and had wide circulation. Indeed, in the years to come it would be accepted as the most accurate recounting of these events, the primary source for anyone studying these Georgia lynchings.

Ida Wells-Barnett was an outspoken, courageous leader in the antilynching movement at the turn of the century. Sam Hose's death proved to her the inhumane extremes to which the South was willing to go in order to maintain its sense of racial superiority. Her outrage is evident in her introduction to the pamphlet. Using the white apologists' own words against them, she tells her readers to "Consider the Facts":

> The real purpose of these savage demonstrations is to teach the Negro that in the South he has no rights that the law will enforce. Samuel Hose was burned to teach the Negroes that no matter what a white man does to them, they must not resist. Hose, a servant, had killed Cranford, his employer. An example must be made. Ordinary punishment was deemed inadequate. This Negro must be burned alive. To make the burning a certainty the charge of outrage was invented, and added to the charge of murder. The daily press offered reward for the capture of Hose and then openly incited the people to burn him as soon as caught. The mob carried out the plan in every savage detail.

Both Wells-Barnett and Le Vin stressed that in this publication they were giving only "the report of the true facts . . . as learned by the investigation." And it is true that Le Vin had obviously dug deeper, talked to a wider variety of witnesses and local blacks, than had Hepworth. And, perhaps not surprisingly, their portrait of "Samuel Hose"—the full name "Samuel" according him a greater degree of respect—and of the other events that made up the "reign of outlawry" in Georgia during these six weeks was quite different from that offered by Hepworth, who had accepted Hose's guilt without question.

Sam Hose had in general been painted as a monster by the southern press, a terrorist, a deep-dyed villain of unspeakable evil. As late as 1907, "black Sam Hose" could be paired without explanation to Jack the Ripper in a *Constitution* book review.[30] In Le Vin's report, Hose, or "Samuel Wilkes," which Le Vin incorrectly gave as his "true name," was presented as a model of rectitude, an innocent brought forth to the slaughter. He came from a family of "hard-working, honest people." He was educated, could read and write, and "was considered a bright, capable man." With an invalid mother and a brother "considered almost an imbecile," he was "the mainstay of the family." After the mother recovered her health to some degree, he had left Marshallville and moved to Coweta County, where he had worked for Alfred Cranford for two years. Le Vin did not dispute that Wilkes had killed Cranford but asserted that it was in self-defense. Both the horrific story of his creeping into the dining room to split Cranford's skull and the accusation of rape were untrue. In Le Vin's version, which he claimed had been related by Wilkes himself after capture, Samuel had received word that his mother's health had again grown worse, and he wanted to visit her. He had asked Cranford for money owed him, Cranford refused, and an argument ensued. Cranford "was known to be a man of quick temper," and the following day he had borrowed his father's revolver and had threatened to kill Samuel if he caused further trouble. On Wednesday, April 12, Wilkes was chopping wood when Cranford approached him. They again argued over the money; Cranford "became enraged and drew his gun to shoot." Wilkes then threw the ax at Cranford and ran toward the nearby woods. According to Le Vin, "He knew the ax struck Cranford, but did not know Cranford had been killed by the blow for several days." After he was captured, Wilkes calmly "told his story in a straightforward way, said he was sorry he had killed Cranford and always denied that he had attacked Mrs. Cranford." He went to his death "free from excitement or terror."[31]

Le Vin further stated that Mattie Cranford had not accused Hose of rape until several days had passed, and he suggested that she had done so at the instigation of her brother-in-law, E. D. Sharkey, "one of the most persistent advocates of the burning." He accused W. A. Hemphill and Clark Howell of the *Atlanta Constitution* of having "contributed more to the burning than any other men and all other forces in Georgia," claiming that they "exaggerated every detail of the killing, invented and published inflammatory descriptions of a crime that was never committed, and by glaring head lines continually suggested the burning of the man when caught." They also offered the five-hundred-dollar "blood money" reward.[32] Le Vin further implicated Governor Candler, stating that he "acquiesced in the burning by refusing to prevent it." In describing Wilkes's death, Le Vin added to the gruesome details already recounted. "They cut off both ears, skinned his face, cut off his fingers, gashed his legs, cut open his stomach and pulled out his entrails, then when his contortions broke the iron chain, they pushed his burning body back into the fire." Throughout it all, however, Wilkes had maintained stoic courage and dignity. "During all the time of his torture he never uttered one cry. . . . Wilkes never once uttered a cry or begged for mercy.

Only once in a particularly fiendish torture did he speak, then he simply groaned, 'Oh, Lord Jesus.'"[33]

Thus, Samuel Hose, or Samuel Wilkes, died a true martyr in Le Vin's account, Christlike in his suffering and his forbearance.[34] But, as Le Vin described it, the same was largely true of the men shot down in Palmetto and of Elijah Strickland. Of the Palmetto fires, he wrote, "It seems that one or two barns or houses had been burned, and it was reported that the Negroes were setting fire to the buildings." But the men arrested "were not men of bad character. . . . They were intelligent, hard-working men, and all declared they could easily prove their innocence." As for Strickland, Le Vin maintained, "I did not talk with one white man who believed that Strickland had anything to do with Wilkes. I could not find any person who heard Wilkes mention Strickland's name. . . . On the other hand, I saw many who knew Strickland, and all spoke of him in the highest terms." Le Vin interviewed Major Thomas, who had tried to save Strickland from the mob, and Thomas had told him that "he never knew a more reliable and worthy man among the colored people. He said that he was always advising the colored people to live right, keep good friends with the white people and earn their respect." On the basis of his investigation, Le Vin returned to Chicago "thoroughly convinced that a Negro's life [was] a very cheap thing in Georgia."[35]

Obviously there were major differences between Le Vin's version of these events and those found in both Hepworth's retelling and in local reports. Le Vin downplayed the damage done by arson in Palmetto, and he presented both the men arrested for the fires and Lige Strickland in the best possible light. Similarly, his Samuel Hose, or Samuel Wilkes, was a man beyond reproach. Le Vin did not mention the rumor that Wilkes had left Marshallville after being accused of raping an elderly woman, and the picture of his brother's being "almost an imbecile" was also disputed by other accounts. He did not relate the local view of Hose as a contentious figure, nor did he mention Mattie Cranford's alleged statements about the family's growing fear of their employee. His version of Cranford's death—an ax thrown in self-defense, followed by a hasty escape, with Wilkes unaware that the blow had proved fatal—was an unlikely explanation and ignored the testimony of Mattie Cranford; of Cranford's father, who claimed to have found his son's body in the dining room; and of the other witnesses. At no previous point had anyone suggested that Cranford's body was discovered in the yard, and it strained credulity to think the family would have moved it inside, there to be found by others. There was not much reason for the family to lie about this: whether Cranford was killed inside the house or out, he was still dead at the hands of a black man. Nor did Le Vin address the issue of the injured baby, whom the papers had at first described as hovering near death. Certainly the melodramatic newspaper accounts of the villainous Hose creeping into the Cranford house had played shamelessly to the fears and prejudices of white southerners, but Le Vin's alternate version was in some ways at least as suspect.

Even more problematic was Le Vin's assertion that there had been no rape:

As soon as her husband was killed [Mattie Cranford] ran to the home of his father and told him that Sam had killed her husband. She did not then say that Sam had assaulted her. She was completely overcome and was soon unconscious and remained so for most of the next two days. So that at the time when the story was started that Sam had added the crime of outrage to murder, Mrs. Cranford, the only one who could have told about it, was lying either unconscious or delirious at the home of her father-in-law, G. E. Cranford.[36]

Le Vin thus asserted that the charge of rape was added later to that of murder in order to incite the white mobs to an even greater fury against Hose. He pointed specifically to Mattie Cranford's brother-in-law, Sharkey: "He claimed that he saw Mrs. Cranford the day after the killing and that she told him that she was assaulted. As a matter of fact, Mrs. Cranford was unconscious at that time. He persistently told the story and urged the burning of Sam as soon as caught."[37] But reports of an assault appeared in the very first accounts of the killing, on Thursday, April 13. If this was a lie, intended to increase white outrage and justify any measure of torture, then it was a lie told from the beginning, not added after a few days' delay as Le Vin maintained. Nor was there any evidence that Mattie Cranford was completely unconscious or delirious for days after her husband's death; both Sharkey and Royal Daniel apparently talked with her during this time.

Nevertheless, Le Vin's report provided a very different portrait of Sam Hose. Then, on June 6, 1899, the *Salt Lake City Broad Ax* confused the issue even more. In a front-page story on Le Vin's investigation titled "Mrs. Alfred Cranford Talks," the paper reported, "The white detective called upon Mrs. Cranford and she informed him that Hose did not attempt to assault her in any manner whatever. She says that her husband and Sam Hose quarreled over wages and her husband ran into the house and went out with his revolver and as he was about to shoot Hose the latter seized an ax and threw it at him. The ax struck her husband in the head and killed him instantly. Then Hose fled from the place." The *Broad Ax* concluded, "Mrs. Cranford's version of the affair no doubt is correct and it certainly puts the Atlanta Constitution and all other advocates of mob and lynch law in a very uncomfortable position."[38]

Although Le Vin's other conclusions were accurately reported in this article, the statement that he had spoken to Mrs. Cranford and that she had given him this version of her husband's death was not. Le Vin had clearly stated that he had never interviewed Mrs. Cranford and that his description of the killing had come from other sources. Nevertheless, the *Broad Ax*'s report that Mrs. Cranford had recanted the original version of the events took root and soon became accepted as fact among other African American newspapers. On June 20, 1899, the *New York Age* published a review of Le Vin's account that repeated the *Broad Ax*'s interpretation, and the *New York Sun* followed two days later. The *Richmond Planet* headlined its October 14, 1899, front-page article "The Detective's Report. The Georgia Burning.—Sam Hose Not Guilty of Rape."[39]

Thus, while Mattie Cranford never publicly or, according to members of her family, privately changed her account, Le Vin's version of the events was taken by many as fact, and Mattie Cranford was named as his primary source for declaring Sam Hose's innocence on the charge of rape. As an example, in late June, the Reverend Charles S. Morris spoke at the People's Temple in Boston, his address meant to rebuke and correct Governor Northen's talk the previous month in the city. Morris first took offense at the more sensationalistic elements of Northen's performance, calling the speech itself a "masterpiece of slander." He explained:

> When Governor Northen came to Boston he described in all its revolting details what purported to be an eye-witness description of how Sam Hose murdered Mr. Cranford and then laid the wife in the warm red blood of her husband and held her there an hour and a half in his brutal embrace.
>
> This was the very climax of his speech, but his description was purely imaginary or deliberately false.

Morris then drew on Le Vin's findings to make his own claims.

> The truth is that Sam Hose never touched Mrs. Cranford nor even spoke to her. Hose had a grudge against Cranford because the latter was the leader of a mob which lynched nine negroes in cold blood a few days previously. Hose never denied the killing of Cranford, but even to his death he asserted his innocence of the crime of outrage.

Morris again repeated the mistaken assertion that Mattie Cranford had denied the rape. "To the detective who investigated the crime, Mrs. Cranford herself said Hose did not say a word or in any way touch her." Furthermore, although Le Vin had described the Palmetto massacre at some length, he had never directly implicated Alfred Cranford in it, much less named him as the "leader" of the mob, nor, of course, had he asserted direct conversation with Mrs. Cranford. Morris was clearly influenced by the *Broad Ax* representation of Le Vin's findings, either in that paper or as repeated in subsequent publications, but he ignored Le Vin's assertion that Hose had accidentally killed Cranford in an act of self-defense. Instead, if Hose were guilty of killing Cranford, as his "confession" seemed to confirm, the murder, as Morris framed it, was an act of revenge and rebellion, a part of an ongoing guerrilla race war.[40]

As if to support this portrait, by early November Hose was claimed as a fellow fighter and martyr by the Filipino rebels in the Philippine-American War. American troops in Angeles, Manila, found a placard written in Spanish nailed to a tree. It was described as "an appeal to the [U.S.] colored troops to join the insurgents in the fight for freedom" and included the admonition: "[Remember] your brothers, Sam Hose and Gray, whose blood calls aloud for vengeance." The placard was sent to Gen. Arthur MacArthur (father of Gen. Douglas MacArthur), who would soon be named military governor of the Philippine Islands, as an illustration of the continued resistance the American forces were encountering. Headlines in the *Atlanta Constitution* emphasized the racial significance of this call for black soldiers to join the rebellion against white colonialism: "Negro Troops Are Asked to Revolt: Spaniards Tell Them to Avenge the Death of Sam Hose."[41]

From this point on, there would be two contending narratives describing the events of spring 1899, sometimes too neatly categorized as the "white" and the "negro" versions. Walter F. Willcox compared these competing stories as early as December 1899 in his essay "Negro Criminality." Willcox, one of the founders of twentieth-century statistical study, was at this time chief statistician at Cornell University. In 1904, he would coauthor with W. E. B. Du Bois the bulletin *Negroes in the United States*, published by the Bureau of the Census, and he would later serve as president of the American Statistical Association. In this article, he pointed out the "incorrectness" of Le Vin's statements concerning the Palmetto fires and the reputation of the men arrested. He repeated the charge that Alfred Cranford was involved in the Palmetto shootings, observing, "The negro version, as set forth by a correspondent, says that Cranford was conspicuous in that region as 'a nigger-hater,' and was probably the leader of the party of lynchers four weeks before. Whether that be true or not, it seems likely that the dominant motive for the murder and rape was revenge." As for the location of Cranford's body, Willcox wrote:

> The negro story also states that Cranford was killed in the yard, and not in the house. To get light upon this radical difference in the two accounts, I wrote to the Atlanta [newspaper] editor . . . asking these questions: "Was the body of Alfred Cranford found in the supper room or in the yard?" He answered, "In the supper room." "Do you know this fact of your own knowledge or by testimony of others?" To this his reply was, "Blood showed position; eye-witnesses testified as to place."

Willcox concluded, "In addition to these errors of statement the negro version reads like a plea, and not an impartial balancing of evidence, and puts aside as untrustworthy the sworn testimony of Mrs. Cranford." He felt certain that the "impartial balancing of evidence" supported the "white" version, even as it implicated Alfred Cranford in the Palmetto shootings.[42]

This "white" version had one last outing as the new century began. In February 1900, Georgia congressman James Griggs spoke before the U.S. House of Representatives. He also made the connection between Sam Hose's death and the war taking place in the Philippines, although his intentions were quite different from those of the Filipino rebels. Following the pattern of Governor Northen's emotional, lurid presentation of the crimes, Griggs first called upon his fellow representatives seated in Washington to picture what had occurred, again representing the events as pure melodrama:

> But let me tell you of a case that happened in Georgia last year. A little family a few miles from the town of Newnan were at supper in their modest dining room. The father, the young mother, and the baby were seated at the table. Humble though it was, peace, happiness and contentment reigned in that modest home. A monster in human form, an employee on the farm, crept into that happy little home and with an axe knocked out the brains of that father, snatched the child from the mother, threw it across the room out of his way, and then by force accomplished his foul purpose.

Griggs repeated the rumor that Hose "was afflicted with the most loathsome disease known to human kind" and increased the duration of the invasion and rape to four hours (Northen had put it at two). With this outrage in mind, the congressman asked his fellow representatives to understand and appreciate the fury of the mob as they took their revenge.

> I do not seek to justify that, but I do say that the man who would condemn those people unqualifiedly under these circumstances has water instead of blood to supply his circulation. (Applause). Not the limpid water that flows from the mountain streams, Mr. Chairman, but the fetid water found in the cesspools of cities. (Applause).

Like Northen, Griggs did not hesitate to magnify Mrs. Cranford's humiliation and shame for his rhetorical purposes. Having not so subtly insulted big-city (read northern) politicos and bleeding hearts, he then made the move in his speech to international events, telling his audience that Georgians' need to protect the sanctity of the southern home was no different from the country's undertaking in the Philippines and elsewhere.

> We propose to fight for and maintain the supremacy of the Anglo-Saxon race—that race which gentlemen have fought to justify here today in shooting brown men in the Philippines in the name of civilization; that race which is today shooting Boers in South Africa in the name of civilization. The people of Georgia, the people of all the south, propose in the name of that same great civilization to stand by their traditions,

to preserve the integrity of the race and to preserve its control everywhere, under all circumstances, whenever it is threatened from any source. (Applause).[43]

Thus, Sam Hose's lynching had now been cheered and applauded in the nation's Capitol. At the same time, Hose had become a symbol of all insurgents, but most specifically of unruly brown men throughout the world, men whose deaths were necessary to preserve the Anglo-Saxon heritage.

Chapter Nine

Sex, Fingers, Toes

In its May 12 edition, the *Newnan Herald and Advertiser* proudly published a poem titled "Sam Holt." Holt was, the poem declared, "The monster fiend of all the fiends / That ever cursed the earth." It further proclaimed,

> 'Twas but right that he should die
>> With lurid fire to light the same.
> 'Twill teach these brute beasts to know
>> That vengeance dire will quickly come;
> God's righteous wrath is never slow
>> To avenge the Christian home.
> And so 'twill be till cause shall cease
>> To blight with crime our Southern land.

The poem, signed with the appellation "Justice," ended with the assurance that God had "ordained" Sam Hose's death.[1] Two months later, C. D. Smith from Atlanta wrote a second poem to honor Newnan for its actions. The town quickly adopted the poem, and it later appeared prominently in *Coweta County Chronicles*, the official history of the region published in 1928.

> Newnan
>
> Enthroned as a Queen, robed in Her beauty
> Fair as the fairest Gem in her Crown
> Faithful to God, to home and to duty
> His blessings forever rest on this town.
>
> Her sons and her daughters, brave-hearted and kind
> With hands ever open to Charity's call
> Peerless in beauty, in culture refined
> Though others may boast, She's Queen over all.

170

Then onward and upward blest be thy name
For all that is great noble and grand
As lasting as time immortal her fame
The brightest and best in a Heaven blest land.[2]

The Sam Hose "affair" was not directly mentioned in the poem, but its unstated presence was clear to the *Herald and Advertiser*'s readers. They had been absolved. Although occasional references to the lynching would continue to appear, most notably in the newspaper squabble between Newnan and Griffin, most people seemed willing to put this event to rest. When Mary G. Jones and Lily Reynolds edited and compiled *Coweta County Chronicles*, covering the county's one-hundred-year history, from the time of "the Indians from Whom the Land was Acquired" to the present day, they made but brief mention of Hose.

> Newnan was given undeserved and undesired nation-wide publicity when a mob brought Sam Hose, caught at Griffin, Georgia, after one of the most fiendish and horrifying crimes at Palmetto in the annals of the State, to one of her suburbs and burned him.[3]

The event was neatly if awkwardly described, packaged into some forty words that deflected guilt from Newnan and onto Griffin, Palmetto, and the entire inquisitive nation. A later history of Newnan failed to mention the lynching at all. This was partly out of respect for the Cranford family, which was prominent in the community, but also out of a greater sense of propriety and the belief that, as the *Macon Telegraph* had noted immediately after the burning, "traces of the tragedy might be demoralizing."[4] Nevertheless, the ghost of Sam Hose could not be so easily exorcised, and the lynching had unexpected consequences in private lives.

W. E. B. Du Bois, for example, identified Sam Hose's torture-death as the event that, as Du Bois put it, "pulled me off my feet," and determined him to take on his lifelong fight against racial injustice. As he put it in one speech:

> A poor Negro in central Georgia, Sam Hose, had killed his landlord in a wage dispute. He could not be found for days; then at last a new cry was raised that he had raped the landlord's wife. It was obviously and clearly a trumped-up charge to arouse the worst passions of the countryside, and the mob roared. I wrote out a careful and reasoned statement concerning the evident facts and started down to *The Constitution*, carrying in my pocket a letter of introduction which I had to Joel Chandler Harris. I did not get there. On the way the news met me: Sam Hose had been lynched and they said that his knuckles were on exhibition at a grocery store on Mitchell Street. I turned back to the university. I suddenly saw that complete scientific detachment in the midst of such a South was impossible.[5]

Du Bois was, of course, correct. How could anyone be detached under these circumstances? The horror of Sam Hose's torture, burning, and dismemberment was already being transformed locally through a kind of grisly southern humor. Pig knuckles were commonly used to add taste to beans and soups. As one present-day correspondent familiar with the events of the Hose lynching has written, "Du Bois apparently never understood the baseness of Southern humor toward blacks and the humor's insight into the fabric of white thinking toward the other race. Butcher shops all around Atlanta and Newnan displayed pig knuckles in their windows under a sign labeling them as the knuckles of Sam Hose. It was a joke and an advertising gimmick. The shop owner would laugh, patrons would laugh, and Papa would laugh at the dinner table when he told his wife and children that the beans were flavored with the knuckles of Sam Hose."[6] As late as 1960, Du Bois, then in his nineties, believed that the charges against Hose were "trumped up," stating in an interview:

> They started then to find Sam Hose and they couldn't find him. And then, suddenly, there was the accusation that Sam Hose had raped [Cranford's] wife. Now, everybody that read the facts of the case knew perfectly well what had happened. The man wouldn't pay him, so they got into a fight, and the man got killed—and then, in order to arouse the neighborhood to find this man, they brought in the charge of rape. Even from the newspapers you could see there was no foundation for it.[7]

Ida Wells-Barnett also supported this version long after the publication of "Lynch Law in Georgia." As perhaps the leading antilynching activist in the country, she had written and spoken with incredible courage against the epidemic of violence that occurred year after year. She knew that charges of a black man's assault on a white woman practically guaranteed mutilation and death, but she also argued, with overwhelming evidence, that such charges were rarely true. Not surprisingly, she had accepted Louis Le Vin's report as further confirmation of what she had long believed. The articles culled from the Atlanta papers that accompanied his report proved to her the barbarism and hysteria of the South.

Wells-Barnett followed up her investigation of the Sam Hose lynching with an exposé of still another episode of racial violence caused, in part, by reaction to Hose's horrible death. In New Orleans, a black laborer named Robert Charles obsessed over the killing of Sam Hose. Charles was a follower of Bishop Henry Turner and worked in the city as subscription agent for Turner's magazine, *Voice of Missions*. According to William Ivy Hair, in his book *Carnival of Fury*, "Reading of the atrocity, knowing that no one would ever be prosecuted for what happened, Robert Charles went into a rage." He declared that "it was the duty of every negro to buy a rifle and keep it ready against the time they might be called

Chapter Nine

upon to act in unison."[8] On July 24, 1900, Charles was accosted by several New Orleans policemen, and in the argument that followed, he shot and killed two of them and wounded a third. Wounded himself, Charles escaped to his home on Saratoga Street and there held off a growing number of policemen and local citizens. By the time the siege was over the next day, Charles had shot twenty-seven whites, seven policemen among them. Four policemen died, as did two other "civilians." Charles was gunned down after his residence was set on fire and he was forced to abandon it. By all accounts he met his death with brave desperation, firing his rifle until he was out of shells. His corpse was then riddled with bullets and beaten and kicked by the crowd. The violence had by this time spilled over into other parts of the city, resulting in indiscriminate attacks on blacks, a number of whom were killed or injured by roving bands of whites.

Using the format employed in "Lynch Law in Georgia," in September 1900, Wells-Barnett produced an account of these events titled "Mob Rule in New Orleans." In her introduction, she made the connection between the Charles killing and the murders of the Palmetto victims, Sam Hose, Elijah Strickland, and unknown others the previous year.

> Immediately after the awful barbarism that disgraced the State of Georgia in April of last year, during which time more than a dozen colored people were put to death with unspeakable barbarity, I published a full report showing that Sam Hose, who was burned to death during that time, never committed a criminal assault, and that he killed his employer in self-defense.

Wells-Barnett made one major distinction between these acts of racial violence in New Orleans and Georgia. In New Orleans, the newspapers had deplored the responses of the city. "In their editorial comment they were at all times most urgent in their defense of law and in the strongest terms they condemned the infamous work of the mob." And unlike the people of Georgia, some in New Orleans had taken a stand against mob rule.

> It is no doubt owing to the determined stand for law and order taken by these great dailies and the courageous action taken by the best citizens of New Orleans, who rallied to the support of the civic authorities, that prevented a massacre of colored people awful to contemplate.[9]

One prominent white Georgian who, some time afterward, did speak publicly against the Hose lynching was Andrew Sledd. Originally from Virginia, Sledd taught at Emory College in Oxford, Georgia. His father-in-law was the Methodist bishop Warren Candler, brother to Judge John Candler, who had briefly led the militia in Palmetto after the shooting of the "firebugs."[10] According to the story that would become a major event in Sledd's biography, he was on a night train passing through Newnan when, as Sledd scholar Terry L. Matthews describes it, "the conductor stopped to allow passengers to view the lynching of Sam Hose."[11] What Sledd saw both angered and sickened him, and three years later he wrote an essay, "The Negro: Another View," published in the *Atlantic Monthly* in 1902.[12] Andrew Sledd was no radical in his concept of blacks. In the article, he recognized as a "fundamental" truth that "*the negro belongs to an inferior race*":

> And this not by reason of any previous condition of servitude or brutal repression on the part of his former master, whether in the days of slavery or since; not on account of his color or his past or present poverty, ignorance, and degradation. These, to be sure, must be reckoned with; but they do not touch the fundamental proposition.

Sledd further stated, "There can hardly be any need to defend this proposition in these days of the boasted universal supremacy of the Anglo-Saxons"; and, indeed, he found hope in the fact that such "ill-advised cant" suggesting that blacks could be the equal of whites had, in his mind, been put to rest.[13]

Nevertheless, Sledd argued as his second point that blacks had "*inalienable rights.*" If the North had foolishly pushed blacks forward as equal to whites, the South, "much more grievously," had "erred in precisely the opposite direction." He observed, "Our society has carried the idea of the negro's inferiority almost, if not quite, to the point of dehumanizing him." Nowhere was this better seen than in the South's "lynching habit."[14]

Sledd went on to use two examples as illustrations of this "wild and diabolic carnival of blood." One came from a personal experience in which he had taken a night train, presumably to Atlanta. A black man in the state had been accused of a murder, and the rumor grew that this man was being transported to jail on the very train Sledd was riding. Sledd observed that "at four stations in less than forty miles, as many mobs were gathered to mete out summary vengeance to the merely suspected black," who, fortunately, was not actually on the train.[15] Sledd's point was that none of these waiting men, anxious to enact their own law, could identify the accused, had proof of his guilt, or could claim any other justification for stopping and searching the train in hopes of finding and killing him. He then, as analogy, moved to the case of Sam Hose.

> The burning of Sam Hose took place on a Sabbath Day. One of our enterprising railroads ran two special trains to the scene. And two train-loads of men and boys, crowded from cow-catchers to the tops of the coaches, were found to go to see the indescribable and sickening torture and writhing of a fellow human being. And souvenirs of such scenes are sought—knee caps, and finger bones, and bloody ears. It is the purest savagery.[16]

In later years, these two episodes discussed by Sledd would be conflated. In fact, in this article, Sledd did not claim to have witnessed Sam Hose's burning. Indeed, the railroad line did not run close enough to Old Troutman Field for anyone on the train to have seen anything from the cars if the train had been stopped. Passengers would have had a long walk to reach the place of execution. We also know that Hose was not, as Matthews describes it, "strung up," and that his death occurred between two thirty and three o'clock in the afternoon, while Sledd rode on a "night train."

But whatever the actual impetus, "The Negro: Another View," calling as it did for fairness under the law regardless of race, resulted in a storm of criticism. Leading the attack against Sledd was Rebecca Latimer Felton. She had, not surprisingly, defended Sam Hose's lynching; indeed, she had helped spread the rumor that Hose was syphilitic and possibly insane from the disease.[17] Thus, Sledd's essay, despite its clear assumption of white racial superiority, was nonetheless an affront and a challenge, and Felton immediately set about having him dismissed from his position at Emory College.

On August 3, 1902, Felton published a letter headlined "The Negro, as Discussed by Mr. Andrew Sledd," in the *Atlanta Constitution*. In the letter, she professed ignorance of Sledd's identity (which Matthews shows to be a pretense on her part) yet states: "But if it should transpire that Mr. Sledd lives in the south, he should be politely compelled to make his assertions good or go to another part of the country—for his health's sake—as his room will certainly be better than his company." The "rot" that he had "vomited" onto the pages of the *Atlantic Monthly* was impossible for a true southerner to bear. She further suggested, "[Sledd] has some sort of phobia. He is afflicted in his mental or moral nature with a disease that it is hardly necessary to name in this connection." That disease would have been, in Felton's opinion, an unnatural affection for the black race.

Turning to Sledd's comments on Sam Hose, Felton grew even more indignant:

> This white man (I presume his color will pass, as he calls this "our" section [of the country]) has not a single word to say of the fiendish murder of a father and husband, of the outrage inflicted on the agonized wife and mother, who was blood covered beside the body of her dead husband, or of the little girls who witnessed the horrible sights, and his logic is only here applied to condemn the white men who put this beast to death!

Felton noted that she had recently "read a circular letter that [was] flooding negro homes" that repeated the conclusions of the Le Vin investigation. "That story is being told all over this union, when we know eye witnesses found that dead body where it was, struck down by the black beast in the dining room, and that poor woman herself told the story of the killing and what she suffered at the hands of the murderer." Sledd's essay would only encourage "the world outside" to "malign the suffering wife still further."[18]

For the next week Sledd came under increasing criticism. When asked to comment on Felton's attack, he told a reporter from the *Constitution*:

> Yes, I wrote the article and I have nothing to retract or explain concerning it. Those who have seen fit to criticize me have been careful to select passages which, when read without the context, make a very different impression from that conveyed by the article as a whole.
>
> I have spent my entire life in the south and the statements made in my article are from observations. I have certain opinions on this subject and I can see no reason why I did not have the right to set them down.[19]

Several black leaders commented on the essay. R. D. Stinson of Morris Brown College in Atlanta felt that Sledd had done harm to the cause of blacks. "If a man persistently tells you what your rights and privileges are according to his ideas and awakes in you all the emotions of your being to the high sense of what belongs to you, and does not tell you how to obtain it, and you cannot do it yourself, I do not see the real good that is accomplished." But Bishop Henry Turner felt that Sledd had "taken a new and novel position for a southern white man" and remarked, "[I hope] that God will raise up other southern men who will speak out along the same lines and who will be even more radical than [Sledd] appears to be."[20]

On the night of Tuesday, August 5, 1902, a crowd of "Bad Boys" in Covington, near where Sledd taught, made two straw dummies representing Sledd and a black man. They drove the two effigies around town, "set up in a wagon showing Professor Sledd with his arms around the negro," and then burned them in front of the courthouse. Although "older citizens" of the town condemned the students' actions, the next day several of them signed a resolution thanking Felton for her comments.[21] On August 8, Sledd resigned from Emory College. In another interview, he told a reporter, "No sane person can claim that I ask for equality with the whites for the negro. I do condemn lynching, but not punishment of crime." He added, "I only claim that the negro has certain fundamental rights, and these should be observed."[22] Sledd also noted that most of those who had condemned him had not read the article itself.

On August 11, the *Constitution* published Sledd's article in its entirety so that its readers could see what Sledd had actually written. It also editorialized on his contentions, arguing that blacks in the South were treated better than in other parts of the country. "It might be said with truth that there [are] not many among them who [have] not felt the touch of a white man's helping hand."

Chapter Nine

While there had been "abuses," most of these "had been the acts of individuals" and did not represent the white race as a whole. Sledd's apology and resignation were appreciated, but the paper felt that he had done great damage in his overall assertions.[23]

One other white Southerner whose life was changed by Sam Hose was Thomas Dixon Jr., the North Carolina minister, playwright, and author. In 1902, the same year the "Sledd affair" took place, Dixon published his novel *The Leopard's Spots*. That novel and his next, *The Clansman* (1905), both as a book and in its later incarnation as a stage play, provided the plot for D. W. Griffith's groundbreaking film *The Birth of a Nation* (1915), for which Dixon received screenplay credit.[24] In his "Historical Note" to *The Leopard's Spots*, Dixon wrote, "The only liberty I have taken with history is to tone down the facts to make them credible in fiction. . . . I tried to write this book with the utmost restraint."[25] A good guess is that Dixon took the title of his novel not only from the original biblical source, Jeremiah 13:23, but from J. M. Early's account of the burning of Henry Smith, *An Eye for an Eye*, in which Early had quoted the verse with a caveat: "'Can the leopard change his spots, or the Ethiopian his skin?' I quote from hearsay; I have not time to look it up."[26] Dixon's "Romance of the White Man's Burden" used the same verse, corrected, as an epigraph: "Can the Ethiopian change his skin or the leopard his spots?" and in this novel he explored further "what virtue there is in fire."

In the third section of *The Leopard's Spots*, titled "The Trial by Fire," Dixon fictionalizes the story of little Myrtle Vance. In the chapter "The Unspoken Terror," little Flora Camp has been warned by her father, Tom, a crippled Confederate veteran, "Run away every time you seed a nigger, unless I was with you! . . . don't you dare go nigh er nigger, or let one get nigh you, no more'n you would a rattlesnake!"[27] Two days later the child is abducted, and a search begins. Dixon's hero, Charlie Gaston, "cool and masterful," organizes the crowd of some one thousand "white people":

> In a moment the white race had fused into a homogeneous mass of love, sympathy, hate and revenge. The rich and the poor, the learned and the ignorant, the banker and the blacksmith, the great and the small, they were all one now. The sorrow of that old one-legged soldier was the sorrow of all; every heart beat with his, and his life was their life, and his child their child.[28]

When Flora's body is found, "her clothes torn to shreds and stained with blood," it is "too plain, the terrible crime that had been committed."[29] In the next chapter, "A Thousand-Legged Beast," a mob has captured Dick, Gaston's black childhood friend, and debates the need for a "fair trial." "Look at the black devil's clothes splotched all over with her blood. . . . Fair trial—hell! We're just waitin' for er can o' oil. You go back and read your law books—we'll tend ter this devil!" they tell Gaston. The mob carries Dick to the place of Flora's assault. "They tied the screaming, praying Negro to a live pine and piled around his body a great heap of dead wood and saturated it with oil. And then they poured oil on his clothes." Gaston argues against death by fire: "Don't disgrace our town, our county, our state and our claims to humanity by this insane brutality. A beast wouldn't do this. You wouldn't kill a mad dog or a rattlesnake in such a way. If you will kill him, shoot him or knock him in the head with a rock—don't burn him alive!" But the mob will not listen, and Dick is set ablaze. "All they would grant [Gaston] was the privilege of gathering Dick's ashes and charred bones for burial." The next morning, a preacher finds Tom Camp, now "a hopeless madman," next to his daughter's grave, from which he has dug out her coffin. He has with him a box of her toys and "a lot of her clothes, a pair of little shoes and stockings, and a bonnet."[30]

This fictional lynching draws on the public executions of both Henry Smith and Sam Hose. Dick's crime is similar to that attributed to Smith, and Dixon's contention that members of the mob "were all one now" and that the old soldier's life "was their life, and his child their child" seems inspired by Early's insistence that his readers should put themselves in the place of Myrtle Vance's parents, should imagine the horror as if the little girl were their own infant daughter. Moreover, the blood on Dick's clothes cites the bloodstained underwear reportedly worn by Henry Smith when captured, and the description of Tom Camp at his daughter's grave recalls the discovery of Myrtle Vance's body, including the stockings and shoes neatly placed nearby.[31] But Dick's death is clearly modeled on Sam Hose's burning. He, like Hose, is bound to a pine tree, wood stacked around his feet and oil poured over his body. Moreover, the figure leading this mob, the man who strikes the match and starts the fire, is identified as a countryman named "Hose Norman." The odd connection by name that Dixon makes between Hose Norman and Sam Hose, in addition to the details of Dick's immolation, show Dixon using Sam Hose for his own literary purposes. As Sandra Gunning has noted, by having Charlie Gaston, like Governor Atkinson, argue against Dick's burning but then rendering him incapable of stopping it—the crowd seizes him, even threatens to knock in *his* head with a rock—Dixon both condemns the act and promotes it and thus implicitly condones the ultimate outcome.[32]

The story of Sam Hose may have influenced other prominent southern writers as well. Margaret Mitchell grew up reading and admiring the novels of Thomas Dixon. In "How Black Was Rhett Butler?" historian Joel Williamson provocatively proposes that Mitchell, who was born in 1900, shortly after Hose's lynching, and who distinctly remembered the Atlanta race riots of 1906, explored the idea of interracial sex between a white woman of a former prominent plantation family and a "mulatto" man in her unfinished and eventually destroyed manuscript "'Ropa Carmagin." Drawing on biography, memory, and pure literary speculation, Williamson suggests that the generally prevalent "Black Beast" rape myth and the specific example of Sam Hose's supposed rape of Mattie Cranford might have inspired Mitchell in this work, at the end of which the "dark lover" is killed and Europa Carmagin is forced by the community to leave her home in shame. Mitchell "liked the story she had written," Williamson observes. "She thought it rich and accurate in historical detail, and, especially, she relished the idea that the theme of 'miscegenation' would raise the story from 'romance' to 'literature.'"[33] Williamson then proposes that Mitchell's later creation Rhett Butler, described in *Gone with the Wind* as "exceedingly dark," can be read as a "hipster-trickster" in the tradition of the "floating black man . . . the Negro loose, the Negro in the woods," in other words, the new generation of black men exemplified in part by scary Sam Hose.[34] One of the most famous scenes in *Gone with the Wind* is Rhett's seduction-rape of Scarlett, after which Butler might easily have repeated the triumphantly villainous boast attributed to Sam Hose: "I have done now what I have always wanted to do."[35]

Although there is clearly quite a distance between Sam Hose and Rhett Butler, Williamson's playful and subversive reading does illuminate that dark suspicion that could not be hidden even as Mattie Cranford lay secluded in her parents' Newnan home and Sam Hose's life was spinning out its last days, the outrageous but intriguing thought that she just might have conspired with the black worker, that the sex was agreeable, the murder plotted. Those voices that dared suggest as much had been quickly silenced, either by the whip or by a form of mass community shaming, but the thought remained, whispered perhaps, waiting for transformation into a more acceptable narrative. If Williamson is correct, if Sam Hose and Mattie Cranford serve as sources twice removed for Rhett Butler and Scarlett O'Hara, if the awful rape is a palimpsest for one of the most famous sex scenes in southern literature and film, then the trickster Sam Hose might well claim, as he is credited with saying, "Now I am through with my work, let them kill me if they can."[36]

Although there is no direct evidence that either William Faulkner or Erskine Caldwell consciously used the Sam Hose story in their fiction, both writers explored the concept of spectacle lynching.[37] In his short story "Dry September," Faulkner examines the psychological basis of mob violence but keeps the actual killing of the black farmer Will Mayes, accused of raping the white spinster Miss Minnie Cooper, "off-screen." However, in both *Sanctuary* and *Light in August*, he includes scenes of horrific intensity. In *Sanctuary*, a white man, Lee Goodwin, is accused of assaulting the coed Temple Drake (with the infamous corncob) and of killing the "feeb" Tommy. The district attorney reminds the jury that Goodwin has defiled "that most sacred thing in life: womanhood" and that "this is no longer a matter for the hangman, but for a bonfire of gasoline." That night, the townspeople of Jefferson, Mississippi, take Goodwin from the jail and both impale and burn him "in the center of a vacant lot where on market day wagons were tethered." A member of the mob is also set ablaze when the fuel can he is using to start the fire explodes. Goodwin's lawyer, Horace Benbow, runs into the crowd gathered around the flames and observes that "from the central mass of fire there came no sound at all. It was now indistinguishable from a white-hot mass out of which there defined themselves faintly the ends of a few posts and planks."[38] Like Charlie Gaston, Benbow is also threatened with death because of his attempts to defend the victim. At the end of *Light in August*, Joe Christmas, who may or may not be mulatto and whose tumultuous sexual entanglement with Joanna Burden exceeds the most feverish and fervid speculations of the white community, is shot and castrated by Percy Grimm. Faulkner then employs one of his most spectacular and audacious images as he describes the "black blood" pulsing from Christmas's mutilated loins:

> It seemed to rush out of his pale body like the rush of sparks from a rising rocket; upon that black blast the man seemed to rise soaring into their memories forever and ever. They are not to lose it, in whatever peaceful valleys, beside whatever placid and reassuring streams of old age, in the mirroring faces of whatever children they will contemplate old disasters and new hopes. It will be there, musing, quiet, steadfast, not fading and not particularly threatful, but of itself alone serene, of itself alone triumphant.[39]

This magnificent scene recalls Royal Daniel's attempts to pen an appropriate conclusion to Sam Hose's burning by describing the red sky, the drifting clouds, the "sparks danc[ing] upward to the sky, fanned by the artificial breeze of the flames. The sparks were as a myriad stars jetting, bursting and falling through space."[40] In Daniel's description, farmers and their wives stand around the still-burning pyre, watching and (as Faulkner suggests) committing to memory events that will pass down to their children and future generations.

Erskine Caldwell, a Georgian who, having lived for a time in the region, was more likely to know the details of the Palmetto-Newnan lynchings, never achieved Faulkner's poetry, but in several stories and a novel he thoughtfully examined the psychology of mob violence. In "Kneel to the Rising Sun," perhaps his best short work of fiction, Caldwell illustrates how good men can be cowed into participating in awful deeds. Although the poor white sharecropper Lonnie is a friend to the black farmer Clem Henry, he betrays him to the mob seeking Clem's death. Surrounding the tree in which Henry has taken refuge, the lynch mob fire their rifles and shotguns until the wounded man falls, "crashing

Chapter Nine

through the lower limbs to the ground. The body, sprawling and torn, landed on the ground with a thud that stopped Lonnie's heart for a moment." Although Henry is now dead, the men again fire round after round into his corpse, which is "tossed" like a "sackful of kittens . . . as charges of lead were fired into it from all sides."[41] Caldwell presents the awful moment in a ritualistic manner so that Clem Henry is brought to earth like a sacrifice demanded by the community.

In "Saturday Afternoon," Caldwell spends much of the story creating a broadly comic portrait of a butcher, Tom Denny, who is too lazy to brush flies off his meat or his own face. When he hears that the "gingerbread Negro" Will Maxie, a respectable farmer, is going to be lynched, he closes his shop and rides with other townspeople to the place where the killing is set to occur. A boy has set up a stand to sell Coca-Colas to the crowd that has gathered to watch, and as Caldwell ironically notes, he does "a good business" although the crowd is small: "There had not been enough time for the word to get passed around." The men bind Maxie to a tree with "a trace chain around his neck and another around his knees." Then they drench him in gasoline and set him afire. "Will Maxie was going up in smoke. When he was just about gone they gave him the lead. . . . They filled him so full of lead that his body sagged from his neck where the trace chain held him up." Once Maxie is dead, Tom Denny returns to town, opens up his store, and prepares to sell his rancid and fly-specked meat to customers for their Sunday meals. Caldwell's brilliance in this story is found in his refusing to distinguish between the butchering of a cow and the murder of a man, and the underlying motif of meat, whether it be for burning or for eating, makes the story a shocking masterpiece.[42]

In his 1940 novel, *Trouble in July*, Caldwell presents his most thorough analysis of communal lynching. He carefully explores all facets of southern society, ranging from the fat sheriff Jeff McCurtain, who sleeps with his black female prisoners and goes fishing when trouble arises; to the self-serving, racist judge Ben Allen, a sick, sadistic old man who condones the extralegal lynching; to Mrs. Narcissa Calhoun, a fictionalized version of Rebecca Latimer Felton, who assumes all black men want to rape white women and spreads the story that results in the killing of the young black man Sonny Clark; to Shep Barlow, the vicious, poor white father of the supposed rape victim Katy and leader of the mob. Caldwell intentionally employs stereotypes but still shocks his readers when the lynching finally occurs. In this novel, everyone plays a predetermined role, even the victim, who passively accepts his own death as his appointed fate. Moreover, Caldwell then has the crowd turn on the girl, whose "assault" set the mob into motion, and stone her to death when she changes her story and protests that Sonny was innocent. Earlier men in the crowd have regaled each other with salacious tales about Katy, reveling in her sexual shame. Whether Caldwell had

Mattie Cranford or Sam Hose in mind is impossible to say, but in broad outline *Trouble in July* follows the lynching narrative established in part by the Sam Hose killing.[43]

Although both Faulkner and Caldwell very likely drew on generic descriptions of mob violence rather than specific details about Sam Hose's death, Michael Harper's poem "Dear John, Dear Coltrane," written in 1966, makes the connection implicitly. It starts with the jazz artist John Coltrane's "himself singing" the first lines of the poem:

> Sex fingers toes
> in the marketplace
> near your father's church
> in Hamlet, North Carolina—
> witness to this love
> in this calm fallow
> of these minds;
> there is no substitute for pain:
> genitals gone or going,
> seed burned out,
> you tuck the roots in the earth,
> turn back, and move
> by river through the swamps,
> singing, a love supreme, a love supreme;
> what does it all mean?

In the poem, Harper blends elements of both men's lives—and deaths. "The first three words in the poem are the fingers and toes of Sam Hose, who was lynched and dismembered. Sam Hose is a very important person," Harper has said. By anachronistically bringing Sam Hose to Hamlet, North Carolina, Coltrane's birthplace, and by having both Sam Hose and John Coltrane sing/play Coltrane's signature piece, "A Love Supreme," while both are dying, Harper establishes Hose/Coltrane as a model for black martyrdom, as inspirations for black striving, as a vehicle for black transcendence:

> Dawn comes and you cook
> up the thick sin 'tween
> impotence and death, fuel
> the tenor sax cannibal
> heart, genitals and sweat
> that makes you clean—
> *a love supreme, a love supreme—*

Hose/Coltrane play through their own dismemberment and immolation on the nightclub stage for the white audience, cooked by drugs as well as fire. They give their body to the crowd for consumption. As their flesh goes down to death, their beauty rises up to "*a love supreme.*"[44] Here, at last, Sam Hose, who is said to have stuttered, who barely spoke before and during his execution, who may have had his tongue cut out, finally finds his voice, sings his death song through Coltrane's tenor sax. The demon-beast of the doggerel poem "Sam Holt" is transformed through Harper's and Coltrane's art into sainthood.

Chapter Ten

Across the Road from the Barbecue House

In all of the United States, I can find only one town called Newnan. Named after Gen. Daniel Newnan (1780–1851), who led volunteers during the Creek Indian War, it was established in 1828 as the county seat of Coweta County, which had been formed two years earlier. Newnan today is known as "The City of Homes" for the antebellum and late-nineteenth-century residences that still line the southern half of its main street. The downtown square, the four one-way roads enclosing at its center a stately courthouse topped by a grand cupola, is a mixture of old and new, but the overall feeling is still that of the small town, a comfortable and pleasant place that has largely resisted change.[1] The courthouse itself is not the one Sam Hose would have seen, the one built in 1828. It was torn down in 1903 by order of the county commissioners, although a bond issue to finance the new construction had been defeated. The commissioners simply imposed a new tax and began demolishing the old building without making their intentions known to the public. By the time anyone could formally or legally object, it was too late. Little Clifford Cranford, blind in one eye, carried water for the construction crew that worked on the new building.[2]

What Sam Hose would recognize is the Confederate War Memorial, erected in 1885. In Hose's time, it stood twenty-two feet high in the middle of Court Square, and the procession that marched him through and around the town passed under the silent view of the stone soldier atop the pedestal, its various inscriptions honoring "Our Confederate Dead / Whom Power Could Not Corrupt / Whom Death Could Not Terrify / Whom Defeat Could Not Dishonor." This memorial has now been moved closer to the new courthouse, where it still keeps watch over the town.

Newnan and Coweta County, however, also reflect change, located as they are within the urban pull of metropolitan Atlanta

184

some forty miles away. While a sign at the southern edge of the city limits invites you to join the Sons of Confederate Veterans, the northern half of the town has slowly bestirred itself in the direction of Hartsfield-Jackson Airport and the clogged freeways and professional sports arenas of the big city, taking on a new complexion as it does. There you find a more modern Newnan, an upscale residential world, still identifiably southern but reflecting the new New South metamorphosis rolling down Highway 29. This part of Newnan is known as Platinum Point, and there you will find what was once the Old Troutman Field. What is left of it is a wooded lot in the shape of a V formed by the convergence of Roscoe Road and Jackson Street and framed by a white wooden fence that, without signs, discourages trespassing. This anonymous place is easily missed. When you ask directions, Newnanites who know give as your landmark the restaurant called Sprayberry's, family owned and operated since 1926 and probably the most popular barbecue house in this part of west Georgia.

After Sam Hose's public burning, the *Newnan Herald and Advertiser* wryly noted, "We want it understood that Newnan's reputation as a barbecue town is not intended to include such functions as that which occurred on Sunday afternoon last. That affair was a rank departure from the orthodox variety made famous in the past by Harry Fisher and Jack Driskill."[3] It is, therefore, somewhat disconcerting that, as you stand in the Sprayberry parking lot, looking across the road at the wooded lot beyond the white fence, the smell of smoked pork, beef, and chicken permeates the air. On the afternoon of April 23, 1899, this lot was filled with onlookers, craning their necks for a better view of the burning man, but today people are here only to eat.

For a long time, Sam Hose was lost to history, as were so many victims of lynching. This shameful period became an embarrassment, and several generations of Americans developed collective amnesia. Although writers like Walter White (*Rope and Faggot: A Biography of Judge Lynch* [1929]) and Arthur F. Raper (*The Tragedy of Lynching* [1933]) wrote books on the phenomenon, the new era of lynching studies began only in the late 1970s and early 1980s with works such as Jacquelyn Dowd Hall's *Revolt against Chivalry: Jessie Daniel Ames and the Women's Campaign against Lynching* (1979), Joel Williamson's *Crucible of Race: Black/White Relations in the American South since Emancipation* (1984), and Trudier Harris's *Exorcising Blackness: Historical and Literary Lynching and Burning Rituals* (1984). More recently, however, the burning of Sam Hose has slowly taken center stage as a primary example of lynching at its worst, and in the process, what Professor Willcox labeled the "negro version" has gained acceptance over the white narrative that explained and attempted to excuse the event. In his own way, Sam Hose has come to represent spectacle lynching in the same way

Emmett Till represents the outrages that fueled the civil rights movement of the 1950s and 1960s. The columnist Leonard Pitts Jr., for example, in decrying the growing cultural acceptance of the word "nigger" among rap artists, filmmakers, and others, observes, "We're talking about the word that was spat out at Sam Hose in 1899 as his face was skinned and his genitals removed by a white mob."[4]

Nevertheless, as revisionist historians have retold and reinterpreted the lynching over the past decade, errors have been introduced and then established as truths in subsequent iterations. W. Fitzhugh Brundage, for example, in his 1993 study *Lynching in the New South: Georgia and Virginia, 1880–1930*, repeated the Le Vin/Wells-Barnett portrait, arguing: "The transformation of Sam Hose, a Georgian who killed his employer in self-defense, from a hard-working tenant to an embodiment of a 'black beast rapist' exposes the power that stereotypical portraits of black criminals had over southern whites. Hose, or at least the portrait whites created of him, became an embodiment of all the southern blacks' alleged failings."[5] Leon Litwack went farther in his 1998 book *Trouble in Mind: Black Southerners in the Age of Jim Crow*, declaring:

> In a subsequent investigation, conducted by a white detective, Cranford's wife revealed that Hose had come to the house to pick up his wages and the two men had quarreled. When her husband went for his revolver, Hose, in self-defense, picked up and hurled the ax, which killed Cranford instantly. Hose then fled the scene. He never entered the house, she told the detective, nor did he assault her. Still another investigation, conducted by Ida B. Wells, a black journalist who had been driven from Memphis in 1892 for her "*incendiary*" editorials on lynching, reached the same conclusion. The results of neither investigation were of any apparent interest to the white press or presumably to the white public.[6]

Thus, both Brundage and Litwack, enormously important and influential historians, opted for the version most sympathetic to Hose without acknowledging the competing narrative, most likely because this was the argument associated with white racists and lynching apologists of the time. Litwack, whose section on Hose also appeared as an introduction to James Allen's *Without Sanctuary: Lynching Photography in America* (2000), went so far as to separate Le Vin's investigation from Wells-Barnett's, giving the impression that two different examinations of the case both came to the same conclusion. Neither historian mentioned the reports of George Hepworth, who interviewed Mattie Cranford (as Le Vin did not) and who accepted Hose's guilt for both murder and rape.

Christopher Waldrep, in his 2002 book, *The Many Faces of Judge Lynch: Extralegal Violence and Punishment in America*, states, "Atlanta newspapers so sensationalized the crime that it seems better to rely on the reports of a white detective named Reverdy C. Ransom hired by a black activist to inquire into the affair. Wells also researched the affair. Ransom and Wells both found that Hose had quarreled with his white employer, Alfred Cranford, killing him only when Cranford threatened to shoot him."[7] Waldrep, like Litwack, made two investigations out of one and further confused the issue by identifying Reverdy Ransom, the black Chicago minister who hired Le Vin, as the detective himself. Shawn Michelle Smith, in her 2004 study, *Photography on the Color Line: W. E. B. Du Bois, Race, and Visual Culture*, again recounts the story, arguing that Sam Hose, "whose real name was Samuel Wilkes" (113), was put to death by a white crowd that included "many of the most prominent citizens, such as E. D. Sharkey, superintendent of Atlanta Bagging Mills, John Hass, president of the Capitol Bank, W. A. Hemphill, president and business manager of the *Atlanta Constitution*, and Clark Howell, editor of the *Atlanta Constitution*," although she does not give a source for this information, which, with the exception of Sharkey's presence in the crowd, seems unlikely. She also states that "several white newspapers embellished the story of Hose's alleged acts with tales of his rape of Mrs. Cranford, and a placard left hanging on a tree near the place of his execution proclaimed: 'We Must Protect Our Southern Women,'" although this sign was pinned to the hanging corpse of Elijah Strickland.[8]

Grace Elizabeth Hale, in her important book *Making Whiteness* (1998), studies the original newspaper accounts but, in keeping with her thesis of "Deadly Amusements," emphasizes the entertainment aspect of the search for and execution of Sam Hose. She, correctly to my mind, points out the morbid sensationalism of the newspaper reporting, the need to "hook their audiences." As she notes, "The Hose murder . . . added a key innovation: local and regional newspapers took over the publicity, promotion, and sale of the event and began the development of a standardized, sensationalized narrative pattern that would dominate reporting of spectacle lynchings through the 1940s." But in making this case, she plays down any individual or community motives, however misguided, other than the basest desire for revenge, punishment, and carnival horrors. Thus, Mattie Cranford becomes simply "exciting copy": "Granting interviews with reporters from both the *Journal* and the *Constitution* [Hale also omits Hepworth's letters in the *New York Herald*], she demanded an active role in planning the lynching, expressing a desire to witness Hose's torture and death and her preference for a slow burning." Hale makes much of Mrs. Cranford's giving Hose Confederate money, "convincing him of its worth," as though she would take satisfaction in "easily outsmarting him" in the middle of such reported terror. The Mattie Cranford pictured in this account is shown as vengeful, manipulative, easily capable of making up a lie of murder and rape to seal the fate of her husband's killer.[9]

Not surprisingly, in this information age, such representations have made their way into popular culture. A recent "Sam Hose" entry in Wikipedia, subsequently updated and corrected, stated that Hose killed "Albert" Cranford and that "Cranford's wife accused Hose of raping her as her husband lay dying, but subsequently admitted to fabricating this claim."[10] "Our Georgia History" reports that, "As the story goes," Hose killed Cranford by accident. "By his own admission, Hose knew he had hit Cranford with the ax but did not know he had killed the man until several days later. Then came the charge of rape. Then a story came out that Mrs. Cranford claimed that her husband's assailant had raped her as her husband lay dying."[11] A Google search of "Sam Hose" brings forth essentially this same story line, no matter the source. The main exception to these constructions is Philip Dray's account in his study of lynching, *At the Hands of Persons Unknown*. Dray notes, "Counter to LeVin's [*sic*] conclusion, a strong argument for the possibility of some kind of sexual assault is the fact that the Cranfords and McElroys [*sic*] were prominent Coweta families and would not have wished to stigmatize Mattie unnecessarily; the accusation that Hose had murdered Alfred Cranford would have been sufficient motivation for any lynch mob."[12]

As we have seen, in her own time Mattie Cranford was portrayed by the white newspapers and her own family and community as shattered, ruined, bordering on madness, a woman lost in the desolation of her horror and grief. Although she, apparently willingly, sat for interviews and photographs, reporters, politicians, and others exploited her tragedy for their own purposes. Locally, the acts committed against her were considered so horrifying that well into the twentieth century the rape remained the unspoken part of the story. For example, in the 1970s, Palmetto historian Carole Harper interviewed the elderly Headden P. ("Bud") Holly, who as a young man had been told not to go into town on the night of the shooting in the warehouse. Holly was in his nineties when he recalled the Cranford murder for Harper, based on what he personally remembered and the stories heard from his father, who had once been mayor of Palmetto. Harper asked him specifically about Mrs. Cranford. "Mr. Bud, did Sam Hose rape Mattie Cranford?" "He could not say the word 'rape,'" Carole Harper recalled. "He could only nod his head. This was not something that he could talk about, even after all that time. He just nodded his head and said, 'Uh, huh.'"[13]

On the other hand, Grace Hale sees Mrs. Cranford, in the beginning, as "the voice of the crime that set the elaborate ritual in motion," as someone who had "claimed the power, possible through her sudden 'fame,' to shape the story." Certainly Mrs. Cranford's professed desire (related by others) to see Sam Hose put to death gives some credence to this reading, as does her willingness to give interviews, to confront her own humiliation publicly, to allow herself and her children to be used as pathetic figures to urge the mobs to greater heights of fury.

But Hale also notes how soon Mattie disappears from the story, "put . . . back on the pedestal" by those men who now carried the narrative forward. "In the end," Hale writes, "Hose was murdered in Newnan. And Mrs. Cranford's desire to see the lynching, for the spectacle to take place near her home in Palmetto, was ignored."[14]

In a sense, Sam Hose has in these recent accounts replaced Mattie Cranford as sympathetic victim. In order to rescue Hose from infamy, to project him as martyr, he must also be "put on a pedestal," and there does not seem to be room for two to share the same space. There is rarely any serious consideration that Hose might have killed Cranford for revenge over the Palmetto shootings or that his motives might have been as base as was represented at the time by apologists for the lynching, and it is easy to understand why. But this desire to redeem Hose from racist constructions comes at a price. Robyn Wiegman, among others, has drawn attention to the "imposition of feminization" on the black male in the lynching ritual, through physical castration (usually the severing of the entire male organ) but also through the "denial of the black male's newly articulated right to citizenship and, with it, the various privileges of patriarchal power that historically accompanied such signification within the public sphere."[15] In effect, Sam Hose has thus been "feminized" by recent history by denying him agency, especially if that agency complicates his image as martyr. Like Mattie Cranford, he has been denied his "voice," his capacity for action, as he is changed from active to passive participant in the drama of his death. While he could once be pictured as a revolutionary, an insurgent fighting against an oppressive and vicious system, today he all too often seems mostly a sad victim of very bad luck.

The scholar who most thoroughly investigated the events surrounding the Sam Hose killing is Mary Louise Ellis. Her 1992 dissertation, "'Rain Down Fire': The Lynching of Sam Hose," is a careful and balanced study of the Palmetto massacre; Hose's alleged crimes, capture, and death; and the hanging of Elijah Strickland. Of Hose's guilt or innocence, Ellis writes:

> It is certain that Alfred Cranford died violently, and it is probable that Hose killed him, as he admitted before he was himself killed. There is less certainty regarding the circumstances of Cranford's death. . . . The only evidence available is in the various newspaper accounts that are largely based on second-hand reports and interviews with people who were by no means objective. The journalistic standards and conventions of the period make such information even less reliable.[16]

Ellis, however, points to "two small details" that she feels are "worth noting." One is the testimony of Grippia Cranford, Alfred's father, who told the reporter Royal Daniel that his son's "blood and brains were scattered all over the dining room—even brain in the plate in which he was eating when the blow was struck." As Ellis summarizes:

> Grippia Cranford's story may have been contrived to disguise the facts, if, for example, the body was actually discovered outside, or if Cranford had managed to make his way into the house after an altercation outdoors. Yet there seems little point in making up a story. Hose "confessed" to the unpardonable crime of killing a white man, whether deliberately or in self-defense. The grisly murder story was, if not true, an unnecessary embellishment. It seems unlikely that Alfred's father would describe such a scene if he had not actually witnessed it.[17]

Her second point concerns the infant Sam Hose is said to have thrown to the floor and injured. This child, Clifford Alfred, blind in one eye, provided compelling evidence of the attack to the local community. As Ellis notes:

> The presence of the children and the fact that some injury was suffered by the baby, lends support to the story that the killing took place in the house, although it does not prove it. The baby might have been injured in some other way, yet it would seem unlikely that a false story would have included the children as witnesses.[18]

As for the accusation of rape, Ellis again is careful to weigh the evidence. She points out that Mattie Cranford never directly stated in print that she had been assaulted, although this was the immediate allegation and was included in the very first reports of the events, suggesting that she did say as much to Grippia Cranford when she appeared at his house to report her husband's death. Her brother-in-law, E. D. Sharkey, reiterated this charge after talking with her, and both Royal Daniel and Dr. Hepworth came away from their interviews with her convinced that the rape had occurred. As Ellis again summarizes:

> Neither she nor anyone in her family ever refuted the rape allegation. The charge was made almost at once after the attack, by an unidentified person, and was never withdrawn. It is certainly possible that it was untrue. Hose would not have been the first or the last black man lynched on a false charge of rape. But under the circumstances, why would such a charge be falsely made? Alfred Cranford's body was death warrant enough for Hose. The rape accusation was not needed to guarantee his punishment. Why would Mattie or her family suggest she had been raped if she wasn't, when rape by a black man was such a dreadful burden for a white woman to bear? Why would they allow others (such as the press) to make such a charge if untrue? Would her family have put a young mother and her children through such humiliation unnecessarily? While it would have been awkward, to say the least, to disavow the rape charge after Hose was killed, it could have been done during the ten days of his pursuit.[19]

Finally, Ellis notes that Louis Le Vin, who represented Hose as an innocent victim, did not interview any of the Cranfords, nor did he talk to the Hose/Wilkes family or to the Jones brothers, who knew and captured Hose. Le Vin did apparently talk to local white men involved in the lynchings—he identified some by name—as well as with "many colored people" whom he would not identify for their own safety. Yet it is Le Vin's account that is now the accepted and most often recounted official version of the events.

Such is not, however, the case in Newnan itself, where the "white" version has, until recently, quietly but defiantly maintained its prominence. In his introduction to the special issue of the *Journal of American History* devoted to memory in the construction of history, editor David Thelen notes, "Since the memory of past experiences is so profoundly intertwined with the basic identities of individuals, groups, and cultures, the study of memory exists in different forms along a spectrum of experience, from the personal, individual, and private to the collective, cultural, and public."[20] Marita Sturken, for example, distinguishes among personal, historical, and cultural recollections in her book *Tangled Memories: The Vietnam War, the AIDS Epidemic, and the Politics of Remembering*. Personal memory, she argues, is individual, short lived, and fragile, easily challenged. Historical memory is "a narrative that has in some way been sanctioned and valorized," while cultural memory is "memory shared in some form, yet not officially sanctioned memory."[21] As most recent theorists in the field of memory observe, while cultural (or collective) memory may not be factually accurate, it is usually driven by social, political, and identity needs. Historical memory is assumed to be "true" in a factual way that cultural memory is not, but cultural memory often exists simultaneously with the historical, each in its own sphere, either ignoring or unaware of the other or simply asserting itself as "truth." While historical memory carries the formal endorsement of the academy, communal memory maintains its own authority, passed down through family story or local lore or legend. As Thelen observes, "individuals, ethnic groups, political parties, and culture shape and reshape their identities—as known to themselves and to others."[22] However, equally important in this process is communal "forgetting," organized or otherwise. As Jonathan Markovitz observes, "Decisions about what and how to remember and forget are far from automatic and are instead always open to contest and based on struggles over meaning and power."[23]

In his effort to examine the relationship between memory and history, the French historian Pierre Nora coined the term *lieux de mémoire*, or "sites of memory," which he defines as a moment or "turning point" where "memory crystallizes and secretes itself." Nora writes:

Memory is life, borne by living societies founded in its name. It remains in permanent evolution, open to the dialectic of remembering and forgetting, unconscious of its successive deformations, vulnerable to manipulation and appropriation, susceptible to being long dormant and periodically revived. History, on the other hand, is the reconstruction, always problematic and incomplete, of what is no longer. Memory is a perpetually actual phenomenon, a bond tying us to the eternal present; history is a representation of the past. Memory, insofar as it is affective and magical, only accommodates those facts that suit it; it nourishes recollections that may be out of focus or telescopic, global or detached, particular or symbolic—responsive to each avenue of conveyance or phenomenal screen, to every censorship or projection. History, because it is an intellectual and secular production, calls for analysis and criticism. Memory installs remembrance within the sacred; history, always prosaic, releases it again.[24]

In his book *Shadowed Ground: America's Landscapes of Violence and Tragedy*, geographer Kenneth Foote examines numerous sites across the nation where violent acts or accidents have "inscribed" the place "with messages that speak to the way individuals, groups, and entire societies choose to interpret their past."[25] Foote suggests four categories for the way these sites are remembered or intentionally forgotten: sanctification, designation, rectification, and obliteration. Of these, the fourth is traditionally associated with scenes of lynching. "Obliteration results from particularly shameful events people would prefer to forget. . . . As a consequence, all evidence is destroyed or effaced," Foote writes.[26]

The people of Newnan set about cleaning up the physical evidence of Sam Hose's execution early on the day following his lynching and sought to bury the public memory soon thereafter, and there is at present no official acknowledgment of Sam Hose's lynching in the vicinity of Troutman Field or anywhere else in Newnan. Nevertheless, his death occupies a site of memory in the community in a way none of the other events examined in this book does. Not the Palmetto Massacre or the hanging of Elijah Strickland or the deaths of still other collateral victims during that convulsive period of violence have yet claimed a place in history or memory as has Sam Hose. Their stories have been omitted or relegated to secondary importance or carelessly blended into other narratives.

But Sam Hose still resonates. Although we have little idea who he really was—hard-working family man caught up in a racial imbroglio that quickly escalated into tragedy, shiftless hired killer with a history of rape, or black insurgent seeking revolutionary justice—over the years, he has been oddly absorbed by the community, entering that magical, sacred realm of memory Nora examines. There Sam Hose abides, often hidden and disguised as he apparently was during so much of his short life. As Palmetto historian Carole Harper puts it, "There are very few people my age who are interested in this. Newcomers to the region, when they hear about it, are blown away. But younger people like my children don't even know about it. There are still prominent families here whose ancestors may have been involved, and you don't want to hurt people's feelings or get them mad at you."[27]

Still, as we have seen, Sam Hose has nevertheless kept residence in these communities, sometimes physically. Judge John Herbert Cranford, great-grandson of Alfred and Mattie Cranford, remembers, as a child in the 1970s, sitting in a barber shop in Newnan one Saturday, the traditional time for boys to get their hair cut. A man talking with the barbers first asked if he was "one of those Cranfords," then came up to the boy to say, "I've got something you want to see. It's in a jar and I'll show it to you." John Herbert Cranford today remembers feeling sick at the suggestion. He refused and left the shop, horrified. "I guess parts of Sam Hose could still be around," he ruefully acknowledges.[28]

Others in Newnan tell similar stories. Robert Wood, who was for a time the only black member of the Coweta County Board of Commissioners, remembers the Newnan of his youth when you could openly identify members of the Ku Klux Klan. He worked for one as a child and was once warned by this man to stay off the street because the Klan would be holding a rally. "So in a way he was looking after me," Wood says. "We all knew, but we worked together, too." He recalls another white man, a "mean" one, who lived at the head of the road where Wood and other black families had their homes. As children they would walk by his house, and the man would sometimes shout at them and threaten: "I'll touch you with my nigger toe!" He carried it with him, and they knew it had come off Sam Hose's foot. "We would run then, I mean it," he says. "We were scared of that toe, lots more than we were scared of him."[29]

So, some forty years ago, at least, parts of Sam Hose's body could still be seen or held, relics preserved in jars or mummified to be carried in pockets and used as a token either of ultimate justice—the man in the barber shop assumed, mistakenly, that a Cranford would feel pride and satisfaction at seeing in this physical evidence that his family's tragedy had been righteously answered—or almost magical power. Perhaps this is true of the photographs as well. At this point of my research, none has come to light, but that doesn't mean they are not hidden away somewhere. As Amy Louise Wood has argued, the conventions of lynching photographs "reproduced and reinforced the ideological role of the lynch mob as determined and heroic" while depicting the black victims as "captive and defiled," and thus served as "visual embodiments of their ideal position in the white supremacist imagination."[30] It is hard to believe that they have all been lost or destroyed.

In a similar fashion, local understanding of the lynching stands at odds with the official historical narrative. As one resident says, "People here believe that

Sam Hose is far from innocent. I have *never* heard anything locally to suggest that Mrs. Cranford ever changed her story. Her descendants definitely believe she was raped by Sam Hose and that the incident ruined the rest of her life. I fear it may be political correctness in our day and time to make the powerful white people the villains."[31] The Cranford family's personal memory and beliefs are more distinct still. When I first began researching this event, Judge John Herbert Cranford told me, "We just don't talk about it [in the family]. It was a dark cloud. Our family did what families do when they experience tragedy. We closed together, and then we moved forward." Another Cranford descendant replied, when I asked if, while growing up, her friends knew of the family history, "Nobody has ever spoken to me about it, ever. And I'd rather you didn't write about it either."

Still, the family has tried to keep up with the way their story has been framed in historical accounts. "So many who write about this tell it as if they knew," John Herbert Cranford says. "There are things that can never be known, but there is still a need for fairness."[32]

There are no known descendants of Sam Hose living in Newnan, but the Cranfords are prominent citizens of the town, a judge and a doctor among them. What is left of Troutman Field is owned by in-laws of one branch of the family, and their imposing brick home sits off to one side of the lot. As a 2007 article in the *Newnan Times-Herald* recalled, "The site where the lynching occurred . . . was vacant for years, and some local residents were astonished when a home was built on the tract—although at some distance from the site of Hose's death."[33] Today this section is still covered by trees and brush. The house at Cranford Mill, the one to which Mattie Cranford never returned, was sold by the family soon after the murder. It stood until the late 1970s, when it burned. The land is now the site of Northgate High School, but although the house is gone, the family cemetery is still there, separated from the surrounding school lot by a locked chain-link fence. Inside are the graves of Alfred Cranford, his father, his murdered uncle, and other relatives. The tombstone placed on Alfred Cranford's grave incorrectly gives his date of death as April 12, 1898, rather than 1899, perhaps reflecting the confusion and anxiety his survivors continued to suffer after his violent passing. At the entrance to this site is a monument placed there by Judge John Herbert Cranford that reads:

> Here Lies Alfred Cranford Who Moved to Coweta County From Cosbie England in 1830. He and His Family Farmed This Very Land and the Old Home Place Sat Approximately Where the School Is Now. His Son, Grippia Elzman Cranford (1838–1909), and His Grandson Alfred L. Cranford (1871–1899) Are Buried in This Same Spot. They Were God Fearing Men. May They Rest in Peace.

There is no mention of Alfred's violent passing.

Mattie Cranford and most of the children are buried in Oak Hill Cemetery in Newnan, further separation from her husband and the place where his death occurred. According to Mary Louise Ellis, Mrs. Cranford and her children at first lived with her husband's parents and then moved back to Newnan, where she lived out the rest of her life. "She never smiled again," her descendants told Ellis.[34]

When Northgate High School, built on the site of the Cranford home, first opened, faculty and students commented on an odd thing. Sometimes in the morning there was the smell of cooking meat, often identified as bacon, wafting through the halls, although there was no source for the odor. Very few who smelled it knew that a terrible death had occurred at this place, and that an even more horrendous death had played out miles away in Troutman Field, but somehow those two violent acts had become conflated in the collective memory of the community. In this fashion, Sam Hose's death had been unconsciously turned into the kind of eerie and anonymous ghost story that the correspondent "Ripples" chuckled about so soon after the lynching. What had remained unspoken, out of shame or guilt or a sense of respect for the descendants of some of those involved, had found other ways to manifest itself. Perhaps it had been forced into Nora's "magical" realm, insisting on its presence through whatever fashion it might.

In 2007, this collective silence came to an end. In February, Richard Rusk, secretary of the Moore's Ford Memorial Committee and a member of the Southern Truth and Reconciliation organization, made contact with a local Newnan group of interracial citizens called Come to the Table (CTTT), which had been formed to bring about greater understanding between the races in Newnan and the surrounding area. The Moore's Ford Memorial Committee had been established ten years earlier to document the lynching deaths in 1946 of two black couples at the Moore's Ford Bridge near Monroe, Georgia, making it one of the few lynching sites to be thus "designated," in Foote's terminology, as a place worthy of official commemoration. As its Web site explained, "The Moore's Ford Memorial Committee is committed to telling the story, honoring the dead, promoting healing and social justice, and creating a living memorial to the victims of this horrible crime."[35] Southern Truth and Reconciliation had been formed in 2003, partly inspired by the Without Sanctuary: Lynching Photography in America exhibit at the Martin Luther King Jr. National Historic site in Atlanta, which had been cosponsored by Emory University. Modeled on Archbishop Desmond Tutu's South African Truth and Reconciliation Commission, this organization has as its mission to "advocate for, and educate communities about, a menu of programs and processes that may contribute to restorative justice and community building." As it further explained, "the trauma that communities and individuals suffer under such circumstances [of racial intolerance and violence] is extremely debilitating, and it resurfaces in future generations if it is not acknowledged and given sufficient attention. S.T.A.R. is about helping communities to 'dig up the past,' but with the intention of helping these communities journey through conflict as a means to becoming more inclusive, whole, and functional." S.T.A.R. was established to aid communities with a history of racial violence to "adapt the truth and reconciliation process to local needs, on the premise that truth-telling and acknowledgement by all stakeholders must precede healing, reconciliation, and justice for the entire community." The four cases or "Issues of Interest" that S.T.A.R. took on as its first objectives were the Sam Hose lynching, the 1906 Atlanta race riots, the Leo Frank lynching in 1915, and the Moore's Ford lynching.[36]

When Rich Rusk first learned of local interest in exploring further the Sam Hose lynching, he contacted the *Newnan Times-Herald* asking that a notice be run in the paper informing its readers of this intention. "I expected that they would run it inside the paper," Rusk later said, "on the fifth or sixth page. Instead, it was a front-page article. When I expressed my surprise, they told me that anything to do with Sam Hose was a front-page story."[37] Under the headline "Memorial to Recall Lynching," the February 6, 2007, article stated, "A group that brought together people of different racial backgrounds by remembering a racially motivated killing in eastern Georgia is helping with plans for a memorial service for Sam Hose, who was lynched in Newnan in 1899." Rusk was quoted as saying, "We hope something good will come after so many years by paying our respects to Sam Hose."[38]

These were, of course, unintentionally inciting words, and the *Times-Herald* article generated a flurry of responses, most of them negative. In the article, the reporter, W. Winston Skinner, had briefly recounted the events that led to Sam Hose's execution. "On April 12, 1899, Hose hit his employer in the head with an axe, killing him," Skinner explained. "He then raped the landowner's wife and injured their infant child." Rusk was concerned that the article failed to acknowledge that Hose might have been innocent or a victim of circumstances, but when he spoke to Skinner about the way the crime had been presented, Skinner told him that, in Newnan, Hose was considered guilty and that, as the hometown paper, the *Times-Herald* would stand by that understanding, in part out of respect for the Cranford descendants who still lived there.[39] Most of the paper's readers who responded to the article were appalled or outraged. "Memorial shameful," one letter stated. "I am amazed there are plans to have a memorial service to show respect and honor for Sam Hose, the man who murdered and raped in our county many years ago. . . . The group proposing to hold this memorial service should truly be ashamed."[40] Another woman wrote, "A man who is an axe murderer and rapist, and whose crimes were described as some of the most violent, needs to be lynched, I don't care the race, sex, orientation, etc. etc." Using arguments similar to those expressed at the time of the lynching, this writer continued, "In fact, maybe if the judicial system actually carried out punishment for crimes committed there might be one person who thinks twice about the crimes instead of looking forward to a cushy life in prison with three squares, cable TV, exercise equipment, libraries and steaks." "Why does this group not seek to honor someone who was just a good, decent person instead of someone who so obviously got what he deserved?" the reader concluded.[41] Yet another respondent, while acknowledging that "Sam Hose was due fair treatment in the American legal system," nonetheless maintained, "Lack of fair legal system treatment . . . is in no way an obligation to 'pay our respects to Sam Hose.' If we start paying our respects to murderers and rapists, then we need to do so for the late Jeffrey Dahmer, Ted Bundy, and John Wayne Gacy."[42]

It is likely that most of those who objected to the proposal to "honor" Sam Hose knew little more about the accused's crimes and his death than was reported in the article. One reader tried to address the issue from a different perspective. "Those folks complaining about the proposed memorial for lynching victim Sam Hose are missing the point," he wrote. "Regardless of whether or not Hose was guilty, his lynching was a horrible crime that was apparently committed with the approval of a large part of the community back in 1899." He felt the Moore's Ford Memorial Committee should be "commended" for its actions, agreeing that "to ignore the past or to sweep it under the rug is what keeps people from getting together in amity and harmony. . . . The bottom line is that addressing an old wrong is the right thing to do."[43]

In an effort to provide a more comprehensive account of the Sam Hose story, the *Times-Herald* next set up a Web site on which it posted a series of articles from the old *Newnan Herald and Advertiser* describing the Cranford murder and rape, the search, and the lynching.[44] The paper also posted a statement from Judge John Herbert Cranford and another from Richard Rusk. Judge Cranford began his comments by noting that the family had never spoken publicly on what they considered to be private matters. "Although generations of my family were affected by the events of April 12, 1899, they did not view themselves as victims or seek attention or publicity in this regard. They allowed the past to be just that and moved on with their lives as best as they could." He furthermore deplored the lynching itself, but noted that most present-day accounts gave little attention to the crimes that precipitated the lynching:

Unfortunately, most who have written on this issue seem to believe that the barbarous acts of a lynch mob seem more atrocious when it can first be established that the individual was innocent of any criminal behavior whatsoever. This action seems somewhat misguided in that the inhumanity and incivility in the acts of a lynch mob remain the same, irregardless of the actual innocence or guilt of the accused. In this quest, it seems that many are willing to accept innuendo, hearsay, intuition and speculation as proof of the innocence of the accused. Their approach usually takes the form of attacking and discrediting the victims of the alleged crime. This rationale seems to me to be far too close to the behavior (i.e. relying on innuendo, speculation, etc.) that we abhor in a lynch mob.

Judge Cranford then took issue with the source of much of what he considered misinformation about his ancestors. He studied the statements of both W. E. B. Du Bois and Louis Le Vin, the Chicago investigator. He noted that Le Vin was the first to assert that Hose had acted in self-defense, and that "numerous books, articles, and papers" now accepted that assertion as fact. "Some even state that Mattie Cranford recanted on her claim of rape. It is with these intuitors and suppositioners that I take issue."

Although Cranford agreed that the complete facts of April 12 could never be known, he defended Mattie Cranford's account: "Based on everything that I was told my entire life, Mattie never changed her version of the events in any manner whatsoever. The story she told family members was consistent with accounts in the papers. She lived a quiet, rather reclusive, life doing the best she could to raise four children as a single parent. I am not certain of the origins of the recanting story; however, I am certain that they have no basis in fact." He concluded by admitting his "partiality on this issue. This is the very reason that relatives are not allowed to sit on juries." He concluded, "This matter should remain what it is, old history. Our family has moved on from this tragedy and I hope others will do so as well."[45]

Rusk's statement took the form of a letter to the editor of the *Times-Herald* in which he acknowledged that he had been unaware of the local conviction of Sam Hose's guilt when he first proposed a memorial to him. "One of the more unfortunate aspects of lynching in Georgia and elsewhere is that many of those killed were innocent of any crime. Hose may indeed be one of the exceptions." Still, he offered, "On several issues many of us can agree. One—whether innocent or guilty, no man deserved to die like Sam Hose. Number two—little lasting good will be achieved if any effort to revisit this horrific event in Newnan is cooked up primarily by 'outsiders.'" Rusk's revised proposal was to hold a public forum rather than an observance to discuss these long-buried sentiments. "Do wounds like Hose's killing really heal by leaving them alone? Or if unaddressed, do they just fester away?" he asked.[46]

On Sunday, March 18, 2007, W. Winston Skinner published a long front-page article titled "Lynching a Tragedy with No Winners." In it he gave a thorough account of the events, including the hanging of Elijah Strickland, although omitting the earlier Palmetto shootings. "The Sam Hose lynching is little known to most Cowetans today," he noted. "There are no markers to tell where any of the events connected with it occurred, and many longtime residents have never heard of the events that unfolded in 1899." Following on Judge Cranford's charges against the investigative work of Louis Le Vin, Skinner observed that Le Vin failed to name "a single person to whom [he] spoke" and that he "repeatedly refers to the town as 'Newman,' raising the question of whether he ever came to Coweta County at all."[47]

In March, Rich Rusk drove from Bishop, Georgia, to Newnan and attended that month's meeting of Come to the Table to discuss the next step. As he had admitted in his letter to the paper, Rusk was discovering that local white animosity toward Sam Hose still ran deep; nevertheless, he was convinced that, as with the Moore's Ford lynchings, something positive could come from facing the truth of the town's history, as best as it could be known. Clearly, many present-day Cowetans had only a sketchy knowledge of the affair, but they were ready to defend their town and county's good name, as well as the good name of the Cranford family, against what they saw as outside pressure to bring up bad memories. But Rusk also understood that his own assumptions, supported by the accounts he had read, might also need to be challenged. These conflicting histories, he felt, offered an opportunity for adherents on both sides to come together in mutual understanding. At the meeting, it was decided that rather than hold a commemoration on the date of Sam Hose's death—April 23 would be the 108th anniversary of the event—Come to the Table would devote that month's meeting to a public forum at St. Paul's Episcopal Church. The Monday, April 9, meeting was announced on the front page of the *Times-Herald*. Rusk, representing the Moore's Ford Committee, and Emory theology professor Thee Smith, a member of Southern Truth and Reconciliation, would each make brief presentations; there would then be open discussion on the lynching. This article, again written by Skinner, provided background on the lynching, but this time the wording was slightly more ambiguous: "Hose, a farmhand, was tortured and burned to death after the murder of his employer, the rape of the farmer's wife and a serious injury of their infant child." Skinner and the paper now carefully avoided taking sides in the debate. Indeed, the moderator of the forum, Marge Zettler, chair of Come to the Table, announced in the article that there would be "ground rules for discussion," a major one being that Hose's guilt or innocence would not be a topic at this time. The article continued, "The discussion is expected to answer such questions as why the Hose lynching should be discussed now and what good could come from that discussion. Zettler indicated the conversation might also examine how Hose's killing impacted the community when it occurred and what impact the incident has today."[48] It would be, as the *Times-Herald* noted, "the first public discussion of the Sam Hose lynching in memory."[49]

The forum ultimately drew only a small crowd of some thirty-five people, including visitors from other counties. Local members of CTTT and representatives from both the Moore's Ford group and S.T.A.R. discussed the need "to get the whole thing out in the open." One CTTT member was quoted as saying that this "hidden history" had been "whitewashed," adding, "It's very important to continue to have these dialogues and decide where we want to go with this." A black participant from nearby Montezuma, Georgia, felt that the Newnan paper had prejudiced the debate with its earlier statement that Hose had killed Cranford and raped his wife. She argued that Hose's guilt or innocence had to be a point of discussion. Marge Zettler, as moderator, again noted that their focus was on "how healing and growth might come from discussion of the lynching and its aftermath." Most agreed that the "context in which lynchings took place" needed to be understood, and that "regardless of guilt, no one deserves what happened to Sam Hose." Others expressed frustration at the lack of community participation, but Penny Young, a member of the Moore's Ford Memorial Committee, urged CTTT to continue its work. "You're not giving yourselves enough credit," she told the group and reminded them that not many people would take this kind of interest in an injustice occurring over a century ago.[50]

After the meeting, Zettler, who is a native of Vermont, recognized the problems facing CTTT, which had already lost membership before the Sam Hose forum was held. Locals who had earlier joined the organization had become disappointed that meeting and talking had not led to concrete developments in the Newnan community. As an interracial group "committed to recognizing and embracing racial and cultural differences in Coweta County," CTTT agreed that it needed a definite focus, but whether Sam Hose could provide that focus was no clearer after the forum than it was before. As Zettler observed, the Moore's Ford Memorial Committee had been formed to bring attention to the 1946 killings, and it had succeeded in part because there were people in the Monroe community who could remember the events and who were closely connected to them. The Palmetto-Sam Hose-Elijah Strickland lynchings had occurred much earlier, and there were no known descendants of the black victims to take up their case. The fact that the Cranfords remained prominent and highly respected members of the community added to the complications. And the further question of Hose's guilt or innocence would surely make any "memorial" to him a point of even greater contention. CTTT, she felt, might be able to use Sam Hose's death as a horrific example of racism that might still exist in the community, but CTTT needed to have a "broader-based purpose."[51] Sam Hose, then, should not once again become a figurehead for any particular political or social purpose, but the community's past involvement in the blatant injustice of his death might yet inspire a renewed commitment to racial understanding and acceptance at the beginning of the twenty-first century. CTTT finally decided to sponsor an annual essay contest for all residents of Coweta County from middle and high school students to adults in the community on the topic "Racial Justice and Reconciliation." Cash prizes would be given in each category. The first awards would be made on April 23, 2008, the anniversary of Sam Hose's death, although no direct connection would, at this time, be made between that event and the contest itself. CTTT also agreed that more needed to be done with "the task of teaching understanding with young children." As the group's new president, Dr. Suzanne Minarcine, put it, "We know racism is there. We're not going to cure it sitting in this room, talking about it."[52]

On Sunday, April 22, 2007, Sam Hose, after more than a century, appeared once again in the Atlanta paper, his image taken from the April 24, 1899, issue of the *Journal*. The reporter, Ernie Suggs, recounted the events of Hose's lynching and examined the efforts of Come to the Table to deal with the community's responsibility. "Our goal is to get it out," Marge Zettler was quoted as saying, "but we're trying to tread lightly. There was just so much negativity around the issue when it was first brought up. But, to us, that's the reason to bring it up."[53]

Today, the site of Sam Hose's death remains unmarked except by the white fence that carefully guards the overgrown pie-slice shape of land that for so long stood anonymous and mute. The local paper has now publicly identified this place, and it is likely that others will come to pause in Sprayberry's parking lot and stare across the busy highway and think for a moment what it must have been like to stand there on that Sunday afternoon in another April in another time. Descendants of some who watched or participated still live in and around Newnan; perhaps they too now come and wonder. It is said that some of those who took part suffered "emotional difficulties" once it was done and regretted their involvement, but these folks are all long gone.[54]

When I first began researching this project, I found a mixture of reticence and support among the people I contacted. Judge John Herbert Cranford met twice with me, quietly expressing his views on this dark episode in his family's past but asking only for "fairness" when I wrote about it. Other members of the family were less encouraging, but none made any attempt to prevent my work. Outside the family, attitudes differed. Some sincerely felt that nothing good would come from bringing up bad memories, that Newnan would be stigmatized once again for this event. It was better, they felt, that this remain "hidden history." But others wanted it told, in all its complexity, for they felt that what was being written in present-day studies was too "one-sided," as I often heard. "It would be so easy to turn all this simply into a racial story," one white resident of Palmetto told me. "But, believe me, it just isn't that simple."

But, of course, although it, indeed, "just isn't that simple," it is, nonetheless, ultimately a "racial story." Despite the protests, made in 1899 and sometimes repeated today, that the magnitude of Sam Hose's crime was so horrible that any perpetrator of such a deed, regardless of his race, would have suffered a similar fate, we surely know this is not true. Although white lynch mobs might occasionally hang white victims, the mockery, the torture, the need to set examples, all derived from racial prejudice and fear.

Over a hundred years ago, Newnan sought to explain itself to the outside world. Today, Newnan is in the process of explaining itself to itself, just as are hundreds of towns across America that are confronting a variety of problematic pasts. Histories, as we have learned, will not stay hidden, no more than Sam Hose could be confined in jars or boxes or faded photographs. Perhaps a marker will one day be posted at the intersection of Jackson Street and Roscoe Road to note what's left of the Old Troutman Field, and perhaps people will journey there, in honor of a black martyr or in expiation of a collective guilt. But for now it remains off-limits, an island of jungle in an urban landscape, a cordoned sanctuary where once none was to be had.

Coda

After it was over and the people of Newnan agreed to forget, Mattie Cranford lived a secluded life in the town raising her children. She died in 1922 of pneumonia, only fifty years old. Her brief, circumspect obituary made no reference to her role in Coweta County history.[1]

Of the children, Mary Estelle, who was four at the time of her father's death and who allegedly was cuffed to the floor by Sam Hose, never married. It was she who told her grandnephews and -nieces about the Cranford tragedy, much to the displeasure of others in the family. She died in 1966. William Herbert Cranford, born in 1892, served in the Marine Corps in France during World War I and was wounded in action, partially blinded by mortar fire. A decorated veteran, he died in 1969. Clestelle (Clessie) Cranford, born in 1896, married Luther Franklin Hancock and had two daughters. Known throughout her adult life as "Doll" Hancock, she lived until 1984.

The baby, Clifford Alfred, became a colorful figure in Newnan. Blind in his left eye, as a result, most believed, of the violence of that evening when Sam Hose was said to have slammed him to the floor or heaved him across the room—still another version had it that Hose tossed him out the window into the bushes, where he suffered the injury—young Cranford grew up working odd jobs such as carrying water during the building of the county courthouse. Mary Louise Ellis describes him as having an "enterprising spirit as a small child," and in later life he owned various businesses including a restaurant, an oil company, and a service station.[2] Judge John Herbert Cranford says of his grandfather, "He was an honest man but very stern, straightforward. People called him 'Tan.' They liked him, but he was not someone to fool with." The nickname

"Tan" derived from his identification by other children as a "Pitty Tan"—
"Pitiful" or "Poor Thing"—due to his bad eye.[3]

Tan Cranford grew up to be a big and sometimes violent man. In 1934,
Newnan, like many textile mill towns throughout the South, was the site of
work strikes that crippled the industry for a time. In September of that year,
Georgia governor Eugene Talmadge made headlines nationwide when he sent
the National Guard to Newnan to round up and arrest the strikers, who were
held without representation at Fort McPherson outside Atlanta.[4] It was during
these "labor wars" that Tan Cranford started his restaurant on Sewell Road off
Highway 29, on the west side of town. The people he hired to build it were non-
union labor, and according to local stories, the pro-union people blew it up before
it was finished. Undeterred, Tan Cranford rebuilt it and audaciously named it the
Dinemite (pronounced "dine-a-mite") restaurant. "So he had a sense of humor,
a wit about him," his grandson recalls. "But he could be a hard man. He had
to be. During World War II, he served a lot of soldiers coming from Fort Benning
or McPherson, and sometimes he had to be rough with them." Soldiers, especially northern ones, who showed disrespect could quickly find themselves the
object of Tan Cranford's wrath. He would toss unruly GIs out of his place or,
as on one occasion, jerk a rude soldier through a car window if the soldier mis-
behaved. Tan was also known for the dog he owned during that time, a Great
Dane that he got from the army, a huge dog that could rise up and place its front
legs on the big man's broad shoulders so that they faced each other in a kind of
dance. Cranford would feed it blood gotten from the local meatpacking company,
and people would come to the restaurant to watch this beast lap the blood from a
bowl. The dog died soon after his master's death in 1952.[5]

Tan Cranford's relationship with blacks reflected the standards of his time.
"He wasn't any more racist than anybody else during that period," his grandson
remembers. "He considered the blacks who worked for the family as a part of the
family." This attitude was also found in his son Clifford Andrew, who served as
court solicitor in Newnan for decades. "He will enforce our laws, showing partiality to none but fairness to all," one of his campaign flyers read. "He has never
loved the dollar more than he has his friends. He will not use his office to mistreat
and unfairly abuse those with whom he comes in contact." These words referred
to members of both races, and such was Clifford Cranford's reputation until his
death in 1988.[6]

Additional figures connected to this history lived little longer than Sam Hose,
while others had long, prosperous lives. The "Great Infidel" Robert Green
Ingersoll was dead by July 1899, of heart failure. Many hoped that in death he
had discovered, to his horror, the errors of his ways. "Ripples," the pseudonym
of Coweta County squire J. P. Reese, died a year later, in May 1900, at the age

of seventy-two. In addition to his fame as correspondent to the *Newnan Herald and Advertiser*, he was also known locally as a songwriter and a vocalist, "perhaps having presided over more singing conventions than any man in Georgia," according to the *Coweta County Chronicles*. Among his original compositions were songs celebrating "Newnan," "Grantville," "Sharpsburg," "Mulberry Grove," and other towns in west Georgia, as well as sentimental and religious tunes such as "Jesus Is My Friend," "Youth Will Soon Be Gone," "Love the Lord," and "My Last Moments."[7] On September 5, 1901, President William McKinley was shot by the anarchist Leon Frank Czolgosz while attending the Pan-American Exposition in Buffalo, New York. McKinley died nine days later, the third U.S. president to be assassinated. Czolgosz was put to death in the electric chair the following month, swift justice indeed. The cantankerous "Country Philosopher Bill Arp," Charles Henry Smith, who had declared, "I will bet on Dixie as long as I've got a dollar," died in 1903, wondering at the direction the New South was heading.

Most shocking, however, was the unexpected passing of Governor William Yeates Atkinson, who unexpectedly died of the results of appendicitis and dysentery in August 1899, just four months after he had faced the lynch mob. He was only forty-four years old. The state mourned the loss, remembering him for his stands against lynching and mob violence, but also for his brave defense of college football. In 1897, after the death of a University of Georgia player, the state legislature had attempted to ban the game, and Atkinson, as governor, had vetoed the bill. Some considered this to be his greatest achievement. For these and other reasons, his adopted town of Newnan accorded him uncommon respect and praise: "The words spoken above his bier were chaplets of love and homage such as are rarely heard on such an occasion," the *Herald and Advertiser* recorded. "All the business houses in Newnan were closed, the court-house portico draped in the emblems of mourning, and such avalanches of flowers and telegrams, as poured into Newnan were never seen before, or since that time."[8]

James E. Brown, who had become editor of the *Newnan Herald and Advertiser* in 1887, continued in that position for forty years until his retirement from the paper in 1928 after being elected mayor of Newnan. He died in May 1939 at the age of eighty-five and was remembered as "one of the most picturesque characters in Georgia politics" and "the sage of political activities in Coweta county."[9] Brown's one-time rival, the cantankerous and unforgiving editor Douglas Glessner of Griffin, had long since passed peacefully in his sleep almost thirty years earlier, in 1910 at the age of fifty-three. A lifelong bachelor, he was found dead in the newspaper office that had essentially been his home.[10] That same year Allen D. Candler also died. After finishing his last term as governor, Candler had devoted himself to compiling and preserving the state's most important historical documents. Most significantly, he and Clement Evans, a Methodist minister, coedited the multivolume *Georgia: Comprising Sketches of Counties, Towns, Events, Institutions, and Persons Arranged in Cyclopedic Form*, published in 1906 and considered the most comprehensive collection of information about the state at that time.[11]

Rebecca Latimer Felton was ninety-four when she died in 1930. By that time she was remembered for her support of women's rights and the fact that she was the first woman to serve in the U.S. Senate, although she was appointed at the age of eighty-seven and her term was brief—one day—and thus largely ceremonial. Her call for mass lynching of black men was carefully elided from most obituaries.[12] She was buried in Oak Hill Cemetery in Cartersville, Georgia, where "Just Plain Sam Jones," the popular preacher, had also been interred. Jones died in 1906 while riding in a Pullman car on the Rock Island Line passing through Arkansas, returning from a revival in Oklahoma City. Over thirty thousand mourners paid their respects as he lay in state in the Georgia capitol.[13]

Felton's one-time adversary Andrew Sledd, after leaving Emory College, served as president of the University of Florida from 1904 to 1909 and then returned to Emory University as a distinguished professor at the Candler School of Theology, where he taught until he fell dead of a heart attack on March 16, 1939. His connection with the Sam Hose lynching, misunderstood though it was, eventually became a part of his official biography, so much so that in April 2002, a hundred years after his resignation, Emory University sponsored the program "Professing Justice: A Symposium on the Civil Rights Legacy of Professor Andrew Sledd," at which time the university attempted "to right a wrong committed a century ago by revisiting the 'Sledd affair' and reflecting on its meaning for Emory today."[14] At the symposium, the story of Sledd's witnessing the death of Sam Hose was retold, and Sledd was honored as a "prophet" who, according to his son, James Sledd, "saw a great evil and saw that good, respectable people tolerated it. . . . At the risk of his career and at the risk of his life, he spoke up."[15] The Pitts Theology Library at Emory set up a special display titled Racial Violence in Our History: Andrew Sledd, Warren Akin Candler and Lynching in Early Twentieth-Century Georgia as part of the university's public apology.

In the same year Sledd died, on June 19, 1939, the newsman Royal Daniel also died of a bad heart. Daniel had become assistant managing editor of the *Journal* before leaving the paper in 1916 and moving to Quitman, Georgia, where he became editor of the *Quitman Free Press*. The reporter had developed a deep interest in psychology, especially in the field of psychic suggestion, and in 1909 he had published his only book, *The Twilight of Consciousness*, exploring this phenomenon. In Quitman, Daniel took on the role of country journalist, but in 1935 he had another dramatic adventure when he was kidnapped by two armed men who forced him into a car and made him drive to Valdosta, some twenty miles away. There his captors had him write a postcard demanding a reward for his release, to be sent to the postmaster in Quitman. At his own suggestion, Daniel was let out of the car in Valdosta to put the card in a mailbox that he had spotted. Next to the box, and unnoticed by the kidnappers, was a fire alarm, which Daniel set off and then ran. The men sped away and were never caught, but Daniel got one final headline.[16]

John S. Candler, who, as colonel, had briefly taken military control of Palmetto after the warehouse shootings, and, as judge, had overseen the trials of some of the surviving defendants, was elected associate justice to the Georgia Supreme Court and served 1902–6. He then retired from the bench and went into private practice in Atlanta. Judge Candler died in 1941.

William Atkinson's widow, Susan Cobb Milton Atkinson, who had caused such consternation with her letter comparing the Hose lynching to both a bull-fight and a Roman extravaganza, became postmistress of Newnan after her husband's death, having met personally with President Theodore Roosevelt and persuaded him to give her the position. She served in this office until 1928. Mrs. Atkinson had earlier encouraged her husband, while he was serving in the legislature, to support public education for women in Georgia and had been a leading force in establishing the first state-sponsored women's college, the Georgia Normal and Industrial College, in Milledgeville, in 1891. Atkinson Hall on campus was named in their honor. In 1941, she was celebrated by the school, now known as the Georgia State College for Women, on its fiftieth anniversary. Susie Atkinson was then eighty and had been flown in for the celebration. At the Milledgeville airport, she and her daughter were met by a horse-drawn carriage. As they paraded through the streets of town, the horses were frightened by the many photographers and bolted, but Mrs. Atkinson, characteristically, later claimed not to have noticed.[17] She died the following year, and in 1996 she was posthumously inducted into the Georgia Women of Achievement, the first Newnanite so honored.[18]

Dr. Hal Johnston, the Palmetto dentist who had figured so prominently in the events of 1899, also went on to have a long and happy life. In October 1899, six months after Sam Hose's capture and death, Johnston and his wife, Ella, celebrated their twenty-fifth wedding anniversary with a lavish party at which "the Doctor, with his noble bearing, graced a handsome dark suit, while Mrs. Johnston was queenly looking in an elegant dress of silver gray satin with a bodice trimming of appliqué and a finishing touch of pink at the throat."[19] He and his sister, India Estes, subsequently opened to the public the Palmetto Hotel, which became a well-known resort lodging in the years that followed. In 1909, as superintendent and general manager of the Palmetto Cotton Mills, Johnston spoke against proposed child-labor laws, arguing that "an idle brain is the devil's workshop" and that children needed to keep busy.[20] By 1906, he was vice president of the Palmetto Cotton Mills, and in that year he welcomed members of the Carriage Builders National Association to Palmetto. "A negro band was on the train and the trip was enlivened with southern melodies which greatly delighted the northern visitors," the *Constitution* reported. The visitors watched "squads" of blacks pick cotton. "In age the negroes ranged from the coonlet who could barely top a cotton stalk to 'Uncle Tom,' who is 80 years of age, has twenty-three children, and is still able to pick 200 pounds of cotton a day." Dr. Hal was presented a gold watch in appreciation by the carriage builders.[21]

Johnston later became president of the mills, a position he held for many years, while also serving four terms in the Georgia legislature as representative of Campbell County. He died on January 19, 1937, at the grand age of eighty-five; his wife, Ella, eighty-two, died four days later, on January 23. They had been married for over sixty-two years and had spent their last years in Atlanta. Nevertheless, in death they were brought back to Palmetto for burial in Floral Hill Cemetery.[22]

Hal Johnston's passing was duly noted in the *Newnan Herald* (the former *Herald and Advertiser*). At the top of the page with the obituary was a comic strip, "Uncle Natchel" (a dramatized version of which played on radio stations throughout the South), in which an elderly black man, so named because "'Natchel' (Natural) Is His Recommendation for Everything," has adventures with his "Little Friend Sonny," a white boy, and the boy's dog, "Nipper." In this strip, the old man and the boy are fishing. "Fishin's Just My Dish," Uncle Natchel tells Sonny with a broad smile, before adding, "Worm, Do Yo Stuff."[23]

It did.

Notes

Introduction

1. Sam Hose was known by several different names, including Sam Holt, Sam Wilkes, and Tom Wilkes. The last is apparently his birth name. The "Sam Holt" identification might well have been influenced by the popular "Sam Holt" brand of firearms, sold by Sears Roebuck at this time. The inexpensive Sam Holt shotgun could be found in many rural homes in Georgia and elsewhere.

2. William Faulkner, *Novels, 1936–1940* (New York: Library of America, 1990), 178.

3. Philip M. Weinstein, *What Else But Love: The Ordeal of Race in Faulkner and Morrison* (New York: Columbia University Press, 1996), xviii.

4. See, for example, Dora Apel, "Torture Culture: Lynching Photographs and Images of Abu Ghraib," *Art Journal* 64, no. 2 (Summer 2005): 88–100.

5. See Michele Faith Wallace, "The Good Lynching and *The Birth of a Nation*: Discourses and Esthetics of Jim Crow," *Cinema Journal* 43, no. 1 (Fall 2003): 85–104, for a discussion of this issue.

6. Grace Elizabeth Hale, *Making Whiteness: The Culture of Segregation in the South, 1890–1940* (New York: Pantheon Books, 1998).

7. Benedict Anderson, *Imagined Communities: Reflections on the Origin and Spread of Nationalism*, rev. ed. (London: Verso, 1991), 35.

Chapter 1. War Fantasies

1. "The Passing Throng," *AC*, September 20, 1899. Further details of Pearl Knott's murder and Kerlin's trial come from articles "Kerlin Makes His Statement to the Jury at Fayetteville," *AC*, September 22, 1899; "Kerlin Goes Up for Life," *AC*, September 23, 1899; and "Is Kerlin Crazy?" *AC*, October 8, 1899. See also Bruce L. Jordan, *Death Unexpected: The Violent Deaths of Fayette* (Atlanta: Midtown, 1997), 6–16.

2. "The Death of Sam Hose," *Athens (Ga.) Weekly Banner*, April 28, 1899.

3. C. Vann Woodward, *Tom Watson: Agrarian Rebel* (New York: Oxford University Press, 1963), 332.

4. "Kerlin Makes His Statement to the Jury at Fayetteville," *AC*, September 22, 1899.

5. George Kerlin died in prison in 1906. See Jordan, *Death Unexpected*, 15–16.

6. "Robert Lewis, Condemned to Death, Is Denied Executive Clemency," *AC*, March 4, 1899; "Sad Day for Two in Tower," *AC*, March 6, 1899; "Expert Declares Lewis Is Sane," *AC*, March 11, 1899; "Murderer Lewis No Longer Feels the Fear He Exhibited Last Week," *AC*, March 13, 1899; "Pardon Board Hears Last Plea," *AC*, March 14, 1899; "Hanging of Lewis in the Tower; Charles Haynes's Murderer Dead," *AC*, March 15, 1899; "Autopsy on Lewis's Brain," *AC*, March 17, 1899.

7. Seventy-five years later, in 2001, the Georgia Supreme Court would declare this form of capital punishment unconstitutional, finding that it "inflicts purposeless physical violence and needless mutilation that makes no measurable contribution to accepted goals of punishment." "Georgia Blocks Electric Chair Use," *AC*, October 5, 2001.

8. Jacquelyn Dowd Hall, *Revolt against Chivalry: Jessie Daniel Ames and the Women's Campaign against Lynching* (New York: Columbia University Press, 1993), 140.

9. Michel Foucault, *Discipline and Punish: The Birth of the Prison*, trans. Alan Sheridan (New York: Vintage, 1995), 33–34. For a more recent discussion of medieval uses of torture, see also Mitchell B. Merback, *The Thief, the Cross, and the Wheel: Pain and the Spectacle of Punishment in Medieval and Renaissance Europe* (Chicago: University of Chicago Press, 1999); and Robert Mills, *Suspended Animation: Pain, Pleasure and Punishment in Medieval Culture* (London: Reaktion Books, 2005), both of which have provided me with ways to think about the Sam Hose execution.

10. David Garland, "Penal Excess and Surplus Meaning: Public Torture Lynchings in Twentieth Century America," *Law & Society Review*, 30, no. 4 (2005): 795, 797, 798, 799, 801.

11. "Not in Position to Give Up the Chase," *Washington Post*, May 1, 1899.

12. Brian McAllister Linn, *The Philippine War, 1899–1902* (Lawrence: University Press of Kansas, 2000), 11.

13. Ibid.

14. I. F. Clarke, *The Pattern of Expectation, 1644–2001* (New York: Basic Books, 1979), 130.

15. Ibid., 131.

16. H. Bruce Franklin, *War Stars: The Superweapon and the American Imagination* (New York: Oxford University Press, 1988), 35–37.

17. Ibid., 31–32.

18. Report available at http://www.ah.dcr.state.nc.us/1898-wrrc/report/front-matter .pdf. See also David S. Cecelski and Timothy B. Tyson, eds., *Democracy Betrayed: The Wilmington Race Riot and Its Legacy* (Chapel Hill: University of North Carolina Press, 1998) for essays on the topic.

19. "Seven Are Lynched," *MT*, March 24, 1899.

20. "Wholesale Lynching," *H&A*, March 31, 1899.

21. "More Dead Bodies," *MT*, March 25, 1899.

22. See David Fort Godshalk, *Veiled Visions: The 1906 Atlanta Race Riot and the Reshaping of American Race Relations* (Chapel Hill: University of North Carolina Press, 2005), and Rebecca Burns, *Rage in the Gate City: The Story of the 1906 Atlanta Race Riot* (Cincinnati: Emmis Books, 2006).

23. Willard B. Gatewood Jr., *Black Americans and the White Man's Burden, 1898–1903* (Urbana: University of Illinois Press, 1975), 140.

24. See, as one example, "Nigger on the Railroad," *MT*, March 7, 1899.

25. Gatewood, *Black Americans*, 140–41.

26. Ibid., 141–43.

27. "The Negro Regiments," *MT*, January 4, 1899.

28. Quoted in Gatewood, *Black Americans*, 149.

29. "To Freeze Out the Negro," *MT*, February 9, 1899; "Negro Voters Barred," *MT*, February 19, 1899; see also "North Carolina Democrats Have Redeemed Every Promise Made," *AC*, March 15, 1899.

30. "The Negro Troops Will Soon Be Out," *AJ*, January 6, 1899; "Macon Will Soon Have No Soldiers," *AC*, February 20, 1899.

31. "Negro Regiments." Also see "Macon Worried about Negroes," *AC*, January 25, 1899.

32. "Will Be Turned Loose in Macon," *AC*, January 10, 1899.

33. "Mustered Out in Installments," *AC*, January 11, 1899.

34. "Macon Would Like Some More Troops," *AC*, January 12, 1899.

35. "Want More Liberty," *MT*, January 15, 1899.

36. Gatewood, *Black Americans*, 132.

37. "Negro Troops Drunk," *MT*, February 1, 1899.

38. "Drunker Soldiers and Police Have Serious Trouble at Depot," *AC*, February 1, 1899.

39. "Police Feared Riot at Depot," *AC*, February 3, 1899.

40. "Police Reserve Was Ordered Out," *AC*, February 4, 1899.

41. "Excitement in Macon Yesterday; Ohio Volunteers Cause Trouble," *AC*, February 11, 1899.

42. "Brandt's Insult to Macon People," *AC*, March 7, 1899.

43. This view of a white southern community's feeling under siege and needing to protect itself became a popular romantic narrative in southern fiction of the late nineteenth and early twentieth centuries. See, for example, Scott Romine's essay "Things Falling Apart: The Postcolonial Condition of *Red Rock* and *The Leopard's Spots*," in *Look Away! The U.S. South in New World Studies*, ed. Jon Smith and Deborah Cohn (Durham, N.C.: Duke University Press, 2004), 175–200. See also Romine's *Narrative Forms of Southern Community* (Baton Rouge: Louisiana State University Press, 1999) and Walter Benn Michaels, *Our America: Nativism, Modernism, and Pluralism* (Durham, N.C.: Duke University Press, 1995) for further analysis of the South's self-image as a colonized territory after the Civil War and into the twentieth century.

44. Gatewood, *Black Americans*, 87, 89.

45. "Immunes Riot at Chattanooga," *AC*, March 8, 1899.

46. "Negroes in Trouble," *AC*, March 8, 1899.

47. "Riotous Colored Troops Cause Trouble by Firing at Citizens," *AC*, March 9, 1899; "Immunes in Fight," *MT*, March 9, 1899.

48. "A Day of Excitement," *Griffin Morning Call*, March 9, 1899.

49. "What City This Is," *GDNS*, March 9, 1899.

50. Quoted in "Riotous Colored Troops."

51. Quoted in "Riotous Immunes," *MT*, March 10, 1899.

52. "Griffin Men Did Their Duty in Checking Drunken Negroes," *AC*, March 10, 1899; see also "Withrow an Unpopular Man," *AC*, March 10, 1899.

53. Gatewood, *Black Americans*, 151.

54. "Negro Volunteers Caused No Trouble," *GDNS*, March 8, 1899.

55. "The Negro as a Soldier," *MT*, March 10, 1899.

56. "A New Crop of Northern Slanderers," *H&A*, December 2, 1898.

Chapter 2. Lynch Sunday

1. "Ripples," *H&A*, May 5, 1899.

2. W. Fitzhugh Brundage records ninety-six lynchings in Georgia between 1890 and 1899. In 1899 there were twenty-six victims of lynchings in the state, including five from the Palmetto shootings (Brundage omits John Bigby, who later died), Sam Hose, and Elijah Strickland. See *Lynching in the New South: Georgia and Virginia, 1880–1930* (Urbana: University of Illinois Press, 1993), 263, 273.

3. Twain's essay with this title was not published until after his death, by Albert Bigelow Paine in a compilation of Twain's writings, *Europe and Elsewhere* (New York: Harper & Bros., 1923).

4. See Joel Williamson, *The Crucible of Race: Black-White Relations in the American South since Emancipation* (New York: Oxford University Press, 1984), 190–95, for a discussion of the McKinley administration's wide-scale appointment of blacks to the offices of postmaster throughout the South. As Williamson notes, "What bothered the whites, of course, was the fact that their womenfolk were forced to do business with black postmasters and clerks, often enough with their political cronies hanging about inside the post office. . . . Physical contact through the mutual handling of mails and monies was bad enough, but even more awful was the prospect that black men in office would make all black men assume themselves more powerful and be led to approach white women sexually" (191).

5. "Buck's Negro Friends," *AC*, March 13, 1890.

6. "Two Sides to the Loftin Shooting," *AC*, September 18, 1897.

7. Ibid.

8. "Negro or Nobody," *Decatur (Ill.) Daily Republican*, September 20, 1897; *History of the Town of Hogansville, 1830–1970*, ed. Jane M. Strain (privately published, ca. 1970), 15.

9. "Hogansville Men to Be Arrested," *AC*, September 20, 1897.

10. "Two Sides."

11. "Negro Postmaster Shot by Citizens," *AC*, September 17, 1897.
12. "Two Sides."
13. Ibid.
14. "Negro or Nobody."
15. The mayor's statement was published throughout the country. One such example is "War on Negro Officials," *New York Times*, September 17, 1897.
16. "Mob Law in the South," *Steubenville (Ohio) Herald-Star*, March 18, 1898.
17. Philip Dray, *At the Hands of Persons Unknown: The Lynching of Black America* (New York: Random House, 2002), 117–19.
18. "Lynchers Indicted," *MT*, April 8, 1899.
19. "Hogansville Men."
20. Ed. M. Durant, "Riot in Fayette," *AC*, July 12, 1890.
21. "Swung Up, Then Shot," *AC*, October 16, 1896.
22. "Armed Men Are in Hot Pursuit," *AC*, July 11, 1897.
23. "Has Williams Been Lynched?" *AC*, July 12, 1897.
24. "Williams Was Not Caught," *AC*, July 14, 1897.
25. "Williams Caught; Troops Save Him," *AC*, July 15, 1897.
26. "Oscar Williams in the Bibb Jail," *AC*, July 16, 1897.
27. Ibid.
28. Tom Allen had killed another man in 1894 while drunk in a Macon saloon. After being found guilty of murder, he escaped from the Bibb County jail in February 1895 and remained at large until he was captured in April of the following year. By that time he had become a local celebrity. See "Wescott Got Him," *MT*, April 22, 1896. Elizabeth Nobles, of Twiggs County, Georgia, was, after a series of trials and appeals, sentenced to be hanged, as was her black accomplice, Gus Fambles, who had shot and killed Nobles's husband for his insurance. When Oscar Williams was placed in the Bibb County jail, Nobles was awaiting a ruling from the U.S. Supreme Court on her request for yet another trial. The court refused this request in November 1897. However, all three of the condemned eventually received executive clemency from Governor Atkinson and were sentenced to life imprisonment. When Nobles died in 1916 at the age of seventy-one, she was deemed "the most notorious woman prisoner in [the] Georgia penitentiary" but was also judged a "much changed" woman who had requested to be buried on the prison grounds in Milledgeville. See "Sentence of Tom Allen Commuted," *AC*, February 10, 1898; "Mrs. Nobles Will Not Be Hanged," *AC*, April 1, 1898; "Mrs. Nobles Will Be Put to Work," *AC*, April 8, 1898; and "Husband-Slayer Dies Much-Changed Woman at Georgia Prison Farm," *AC*, February 7, 1916.
29. "Ryder Hanged by Citizens of Talbot," *AC*, July 20, 1897; "Thrilling Story of the Hanging," *AC*, July 21, 1897; "Ryder Lynched," *MT*, July 20, 1897; "Dr. W. L. Ryder Is Lynched by a Mob of Fifteen Men," *AJ*, July 20, 1897.
30. "Why Williams Was Moved from Macon," *AC*, July 23, 1897.
31. Ibid.
32. "Mob to Attack Bibb Jail?" *AC*, July 22, 1897.
33. "Why Williams Was Moved."

34. "Quiet Mob Hangs Oscar Williams," *AC*, July 23, 1897.

35. Ibid. See also "Hemp and Lead," *MT*, July 23, 1987; "Oscar Williams Lynched at Griffin," *AJ*, July 23, 1897.

36. "The Williams Lynching," *AC*, July 23, 1897.

37. "Dr. Ryder's Death Will Be Avenged," *AC*, July 24, 1897; "Governor Knows the Names of Men Who Lynched Ryder," *AC*, July 25, 1897.

38. "Quiet Mob Hangs Oscar Williams."

39. "Will Stretch Rope If He Is Caught," *AC*, December 20, 1898.

40. "Lynched Three," *MT*, February 12, 1899.

41. "Will Stretch Rope."

42. Ibid.

43. "Surround Him in Swamp," *AC*, December 23, 1898.

44. "'Cupid' Confessed It," *MT*, February 16, 1899; see also "Some Confusion," *MT*, February 13, 1899.

45. "Lynched Three," *MT*, February 12, 1899.

46. Ibid.

47. "Reward for Lynchers," *MT*, February 13, 1899.

48. "Some Confusion."

49. "Reward for Lynchers."

50. "That Lynching at Leesburg," *AC*, February 13, 1899; see also "Three Men Implicated in Maroney Outrage Are Lynched at Leesburg," *AC*, February 12, 1899.

51. "Reward for Lynchers"; "Lynched Three."

52. In the appendix "Lynching Victims in Georgia, 1880–1930," Brundage identifies the three victims as George Bivins, William Holt, and George Foot. See *Lynching in the New South*, 273.

53. "Georgia Negro Shot Down," *AC*, April 28, 1899.

Chapter 3. The Palmetto Massacre

1. *Palmetto: A Town and Its People*, ed. Barbara Crisp and Teresa Daugherty (n.p.: n.d.), 4.

2. Ibid. The regiment played an important role in the Mexican War. Placed under the command of Gen. Winfield Scott, the men from South Carolina took part in the siege of Vera Cruz and the capture of Mexico City. Their flag was one of two flown above Chapultepec Castle, the entrance to the city. But the regiment also suffered the highest death rate in Scott's army. http://www.state.sc.us/crr/mexwar.htm.

3. *Palmetto*, 5.

4. Ibid., 6.

5. "Palmetto Badly Damaged by Fire," *AC*, January 25, 1899.

6. "Torch of Incendiary at Palmetto Again," *AJ*, January 28, 1899.

7. Ibid.

8. "Another Fire at Palmetto, Ga.," *AC*, January 29, 1899.

9. "Torch of Incendiary."

10. "Palmetto Again Swept by Fire," *H&A*, February 3, 1899.

11. "Great Slaughter at Palmetto," *MT*, March 16, 1899.

12. Royal Daniel, "4 Dead, 1 Dying, 2 Wounded," *AJ*, March 18, 1899.

13. Much of this informal history comes from Carole Harper, local historian, who interviewed elder residents of Palmetto in the 1970s and 1980s, gathering their memories of the Palmetto burning and subsequent shootings. Telephone interview with Carole Harper, November 17, 2006.

14. Ibid.

15. While Sam Hose was at large, rumors of intended black assassinations of prominent whites in Palmetto were reported in the local papers. An article, "Palmetto's Reign of Terror," datelined April 22, gave as one example a plot against Tom Daniel, who was warned that an ambush had been set for him. The *Newnan Herald and Advertiser* related that "several nights ago . . . [f]our negroes waited several hours for him to pass the place where they were concealed, but by accident the negroes were discovered" (*H&A*, April 28, 1899). It seems likely that this story is the source of the variant explanation of the arrests.

16. "Nine Negroes Shot Down at Palmetto, Ga., This Morning," *AC*, March 16, 1899.

17. "Great Slaughter at Palmetto."

18. "Night of Horrors at Palmetto," *MT*, March 17, 1899.

19. Frank Fleming, "Scenes and Incidents at Palmetto, Ga., Yesterday," *AC*, March 17, 1899.

20. Ibid.

21. Daniel, "4 Dead, 1 Dying."

22. "Night of Horrors."

23. Daniel, "4 Dead, 1 Dying."

24. "A Massacre of Negroes," *Columbus (Ga.) Enquirer-Sun*, March 17, 1899.

25. Fleming, "Scenes and Incidents."

26. Ibid.

27. Ibid.

28. Telephone interview with Carole Harper, December 8, 2006.

29. "Reward Is Offered for the Murderers," *AJ*, March 16, 1899.

30. "Governor Candler Talks of the Palmetto Trouble," *AC*, March 17, 1899.

31. "Governor Candler Takes Prompt Action," *AJ*, March 17, 1899.

32. Royal Daniel, "Martial Law Ruled Palmetto Last Night," *AJ*, March 17, 1899. See also "A Cloud of Gloom over Palmetto," *AC*, March 17, 1899; and "More Troops Go to Palmetto," *AC*, March 18, 1899.

33. For a discussion of such a "black exodus," see Stewart E. Tolnay and E. M. Beck, *A Festival of Violence: An Analysis of Southern Lynchings, 1882–1930* (Urbana: University of Illinois Press, 1995), 218.

34. See Andrew Silver, *Minstrelsy and Murder: The Crisis of Southern Humor, 1835–1925* (Baton Rouge: Louisiana State University Press, 2006), 58. Silver's chapter "Making Minstrelsy of Murder: George Washington Harris, the Ku Klux Klan, and the Reconstruction Aesthetics of Fright" is especially relevant to this discussion.

35. Daniel, "4 Dead, 1 Dying."

36. Fleming, "Scenes and Incidents."

37. Ibid.

38. Daniel, "Martial Law Ruled Palmetto."

39. Ibid.

40. Ibid.

41. Fleming, "Scenes and Incidents."

42. "Cloud of Gloom."

43. Fleming, "Scenes and Incidents."

44. Ibid. See also account given by Daniel, "4 Dead, 1 Dying."

45. Fleming, "Scenes and Incidents."

46. "Cloud of Gloom."

47. Quoted in Daniel, "4 Dead, 1 Dying."

48. "Palmetto Preacher Leaves in Haste," *AC*, March 21, 1899.

49. "Bigby, Mob's Victim, Dead," *AJ*, March 21, 1899.

50. "More Troops Go to Palmetto."

51. "Palmetto Preacher."

52. "Cloud of Gloom."

53. "They Had Very Bad Records," *AC*, March 18, 1899; "Palmetto Organizes a Military Company," *AC*, March 22, 1899.

54. "Palmetto Organizes."

55. "Cloud of Gloom."

56. "Uncalled For Lynching of Several Negroes," *Augusta Chronicle*, March 17, 1899; "The Palmetto Lynching," *Savannah Morning News*, March 17, 1899.

57. "The Palmetto Mob," *AC*, March 17, 1899.

58. "The Palmetto Affair," *MT*, March 17, 1899.

59. "The Negro South," *Washington Bee*, March 18, 1899.

60. "The Palmetto 'Affair,'" *H&A*, March 24, 1899.

61. "Tower a Haven for Criminals," *AC*, August 4, 1899.

62. "Candler Denies Advocating Lynching," *AC*, May 24, 1899.

63. "The Passing Throng," *AC*, September 30, 1899.

64. "Palmetto Fire Bugs," *AC*, August 23, 1899.

65. "Passing Throng."

66. "Big Fight over Palmetto Reward," *AC*, October 14, 1899.

67. "Dr. Hal Johnson [sic] Will Get Reward," *AC*, January 6, 1900.

68. Isabella Webb Parks, "Our Responsibility to the American Negro," *Methodist Review* 15, no. 5 (September 1, 1899): 713–26. In an article, "Negro Criminality," published in the *Journal of Social Science* in December 1899, Walter F. Willcox related the story sent to him by an "editor of an Atlanta daily paper, who made a special investigation of the facts after the terrible climax." According to Willcox, the evidence against the men "consisted in conversation heard by a reputable white citizen while in hiding under the house of a negro, and in a confession of the ringleader." He also repeated the story that "the nine had been examined, released for lack of evidence, and subsequently rearrested." See Willcox,

"Negro Criminality," *Journal of Social Science, Containing the Proceedings of the American Association (1869–1909)* 37 (1899): 78–98. *APS Online* ProQuest.

Chapter 4. A Carnival of Blood and Lust

1. "President's Trip to Thomasville: Party Will Leave on Next Monday," *AC*, March 11, 1899.
2. "Mr. McKinley in Thomasville," *AC*, March 16, 1899.
3. "McKinley Has Day of Driving," *AC*, March 16, 1899.
4. "The Nation's Chief Is Fond of Georgia," *AJ*, March 18, 1899.
5. "Warren Leland's Windsor Proves a Death Trap; Governor Candler's Sister-in-Law Is a Victim," *AC*, March 18, 1899.
6. The disaster was also recorded by a new medium of communication. J. Stuart Blackton and cameraman Albert E. Smith filmed the scene shortly after the fire was contained. They then returned to their studio, built a miniature of the building and area, set it on fire, and filmed that as well. The resulting "Windsor Hotel Fire" showed the obviously simulated burning and then cut to footage of removal of corpses from the actual building's ruins. The combination of fakery and truth proved enormously effective to naive viewers, who had not yet learned to distinguish between filmed "reality" and special effects, no matter how crudely done. Like contemporary newspaper accounts, this "newsreel" created its own astonishing and entertaining truth.
7. "Death and Devastation Mark Path of Cyclone at Edwardsville, Ala.," *AC*, March 19, 1899.
8. "The Ante-bellum Darkey," *H&A*, April 7, 1899.
9. "Assassination near Palmetto; Mr. Cranford Brained with Axe," *AJ*, April 13, 1899.
10. "Murder and Rape," *H&A*, April 14, 1899.
11. "Cranford Murdered; His Wife Assaulted," *AJ*, April 13, 1899.
12. "Determined Mob after Hose; He Will Be Lynched If Caught," *AC*, April 14, 1899.
13. "The Hose Will Not Put Out This Fire," *GDNS*, April 15, 1899.
14. "Tracked by Bloodhounds," *Washington Post*, April 14, 1899; "Hunt for a Georgia Negro," *New York Times*, April 14, 1899.
15. "Mr. Sharkey Tells of Crime," *AC*, April 14, 1899.
16. Jacquelyn Dowd Hall, *Revolt against Chivalry: Jessie Daniel Ames and the Women's Campaign against Lynching* (New York: Columbia University Press, 1993), 151, 150.
17. Daniel Carey, "Capture of Sam Hose Seems to Be Matter of Only a Few Hours," *AC*, April 15, 1899.
18. Royal Daniel, "Hose Yet at Large; Mrs. Cranford Tells Story of the Crime," *AJ*, April 15, 1899.
19. "Murder and Rape."
20. Carey, "Capture of Sam Hose."

21. "Reward of $250 Offered," *AJ*, April 14, 1899.

22. Daniel, "Hose Yet at Large."

23. Carey, "Capture of Sam Hose."

24. Ibid.

25. Daniel, "Hose Yet at Large."

26. "Hose Almost in Their Grasp," *AC*, April 16, 1899; "Dispatch Stopped Chase," *Savannah Morning News*, April 16, 1899.

27. Mason Stokes, *The Color of Sex: Whiteness, Heterosexuality, and the Fictions of White Supremacy* (Durham, N.C.: Duke University Press, 2001), 81–107.

28. Chas. Carroll, *"The Negro a Beast" . . . or . . . "In the Image of God"* (Miami: Mnemosyne, 1900).

29. Ibid., 45, 165.

30. Carey, "Capture of Sam Hose."

31. "The Negro Must Die," *MT*, April 16, 1899.

32. "Something Must Be Done," *MT*, April 16, 1899.

33. Daniel Carey, "Hose Is a Will O' the Wisp to His Determined Pursuers," *AC*, April 16, 1899.

34. Ibid.

35. Carey, "Hose Is a Will O' the Wisp."

36. Ibid.

37. "Searching for Sam Hose," *LaGrange Graphic*, April 18, 1899.

38. "Sam Hose Was Shot," *MT*, April 18, 1899.

39. "Circle of Vengeance Slowly Closing on Fleeing Sam Hose," *AC*, April 18, 1899.

40. Ibid.

41. "Letters from the People: Silence of the Anti-Lynchers," *AC*, April 20, 1899.

42. "The Trouble at Palmetto," *LaGrange Graphic*, April 18, 1899.

43. "Reward for Sam Hose Is Increased to $500," *AJ*, April 18, 1899.

44. "Something Must Be Done."

45. "Circle of Vengeance."

46. Hose's supposedly exhausted state was reported in "Thought to Be at Taylor," *MT*, April 19, 1899; report of his alleged arrest appears in "Thinks Hose in Jail," *AJ*, April 18, 1899; "May Be Sam Hose," *MT*, April 21, 1899.

47. "Chase Still Continues," *AJ*, April 18, 1899.

48. "Excitement Prevails at Griffin," *MT*, April 18, 1899.

49. "Tramped over 200 Miles," *MT*, April 19, 1899.

50. "Hot after Sam Hose," *MT*, April 19, 1899.

51. "Reward for Sam Hose."

52. "Whipping of Henry Harris," *AC*, April 22, 1899.

53. "Badly Beaten by a Mob," *MT*, April 21, 1899; see also "Negro Beaten by a Mob," *AJ*, April 21, 1899.

54. "Griffin Negro Badly Whipped," *Columbus (Ga.) Enquirer-Sun*, April 23, 1899; "The Lash in Griffin Again," *AC*, April 23, 1899.

55. "Talked about Holt's Victim," *AC*, April 24, 1899.

56. "Reward for Sam Hose."

57. Telephone interview with Carole Harper, November 17, 2006.

58. "Dr. Hal L. Johnson [*sic*] Tells of Hose Chase," *AJ*, April 21, 1899.

59. Stephen Ward Angell, *Bishop Henry McNeal Turner and African-American Religion in the South* (Knoxville: University of Tennessee Press, 1992).

60. Ibid., 236.

61. Ibid., 267–68.

62. "Dr. Hal L. Johnson."

63. Ibid.

64. "Palmetto Appeals for Aid; Description of Sam Hose," *AJ*, April 22, 1899.

65. "Negroes Vow to Revenge," *AJ*, April 22, 1899.

Chapter 5. The Wild Ride

1. "Story of the Capture of Sam Holt by the Jones Brothers," *AC*, April 25, 1899.

2. "Captors Tell Their Story," *AJ*, April 24, 1899.

3. "On the Scene," *MT*, April 25, 1899. Mary Louise Ellis, citing the *Crawford County (Ga.) Correspondent*, identifies a "Mr. Petterman, of Marshallville," who assisted in disguising Sam Hose. See Ellis, "'Rain Down Fire': The Lynching of Sam Hose" (PhD diss., Florida State University, 1992), 100.

4. "Denied His Identity," *MT*, April 24, 1899.

5. Grace Elizabeth Hale, Making Whiteness: The Culture of Segregation in the South, 1890–1940 (New York: Pantheon Books, 1998), 212.

6. Eric Lott, *Love and Theft: Blackface Minstrelsy and the American Working Class* (Oxford: Oxford University Press, 1995), 148.

7. "On the Scene."

8. In addition to its recent encounters with black militia and the general commotion Sam Hose's pursuit had caused, yet another embarrassing race "sensation" had gripped the city of Griffin. In early January, an eighteen-year-old white man named Jerry W. Rhoades had accused a black man, Percy Campbell, of killing another black man named Bud Dickinson, and Campbell had been jailed along with yet another black, Mose Ager, who had discovered Dickinson's body. But while waiting to testify against Campbell, Rhoades had admitted to a white friend, "I hate to swear in this case, for I know he [Campbell] had nothing to do with it." When asked why, Rhoades supposedly admitted, "If I tell I might go to the chaingang for life or have my neck broken. . . . By ——, I killed him myself, but the man who gives me away I'll kill him as sure as ——. If I am ever arrested I'll lay it on Mose Ager or Bob Williamson [a white man and a justice of the peace in Griffin], and if that won't do, I'll go as crazy as a bed bug." After much consideration, the friend had gone to the authorities, and on March 16, 1899, the same day of the Palmetto massacre, Rhoades had been arrested and charged with Dickinson's murder, while Campbell was released. Adding to the commotion was the rumor that Rhoades and Dickinson had earlier fought over a black woman named Taylor, and that Rhoades's killing of Dickinson was motivated by jealousy. "Did the Negro or White Boy Do It?" the *Macon Telegraph* wondered, and

this frank admission of interracial sexual companionship further stirred the racial frenzy gripping the town. "Rhodes Arrested," *GDNS*, March 17, 1899; "An Accuser Accused," *MT*, March 17, 1899.

9. "Story of the Capture of Sam Holt"; "The Black Beast Burned at the Stake," *MT*, April 24, 1899.

10. "Story of the Capture."

11. "The Wild Ride from Griffin," *AJ*, April 24, 1899.

12. Ibid.

13. "Black Beast." Some of the law officers are misidentified in this article.

14. "Story of the Capture."

15. "Wild Ride from Griffin."

16. "Hose Admits All," *MT*, April 24, 1899.

17. "Wild Ride from Griffin."

18. "Story of the Capture."

19. "Black Beast."

20. "Burned at the Stake," *H&A*, April 28, 1899.

21. "Howling Mob in Newnan," *AJ*, April 24, 1899.

22. Ibid.; see also "Burned at the Stake," *H&A*.

23. "Howling Mob in Newnan."

24. "Burned at the Stake," *H&A*.

25. "Howling Mob in Newnan."

26. "Black Beast."

27. Receipt reprinted on front page of *AC*, April 25, 1899.

Chapter 6. A Holocaust of Human Flesh

1. "Howling Mob in Newnan," *AJ*, April 24, 1899.

2. Barton K. Shaw, *The Wool-Hat Boys: Georgia's Populist Party* (Baton Rouge: Louisiana State University Press, 1984), 110.

3. Ibid., 118.

4. Ibid., 136–37.

5. October 3, 1896; quoted in Shaw, *Wool-Hat Boys*, 156.

6. *Journal of the House of Representatives of the State of Georgia . . . at Atlanta, Wednesday, October 27, 1897* (Atlanta: Franklin Printing and Publishing, 1897), 40–41.

7. "The Black Beast Burned at the Stake," *MT*, April 24, 1899.

8. "Governor Atkinson on Lynching of Hose," *AC*, April 24, 1899.

9. "Black Beast."

10. "Burned at the Stake," *H&A*, April 28, 1899.

11. "Howling Mob in Newnan."

12. "Governor Atkinson on Lynching."

13. "Howling Mob in Newnan."

14. "Burned at the Stake," *H&A*.

15. Ibid.

16. "Howling Mob in Newnan."

17. "Mrs. Cranford's Condition," *MT*, April 24, 1899.

18. "Burned at the Stake," *H&A*.

19. "Howling Mob in Newnan."

20. "Black Beast."

21. Ibid.; "Howling Mob in Newnan."

22. "Burned at the Stake," *H&A*.

23. "Howling Mob in Newnan."

24. Ellis quotes the Pennsylvanian as telling a Knoxville reporter that he "begged for and was granted the privilege of pouring the oil as an expression of a Northern man's commendation of the [lynching]." See Mary Louise Ellis, "'Rain Down Fire': The Lynching of Sam Hose" (PhD diss., Florida State University, 1992), 119n30.

25. "Black Beast."

26. "Pinned to Earth; Roasted to Death," *AC*, March 11, 1899.

27. There is an obvious emotional connection here with the destruction of the World Trade Center in 2001. One further wonders if the citizens of Palmetto enacted such rough justice against the accused arsonists in part because of the manner in which their town was supposedly threatened.

28. Stuart Banner, *The Death Penalty: An American History* (Cambridge, Mass.: Harvard University Press, 2002), 70–71.

29. "To Be Burned Alive," *New York Times*, February 2, 1893. I draw on the research of Kathryn Langston for information on the Henry Smith lynching. Her unpublished paper "Did the Punishment Fit the Crime? The Lynching of Henry Smith, Paris, Texas, February 1, 1893" introduced me to J. M. Early's *"An Eye for an Eye"; or, The Fiend and the Fagot*.

30. "Relic of Barbarism," *Fitchburg (Mass.) Daily Sentinel*, February 2, 1893. See also "Another Negro Burned: Henry Smith Dies at the Stake," *New York Times*, February 2, 1893.

31. An obvious reference for this kind of communal performance is Mikhail Bakhtin's analysis of carnival and the grotesque in *Rabelais and His World*, trans. Hélène Iswolsky (1941; Cambridge, Mass.: MIT Press, 1965).

32. See Joel Williamson, *The Crucible of Race: Black-White Relations in the American South since Emancipation* (New York: Oxford University Press, 1984), 185–86, for another description of the torture and death of Henry Smith.

33. Mertins took a series of photographs that recorded the case, from the discovery of Myrtle Vance's body to the parading of Smith through the town to his death by burning. According to Jacqueline Goldsby, Mertins "took the precautionary step of depositing his work with the Library of Congress to ensure his copyright control over the images" (240). Furthermore, Goldsby notes that a gramophone recording was made of Smith's interrogation, torture, and death in which Smith could be heard begging and groaning. She refers her readers to Samuel Burdett's *Test of Lynch Law: An Expose of Mob Violence and the Courts of Hell* (Seattle: n.p., 1904), in which Burdett, a black man, relates having come across a display of Mertins's photographs accompanied by the sound recording in Seattle

several months after Smith's lynching. See Goldsby, *A Spectacular Secret: Lynching in American Life and Literature* (Chicago: University of Chicago Press, 2006), esp. 13–15, 38–40, 239–41.

34. J. M. Early, *"An Eye for an Eye" or The Fiend and the Fagot* (n.p.: n.d.), 3.

35. Ibid., 6.

36. Ibid., 6, 9, 11.

37. Ibid., 15.

38. Ibid., 17–18.

39. Ibid., 18.

40. Ibid., 20–21.

41. Ibid., 32. Regarding the authenticity of the statements attributed to Smith, if there was indeed a sound recording of the interrogation as Samuel Burdett describes in *A Test of Lynch Law*, then Early might have used it in constructing his account, however much he might have polished it.

42. Ibid., 20.

43. Ibid., 46–48.

44. In his study of the French Revolution, David Andress points out that in prerevolutionary eighteenth-century France, death decrees were a normal part of the justice system, and executions were carried out in an orderly fashion. "Even if, as in Paris, it was part of the hangman's duties to flog, brand, and sometimes beat the condemned to death, he was always just doing his job, in his sinister, otherworldly, but almost gentlemanly way" (*The Terror: The Merciless War for Freedom in Revolutionary France* [New York: Farrar, Straus, and Giroux, 2005], 110). When the madness of the Terror took over, Andress notes, and victims were being slaughtered by the thousands, the need for a "good death" was still required: "There was nothing the crowd liked better than a brave and well-spoken final speech—even if at the height of Terror that might be reduced to a few bantering words from the tumbril." Victims "sometimes rehearsed the whole ritual of execution, anxious to accustom themselves to its manoeuvres and not lapse into humiliating confusion at their last public appearance" (322–23).

45. "Burned at the Stake," *H&A*.

46. "Sam Hose Burned," *GDNS*, April 24, 1899.

47. The estimated size of the crowd is based on local memory. See W. Winston Skinner, "Lynching a Tragedy with No Winners," *Newnan Times-Herald*, March 18, 2007.

48. "Sam Holt, Murderer and Assailant, Burned at the Stake in Newnan," *AC*, April 24, 1899.

49. Royal Daniel, "While Hose Is Tortured the Multitude Applauds," *AJ*, April 24, 1899.

50. "Shocking Details of the Brute's Last Minutes," *MT*, April 24, 1899.

51. Daniel, "While Hose Is Tortured."

52. "Black Beast"; Daniel, "While Hose Is Tortured"; "Sam Hose, Captured and Burned," *AJ*, April 24, 1899.

53. Daniel, "While Hose Is Tortured."

54. "Mutilated and Burned," *Savannah Morning News*, April 24, 1899.

55. Daniel, "While Hose Is Tortured."

56. Ibid.

57. "Murderer and Rapist Burned at the Stake," *Griffin Evening Call*, April 24, 1899; "Burned at the Stake," *H&A*.

58. Daniel, "While Hose Is Tortured."

59. "Burned at the Stake," *H&A*.

60. See Christopher Waldrep, "'Raw, Quivering Flesh': John G. Cashman's 'Pornographic' Constitutionalism Designed to Produce an 'Aversion and Detestation,' 1883–1904," *American Nineteenth Century History* 6, no. 3 (September 2006): 295–322, for a defense of such lurid, horrific reporting as Daniel's.

61. "Burned at the Stake," *H&A*.

62. Banner, *Death Penalty*, 75.

63. Daniel, "While Hose Is Tortured."

64. "Handy," *H&A*, May 12, 1899.

65. Banner, *Death Penalty*, 77–78.

66. "Hanging of Lewis in the Tower; Charles Haynes's Murderer Dead," *AC*, March 15, 1899.

67. Daniel, "While Hose Is Tortured."

68. "Mrs. Cranford's Condition."

69. "Dr. Hal L. Johnston Returns, Tells of His Weary Chase," *AJ*, April 24, 1899.

70. "How It Is Viewed in North and West," *AJ*, April 24, 1899.

Chapter 7. Beware, All Darkies!

1. "Five Others Wanted," *MT*, April 24, 1899.

2. "The Third Victim," *GDNS*, April 24, 1899.

3. "Burned at the Stake," *LaGrange Graphic*, April 25, 1899.

4. "How the Journal Printed the News," *AJ*, April 24, 1899.

5. "News and Gossip of the Railroads," *AJ*, April 24, 1899.

6. "Crowds Leave for Lynching," *AC*, April 24, 1899.

7. "Palmetto Was Disappointed," *AC*, April 24, 1899.

8. "Strickland Meets Death Saying He Is Innocent," *AJ*, April 24, 1899.

9. "Lige Strickland Lynched," *H&A*, April 28, 1899.

10. "Major W. W. Thomas Pleaded in Vain for Lige Strickland's Life," *AC*, April 25, 1899.

11. Ibid.

12. "Lige Strickland Lynched"; see also "Strickland Meets Death"; "Major W. W. Thomas Pleaded."

13. "Strickland Strung Up," *Columbus (Ga.) Enquirer-Sun*, April 25, 1899.

14. "Another Lynching," *MT*, April 25, 1899.

15. "Major W. W. Thomas Pleaded."

16. "Another Lynching."

17. "Lige Strickland Lynched."

18. "Another Lynching."

19. Ibid.

20. "A Conjure Bag," *MT*, April 25, 1899.

21. "Hose's Motive," *MT*, April 25, 1899.

22. "Another Lynching."

23. "Lige Strickland Lynched."

24. "Sought No Evidence," *MT*, April 25, 1899.

25. "Gives Strickland a Bad Name," *AC*, April 25, 1899, reprinted in *H&A*, April 28, 1899. James Madison Quigley was married to Mary Jane Strickland, from whose family Elijah Strickland took his name. The father-in-law mentioned is Ephraim Strickland, whose father was one of the earliest settlers of the region. A Stricklandtown community is still located in Meriwether County. Information provided by W. Winston Skinner.

26. "Arp Has Sworn Off," *AC*, May 28, 1899.

27. Telephone interview with Carole Harper, December 8, 2006.

28. "Negro Dies at the Stake," *New York Times*, April 24, 1899.

29. "Stoned the Train," *MT*, April 24, 1899.

30. "Cranford Home Deserted," *MT*, April 25, 1899.

31. "Negroes Are Wrought Up," *MT*, April 26, 1899.

32. "No Danger of Race Trouble," *AC*, April 26, 1899.

33. "Quiet at Palmetto," *MT*, April 25, 1899.

34. "At Newnan," *MT*, April 25, 1899.

35. "What the Press and People Say about the Lynchings in Georgia," *AC*, April 25, 1899.

36. "Cruelties More Revolting Than Those of the Apaches," quoted in *AC*, April 25, 1899.

37. "What the Savannah Press and People Say of the Lynching," quoted in *AC*, April 25, 1899.

38. "Despicable Journalism," *Savannah Morning News*, April 28, 1899.

39. "The Reward Paid," *AC*, April 25, 1899.

40. "Constitution Pays Its Reward of $500 for Capture of Holt," *AC*, April 25, 1899.

41. "Death to All Ravishers," *Rome (Ga.) Tribune*, quoted in *H&A*, April 28, 1899.

42. "Will Go around Palmetto," *Americus (Ga.) Investigator*, quoted in *AC*, April 29, 1899.

43. Item, *H&A*, May 12, 1899.

44. "Lynchers Are Savages, Says Colonel Ingersoll," *AJ*, April 25, 1899.

45. "As to Infidel Bob," *Augusta (Ga.) Tribune*, quoted in *AC*, April 29, 1899.

46. "From the Ashes of Hose Rises a Terrible Warning," *AJ*, April 29, 1899.

47. "Burned at the Stake," *H&A*, April 28, 1899.

48. "Atlanta Ministers," *MT*, April 25, 1899.

49. "Ministers Talk of the Lynching," *AJ*, April 24, 1899.

50. Sam P. Jones, "Burning of Sam Hose, Anti-Spitting Law," *AJ*, April 29, 1899.

51. "Mob Sympathy in Atlanta," *Washington Post*, May 1, 1899.

52. "Lyncher's Horrible Gift," *Nagatuck (Conn.) Daily News*, April 28, 1899; "Piece of Sam Hose's Flesh," *Savannah Morning News*, April 29, 1899.

53. "Vandals Damage the Tabernacle," *AC*, May 2, 1899.

54. Darren E. Grem, "Sam Jones, Sam Hose, and the Theology of Racial Violence," *Georgia Historical Quarterly* 90, no. 1 (Spring 2006): 35–61. See also Kathleen Minnix, *Laughter in the Amen Corner: The Life of Evangelist Sam Jones* (Athens: University of Georgia Press, 1993), esp. 200–201.

55. Sam Jones, "Letter," *AJ*, August 19, 1899.

56. "Vandals Damage the Tabernacle."

57. "News from Atlanta," *Arizona Republican*, May 10, 1899.

58. Quoted in David B. Parker, *Alias Bill Arp: Charles Henry Smith and the South's "Goodly Heritage"* (Athens: University of Georgia Press, 1991), 113.

59. Ibid., 114.

60. Ibid., 126.

61. "Bill Arp Grows Caustic about the Critics of Lynching," *AC*, April 30, 1899.

62. Quoted in "Mrs. Felton's Views," *Griffin (Ga.) Evening Call*, April 25, 1899.

63. "A Voice from the South," *Salt Lake City Broad Ax*, May 9, 1899.

64. "Mrs. Atkinson on the Burning," *AC*, April 26, 1899.

65. "A Mighty Protest," *Portsmouth (N.H.) Herald*, June 16, 1903.

66. "Hypocrisy of the Press," *GDNS*, April 25, 1899.

67. "The News in Griffin," *AJ*, April 24, 1899.

68. "Two Ex-Governors," *GDNS*, April 24, 1899.

69. "Burned at the Stake," *H&A*.

70. Quimby Melton, *History of Griffin, Georgia 1840–1940* (Griffin, Ga.: Hometown Press, 1961), 138

71. "An Unjust Imputation," *GDNS*, March 26, 1899.

72. "'An Unjust Imputation'," *H&A*, March 31, 1899.

73. "AN UNJUST IMPUTATION," *GDNS*, April 7, 1899.

74. "Burned at the Stake," *H&A*.

75. "Two Ex-Governors," *GDNS*.

76. Ibid. Grace Elizabeth Hale, in her study *Making Whiteness: The Culture of Segregation in the South, 1890–1940* (New York: Pantheon, 1998), represents Atkinson as something of a posturer, a slightly buffoonish character who, after the events, "bragged that though he had not prevented the lynching he had at least succeeded in persuading them to move the spectacle out of Newnan's town square and away from the white women and children" (213). He was, however, a man who long spoke out against lynching and was severely criticized and at times ostracized by his society. It was also evident in this editorial that Atkinson had made efforts to bring at least some of the men he identified in the mob to justice, although he was never successful in doing so.

77. "An Example to the State," *GDNS*, April 30, 1899.

78. "The Newnan Lynching," *GDNS*, May 2, 1899.

79. "Captors Get $600 Reward," *AJ*, April 25, 1899.

80. "Newnan Lynching."

81. "The 'Flower of Chivalry,' Etc.," *H&A*, May 5, 1899.

82. "The Statesman and the Editor," *GDNS*, May 9, 1899.

83. "Col. Duggy Glessner *Et Al*," *H&A*, May 19, 1899.

84. Items, *H&A*, May 19, 1899.

85. "Candler Talks of Lynching," *AJ*, April 25, 1899.

86. "What Governor Candler Says," *AC*, April 24, 1899.

87. "Governor Candler Denies That He 'Fiddled' While Sam Hose Was Burning," *AJ*, April 29, 1899.

88. John J. Ingalls, "The Negro Question," *H&A*, May 12, 1899; "Fagots and Fiends," *H&A*, May 12, 1899.

89. "Aid Is Being Sent Palmetto People," *AJ*, April 28, 1899.

90. "Flowers for Dead," *MT*, April 27, 1899.

91. "Unique Contests for the Negroes," *AC*, April 25, 1899.

92. "Great Day at Grantville," *H&A*, May 12, 1899.

93. "Two Negroes Whipped for Using Wrong Language about the Hose Crime," *GDNS*, April 22, 1899.

94. "A Card," *H&A*, May 5, 1899.

95. "Leading Negro Talks," *MT*, April 26, 1899.

96. Item, *Salt Lake City Broad Ax*, April 25, 1899.

97. "Lawlessness in the South," *Salt Lake City Broad Ax*, May 2, 1899.

98. I have found no other mention of Griggs or of any other victim burned and dismembered, although, as discussed earlier, there is the possibility that someone was killed in the bonfire in Palmetto.

99. "A Wild-Eyed Anarchist," *Salt Lake City Broad Ax*, May 30, 1899.

100. "From the Ashes."

101. Item, *H&A*, April 28, 1899. I have found no copies of this photograph.

Chapter 8. Lynch Law in Georgia

1. Item reprinted from *The Freeman* in *Salt Lake City Broad Ax*, June 6, 1899.

2. "Negro Imposter Believed," *AC*, May 5, 1899.

3. "Sam Hose's Alleged Son," *AC*, May 5, 1899; also "Negro Imposter Disappears" *Washington Post*, May 8, 1899.

4. "Negro Imposter Believed."

5. "Victims of Credulity," *AC*, August 19, 1899.

6. "Miss Jewett to Come South," *AC*, August 16, 1899.

7. "Victims of Credulity."

8. "Negroes Vow to Revenge," *AJ*, April 22, 1899; "Each Swore to Kill a Man," *Washington Post*, April 24, 1899.

9. "Holt Killed an Old Couple," *AC*, April 28, 1899; "Mutilated and Burned," *Savannah Morning News*, April 24, 1899.

10. "Protection for Women," *Washington Post*, April 25, 1899.

11. In May 1899, *Harper's Weekly* discussed a legal solution that Northen might well have supported: "drum-head courts." The magazine explained that under this process, southern governors could appoint an officer in every "township." If an assault occurred, the officer should "summon six citizens who live conveniently near, constitute them a special jury, preside over them himself, hold a summary trial, and, if guilt is proved, give sentence, and execute it without further delay." *Harper's* further explained, "Negro criminals of the sort these courts would deal with do not greatly object to being hanged, provided they have plenty of time to get ready, and especially to repent and get religion. Where the criminal, after a life of vice ending in some hideous crime of violence, is given time to become a happy convert, so that he steps confidently from the gallows trap into eternal bliss, the effect of his punishment upon other evil-doers is almost nullified. When he is sped into the unknown without unwashed hands [*sic*], the example is held to be more salutary."

12. "Ex-Governor Northen, of Georgia, Meets Colored Bishop in Debate," *AC*, May 23, 1899.

13. See "The Truth Plainly Stated," an editorial in *AC* that supported Northen's argument, which was reprinted in the same edition, May 23, 1899; see also "Deep Interest in Northen's Address," *AC*, May 24, 1899.

14. "Law in the South," *North Adams (Mass.) Evening Transcript*, June 19, 1899.

15. "Northen Tells of Boston Trip," *AC*, May 25, 1899.

16. "Arp Has Sworn Off," *AC*, May 28, 1899.

17. George H. Hepworth, "First of the Letters by Dr. Hepworth on Lynching in the South and the Remedy," *AC*, May 14, 1899.

18. "A New York Editor," *H&A*, May 12, 1899.

19. George H. Hepworth, letter 1, "Southern Lynchings, Their Causes and the Only Remedy," *New York Herald*, May 14, 1899; Hepworth, "First of the Letters."

20. "Dr. Hepworth's Visit," *MT*, May 10, 1899. Atkinson repeated these sentiments in a letter to Walter F. Willcox "written shortly before [Atkinson's] death." Willcox had asked Atkinson whether local blacks believed Hose was guilty of murder and rape. Atkinson replied that he had made further investigation by talking "with some of the white and colored people from that section of the county in a confidential way." He insisted that the blacks with whom he talked would not have hesitated to tell him that "the negroes doubted Hose's guilt if such doubts had existed" and concluded, "There is no reason for the doubt expressed by you in your letter." Willcox, however, still felt "that a large proportion of the negroes of Georgia [did] not share the belief of their white neighbors about the guilt of Sam Hose." Walter F. Willcox, "Negro Criminality," *Journal of Social Science, Consisting of the Proceedings of the American Association (1869–1909)* 37 (1899): 78–98, here 94. *APS Online* Proquest.

21. Mary Louise Ellis cites an April 25, 1899, letter from Wells B. Whitmore to Rebecca Felton's husband, Dr. William B. Felton, in which Whitmore writes that Hose "carried [Mrs. Cranford's] helpless body to another room, and there he *stripped* her person of every thread and vestige of clothing, there keeping her till time enough had elapsed to

permit him to accomplish his fiendish offense twice more and again. And, as to render all still more horrible and horrifying, he was afflicted with loathsome 'S******s' [syphilis], for which Mr. *Cranford was having him treated.*" See Ellis, "'Rain Down Fire': The Lynching of Sam Hose" (PhD diss., Florida State University, 1992), 82–83.

22. Letter 1.

23. George H. Hepworth, letter 2, "How Lynching May Be Stopped," *New York Herald*, May 14, 1899; *AC*, May 14, 1899.

24. George H. Hepworth, letter 4, "Conflict of Races," *New York Herald*, May 21, 1899.

25. "Dr. Hepworth's Letters," *AC*, May 14, 1899.

26. "Ripples," *H&A*, May 19, 1899.

27. Item, *Chicago Tribune*, May 1, 1899.

28. Ellis, "'Rain Down Fire,'" 201; item, *Galveston Daily News*, June 5, 1899; Ida B. Wells-Barnett, "Lynch Law in Georgia" (Chicago: Chicago Colored Citizens, 1899), 13.

29. Wells-Barnett, "Lynch Law in Georgia," 1.

30. "Literary News and Comment," *AC*, November 30, 1907. On the other hand, in 1909 there was also a "droll" comedian named Sam Hose, whose "clever antics and smart sayings . . . made thousands laugh," listed on the same page advertising an appearance by W. S. Hart, the stage version of *Ben Hur*, and a blackface duo called "The Bimbos." "The Theater," *Oshkosh (Wis.) Daily Northwestern*, March 20, 1909.

31. Wells-Barnett, "Lynch Law in Georgia," 14–15.

32. Five years later, the *Constitution* would again put up five hundred dollars as a reward for the capture of the murderer of a young white woman named Sophie Kloeckler found drowned at the Lakewood resort near Atlanta. At that time, the paper recalled the Sam Hose reward and carefully explained that it was intended to ensure Hose's safe delivery to the proper authorities since a receipt from the sheriff was required as proof in order to collect the payment. See "Constitution Paid $500," *AC*, June 5, 1904.

33. Wells-Barnett, "Lynch Law in Georgia," 15–16.

34. In his article "Negro Criminality," Walter F. Willcox notes, "The stoical silence with which Hose bore his tortures, and the evident pride of the negroes in that silence, receive new meaning. It was the weapon whereby, even in death, they felt that he triumphed over their enemies and his."

35. Wells-Barnett, "Lynch Law in Georgia," 17–18.

36. Ibid., 15.

37. Ibid.

38. "Mrs. Alfred Cranford Talks," *Salt Lake City Broad Ax*, June 6, 1899.

39. Item, *New York Age*, June 20, 1899; "The Detective's Report. The Georgia Burning.—Sam Hose Not Guilty of Rape," *Richmond (Va.) Planet*, October 14, 1899.

40. "A Reply to Northen," *North Adams (Mass.) Evening Transcript*, June 26, 1899.

41. "Negro Troops Are Asked to Revolt: Spaniards Tell Them to Avenge the Death of Sam Hose," *AC*, November 2, 1899.

42. Willcox, "Negro Criminality," 90–92.

43. "Griggs Defends South for Lynching of Negroes," *AJ*, February 5, 1900.

Chapter 9. Sex, Fingers, Toes

1. "Sam Holt," *H&A*, May 12, 1899.

2. "Newnan," *H&A*, July 22, 1899.

3. *Coweta County Chronicles*, ed. and comp. Mary G. Jones and Lily Reynolds (Newnan: Coweta County Historical Society, 1928), 336.

4. "At Newnan," *MT*, April 25, 1899.

5. W. E. B. Du Bois, *A Pageant in Seven Decades, 1868–1938* (Atlanta, 1938), 254; see a slightly different version of this memory in *Dusk of Dawn: An Essay toward the Autobiography of a Race Concept* (1940), in *W. E. B. Du Bois: Writings*, ed. Nathan Huggins (New York: Library of America, 1986), 602–3, and in *The Autobiography of W. E. B. Du Bois* (n.p.: International Publishers, 1968), 221–22. Joel Chandler Harris's son Evelyn, a reporter for the *Constitution*, was present at Hose's execution. Mary Louise Ellis quotes a letter from Harris to his daughter Lillian, written on the day of the burning, telling her, "[Evelyn] went to the cremation of Sam Holt and I expect to see a badly shaken young man tomorrow." See Ellis, "'Rain Down Fire': The Lynching of Sam Hose" (PhD diss., Florida State University, 1992), 134.

6. E-mail correspondence with John Strain, March 21, 2007.

7. Quoted in Philip Dray, *At the Hands of Persons Unknown: The Lynching of Black America* (New York: Random House, 2002), 7.

8. William Ivy Hair, *Carnival of Fury: Robert Charles and the New Orleans Race Riot of 1900* (Baton Rogue: Louisiana State University Press, 1976), 108.

9. Ida B. Wells-Barnett, "Mob Rule in New Orleans" (1900), reprinted in Wells-Barnett, *On Lynching*, intro. Patricia Hill Collins (Amherst, N.Y.: Humanity Books, 2002), 153–203, here 153. See also Joel Williamson, *The Crucible of Race: Black-White Relations in the American South since Emancipation* (New York: Oxford University Press, 1984), 201–9.

10. Ellis, "'Rain Down Fire,'" 62; see also "Warren Akin Candler," http://www.georgiaencyclopedia.org/nge/Article.jsp?id=h-754&hl=y.

11. Terry L. Matthews, "The Voice of the Prophet: Andrew Sledd Revisited," *Journal of Southern Religion* 6 (December 2003): 5.

12. See Williamson, *Crucible of Race*, 259–61.

13. Andrew Sledd, "The Negro: Another View," *Atlantic Monthly*, 90, no. 537 (July 1902): 66.

14. Ibid., 67–68.

15. Ibid., 70.

16. Ibid., 71.

17. See chap. 8, note 21.

18. Mrs. W. H. Felton, "The Negro, as Discussed by Mr. Andrew Sledd," *AC*, August 3, 1902.

19. "Indignation at Covington," *AC*, August 5, 1902.

20. "Leaders of the Race Differ in Their Views," *AC*, August 6, 1902.

21. "Bad Boys Burn Sledd in Effigy," *AC*, August 7, 1902.

22. "To Protect Emory Sledd Will Leave," *AC*, August 9, 1902.

23. "Professor Sledd's Article," *AC*, August 11, 1902.

24. For a comprehensive study of Dixon, see Anthony Slide, *American Racist: The Life and Films of Thomas Dixon* (Louisville: University of Kentucky Press, 2004). See also Williamson's chapter "Thomas Dixon and *The Leopard's Spots*," in *Crucible of Race*, 140–79.

25. Thomas Dixon Jr., *The Leopard's Spots: A Romance of the White Man's Burden* (New York: Doubleday Page, 1902), iv.

26. J. M. Early, *"An Eye for an Eye" or The Fiend and the Fagot* (n.p.: n.d.), 10.

27. Dixon, *Leopard's Spots*, 370. See also Williamson, *Crucible of Race*, 148–49.

28. Dixon, *Leopard's Spots*, 372.

29. Ibid., 375.

30. Ibid., 382–84.

31. See "Another Negro Burned: Henry Smith Dies at the Stake," *New York Times*, February 2, 1893.

32. Sandra Gunning, *Race, Rape, and Lynching: The Red Record of American Literature, 1890–1912* (New York: Oxford University Press, 1996), 41–42. Glenda Elizabeth Gilmore finds connections between this episode and events closer to home for Dixon: the Wilmington race riots and a murder and rape that occurred in Concord, N.C., in 1898. See *Gender and Jim Crow: Women and the Politics of White Supremacy in North Carolina, 1896–1920* (Chapel Hill: University of North Carolina Press, 1996), 82–89, 135.

33. Joel Williamson, "How Black Was Rhett Butler?" in *The Evolution of Southern Culture*, ed. Numan V. Bartley (Athens: University of Georgia Press, 1988), 103.

34. Ibid., 98–99.

35. Ibid., 101.

36. In his book *Southern Daughter: The Life of Margaret Mitchell* (New York: Oxford University Press, 1991), biographer Darden Asbury disputes Williamson's reading and denies Mitchell's suggested "latent fascination with black men" (216). Although correctly pointing out that the manuscript no longer exists and that much of Williamson's speculation is based on the faulty memory of several who had read it long ago, Asbury is perhaps overly protective of Mitchell and her creative imagination.

37. Although I discuss only Faulkner and Caldwell, I could easily extend this section to include others, especially black writers. Ralph Ellison's story "A Party Down at the Square," for example, presents a public burning, as does James Baldwin's "Going to Meet the Man." See Ellison, *Flying Home and Other Stories* (New York: Random House, 1996), 3–11; Baldwin, *Going to Meet the Man* (New York: Dial, 1965), 229–49. See also Trudier Harris, *Exorcising Blackness: Historical and Literary Lynching and Burning Rituals* (Bloomington: Indiana University Press, 1991) for a comprehensive examination of literary lynchings.

38. William Faulkner, *Sanctuary* (1931), in *William Faulkner: Novels 1930–1935* (New York: Library of America, 1985), 284, 296.

39. William Faulkner, *Light in August* (1932), in *William Faulkner: Novels 1930–1935*, 743.

40. Royal Daniel, "While Hose Is Tortured the Multitude Applauds," *AJ*, April 24, 1899.

41. Erskine Caldwell, "Kneel to the Rising Sun," in *The Stories of Erskine Caldwell* (Athens: University of Georgia Press, 1996), 663.

42. Erskine Caldwell, "Saturday Afternoon," in *Stories of Erskine Caldwell*, 30, 31, 32. This idea of meat as metaphor for lynching victims inspires an ironic, though unintended, reading of certain newspaper reports. One of the major stories of 1899 concerned the U.S. Army's purchase of "bad meat" from meatpackers such as Armour. These putrid supplies sickened thousands of soldiers fighting in Cuba and the Philippines. In 1898, President McKinley appointed Maj. Gen. Grenville M. Dodge to investigate, and although the Dodge Commission's final report in 1899 exonerated the meat industry (Upton Sinclair, for one, would assail the findings in such works as *The Jungle* [1906]), the proceedings were sometimes reported on the same pages with articles describing lynching events such as the Palmetto massacre. For example, on March 16, the *Macon Telegraph* ran the story "Great Slaughter at Palmetto" juxtaposed to another titled "Looks Bad for Beef." In "Saturday Afternoon," Caldwell boldly draws the connection between slaughtered men and butchered animals.

43. See the discussion of this novel in Sylvia Jenkins Cook, *Erskine Caldwell and the Fiction of Poverty* (Baton Rouge: Louisiana State University Press, 1991), 141–51. See also Edwin T. Arnold, "Erskine Caldwell and Judge Lynch: Erskine Caldwell's Role in the Anti-Lynching Campaign of the 1930s," in *Reading Erskine Caldwell: New Essays*, ed. Robert L. McDonald (Jefferson, N.C.: McFarland), 183–202.

44. http://www.jerryjazzmusician.com/mainHTML.cfm?page=harpercoltrane.html.

Chapter 10. Across the Road from the Barbecue House

1. Exteriors for a popular television show used this homey aspect of Newnan to create a sense of the generic American village. Filming on the ABC/Touchstone series *October Road* began in March 2006. Although set in a fictional New England town, the series used the city square and some of the scenic homes as backdrops. As one article reported, "Crews transformed Newnan's Court Square into a fall season look for filming earlier this year, including fall-colored leaves tied to the trees." Latina Emerson, "'October Road' TV Filming Will Resume in Newnan," *Newnan Times-Herald*, October 24, 2006.

2. Newnan-Coweta Historical Society, *A History of Coweta County, Georgia* (Roswell, Ga.: W. H. Wolfe, 1988), 136; see also Mary Louise Ellis, "'Rain Down Fire': The Lynching of Sam Hose" (PhD diss., Florida State University, 1992), 232.

3. "Burned at the Stake," *H&A*, April 28, 1899.

4. Leonard Pitts Jr., "What's in a Name? Something Old and Deep and Rancid," *Jewish World Review*, September 20, 2005. http://www.jewishworldreview.com/0905/pitts091905.php3.

5. W. Fitzhugh Brundage, *Lynching in the New South: Georgia and Virginia, 1880–1930* (Urbana: University of Illinois Press, 1993), 82.

6. Leon Litwack, *Trouble in Mind: Black Southerners in the Age of Jim Crow* (New York: Alfred A. Knopf, 1998), 283.

7. Christopher Waldrep, *The Many Faces of Judge Lynch: Extralegal Violence and Punishment in America* (New York: Palgrave Macmillan, 2002), 119.

8. Shawn Michelle Smith, *Photography on the Color Line: W. E. B. Du Bois, Race, and Visual Culture* (Durham, N.C.: Duke University Press, 2004), 114.

9. Grace Elizabeth Hale, *Making Whiteness: The Culture of Segregation in the South, 1890–1940* (New York: Pantheon Books, 1998), 210–11.

10. "Sam Hose" entry in Wikipedia, http://en.wikipedia.org/wiki/Sam_Hose.

11. "Sam Hose" entry in "Our Georgia History," http://ourgeorgiahistory.com/chronpop/933.

12. Philip Dray, *At the Hands of Persons Unknown: The Lynching of Black America* (New York: Random House, 2002), 16.

13. Telephone interview with Carole Harper, November 17, 2006.

14. Hale, *Making Whiteness*, 211.

15. Robyn Wiegman, *American Anatomies: Theorizing Race and Gender* (Durham, N.C.: Duke University Press, 1995), 83.

16. Ellis, "'Rain Down Fire,'" 236.

17. Ibid., 237.

18. Ibid., 238.

19. Ibid., 238–39.

20. David Thelen, ed., "Memory and American History," *Journal of American History* 75, no. 4 (March 1989): 1117–29, here 1117.

21. See introduction to Marita Sturken, *Tangled Memories: The Vietnam War, the AIDS Epidemic, and the Politics of Remembering* (Berkeley: University of California Press, 1997), 1–17. See also Jonathan Markovitz, *Legacies of Lynching: Racial Violence and Memory* (Minneapolis: University of Minnesota Press, 2004), in which Markovitz quotes Sturken and examines lynching as metaphor in modern society.

22. Thelen, "Memory and American History," 1118.

23. Markovitz, *Legacies of Lynching*, xxii.

24. Pierre Nora, "Between Memory and History: *Les Lieux de Mémoire*," in *History and Memory in African-American Culture*, ed. Geneviève Fabre and Robert O'Meally (Oxford: Oxford University Press, 1994), 285–86.

25. Kenneth E. Foote, *Shadowed Ground: America's Landscapes of Violence and Tragedy* (Austin: University of Texas Press, 1997), 5.

26. Ibid., 7–8.

27. Interview with Carole Harper, December 8, 2006.

28. Interview with John Herbert Cranford, August 2, 2005.

29. Interview with Robert Wood, August 3, 2005.

30. Amy Louise Wood, "Lynching Photography and the Visual Reproduction of White Supremacy," *American Nineteenth Century History* 6, no. 3 (September 2005): 375.

31. W. Winston Skinner, e-mail correspondence, February 12, 2005.

32. Interview with John Herbert Cranford.

33. W. Winston Skinner, "Lynching a Tragedy with No Winners," *Newnan Times-Herald*, March 18, 2007.

34. Ellis, "'Rain Down Fire,'" 232.

35. http://www.mooresford.org/index.html. For a thorough study of the Moore's Ford lynching, see Laura Wexler, *Fire in a Canebrake: The Last Mass Lynching in America* (New York: Scribner, 2003).

36. http://www.southerntruth.org/aboutus.htm.

37. Telephone interview with Richard Rusk, March 18, 2007.

38. W. Winston Skinner, "Memorial to Recall Lynching," *Newnan Times-Herald*, February 6, 2007.

39. Interview with Richard Rusk.

40. Dianne Webb, "Memorial Shameful," *Newnan Times-Herald*, February 22, 2007.

41. Lisa Pitts, "Honoring Murderer Wrong," *Newnan Times-Herald*, February 21, 2007.

42. Michael Stringfellow, "No Memorial for Rapist," *Newnan Times-Herald*, February 18, 2007.

43. Steven R. Harbin, "Memorial the Right Thing to Do," *Newnan Times-Herald*, February 17, 2007.

44. http://times-herald.com/samhose.

45. http://times-herald.com/samhose/pdfs/01–03.pdf.

46. http://times-herald.com/samhose/pdfs/03a.pdf.

47. Skinner, "Lynching a Tragedy."

48. W. Winston Skinner, "Sam Hose Lynching to Be Topic of Community Forum," *Newnan Times-Herald*, April 6, 2007.

49. W. Winston Skinner, "Group Looks to Reach Out to Local Youth," *Newnan Times-Herald*, October 10, 2007.

50. W. Winston Skinner, "35 Discuss Hose 1899 Lynching: Ordeal Subject of Come to the Table," *Newnan Times-Herald*, April 10, 2007.

51. W. Winston Skinner, "What's Next for CTTT?" *Newnan Times-Herald*, April 11, 2007.

52. Skinner, "Group Looks to Reach Out."

53. Ernie Suggs, "The Lynching of Sam Hose," *Atlanta Journal-Constitution*, April 22, 2007, D1, 12.

54. Skinner, "Lynching a Tragedy."

Coda

1. Obituary, Mrs. M. E. Cranford, *Newnan Herald*, January 27, 1922.

2. Mary Louise Ellis, "'Rain Down Fire': The Lynching of Sam Hose" (PhD diss., Florida State University, 1992), 232.

3. Interview with John Herbert Cranford, August 2, 2005.

4. See "The Uprising of '34," video recording (New York: First Run/Icarus Films, 1995), for a fascinating account of the series of textile mill strikes throughout the South at

this time. The film contains interviews with mill workers from Newnan, Grantville, and Hogansville, among other places.

5. Interview with John Herbert Cranford.

6. "Elect Clifford Cranford, " *Newnan Herald*, January 10, 1952.

7. *Coweta County Chronicles*, ed. and comp. Mary G. Jones and Lily Reynolds (Newnan: Coweta County Historical Society, 1928), 343–44.

8. "A Great Man Has Died," *H&A*, August 11, 1899.

9. "Octogenarian Mayor of Newnan Reminisces on Old-Time Politics," *AC*, May 17, 1938. Also see "Mayor J. E. Brown Dies in 86th Year," *AC*, May 15, 1939.

10. "Douglass [*sic*] Glessner Claimed by Death," *AC*, July 12, 1910.

11. "Allen D. Candler Called by Death," *AC*, October 27, 1910.

12. "Mrs. Rebecca Felton, Only Woman Senator, Dies," *AC*, January 25, 1930.

13. "The Passing of Rev. Sam Jones," *AC*, October 16, 1906.

14. Terry L. Matthews, "The Voice of the Prophet: Andrew Sledd Revisited," *Journal of Southern Religion* 6 (December 2003): 1. See also John E. Talmadge, *Rebecca Latimer Felton: Nine Stormy Decades* (Athens: University of Georgia Press, 1960), 116–17. Talmadge misidentifies Sam Hose as "Sam Horse" and the Cranfords as the "Crandalls," and therefore should be used cautiously.

15. Eric Rangus, "Reverence, Emotion Run High at Sledd Symposium," *Emory Report*, April 29, 2002. http://www.emory.edu/EMORY_REPORT/erarchive/2002/April/erApril.29/4_29_02sledd.html.

16. "Quitman Editor Escapes Abductors by Ruse," *AC*, June 3, 1935; "Royal Daniel Dies of Heart Attack," *AC*, June 19, 1939.

17. "Georgia College: Existence Owed to Newnan's Susie Atkinson," *Newnan Times-Herald*, December 5, 1989.

18. W. Winston Skinner, "Mrs. Susan Atkinson Named to Georgia Women of Accomplishment," *Newnan Times-Herald*, March 23, 1996.

19. "Silver Wedding of Dr. and Mrs. Hal Johnston," *AC*, October 20, 1899.

20. "Child Labor Laws Objected To," *AC*, November 20, 1902.

21. "Watch for Dr. Hal Johnson [*sic*]," *AC*, December 9, 1906.

22. Obituary, *Newnan Herald*, January 29, 1937.

23. "Uncle Natchel and Sonny," *Newnan Herald*, January 29, 1937.

Index

P8/14